IMAGES
of America

ADRIAN

On the Cover: This 1889 photograph shows a group of young people enjoying the Lenawee County Fair. This county fair has been held in Adrian since 1839 and still serves as a highlight of the summer. (Courtesy of the Lenawee Historical Society Museum.)

IMAGES
of America

ADRIAN

Julieanna Frost

ARCADIA
PUBLISHING

ISBN 978-0-7385-8282-5

Published by Arcadia Publishing
Charleston, South Carolina

Printed in the United States of America

Library of Congress Control Number: 2010941560

For all general information, please contact Arcadia Publishing:
Telephone 843-853-2070
Fax 843-853-0044
E-mail sales@arcadiapublishing.com
For customer service and orders:
Toll-Free 1-888-313-2665

Visit us on the Internet at www.arcadiapublishing.com

*To Lynn Frost, my favorite blue-ribbon winner
at the Lenawee County Fair.*

Contents

ACKNOWLEDGMENTS

This work would not have been possible without the resources at the Lenawee Historical Society Museum. Opened in 1972, this museum has faithfully conserved this county's history and graciously provided the majority of the photographs included in this book. I am very thankful to the members of the Lenawee County Historical Society for their dedication to local history. Unless otherwise noted, all images appear courtesy of the museum.

I am also indebted to a host of individuals for their encouragement and advice, specifically Kathyrn Alexander, Cindy Anderson, Sr. Mary Beaubien, Dan Cherry, Kathryn Galchutt, Robert Gordon, Mike Griffin, Kassandra Frost, Lynn Frost, Gina Kemerer, Ben Mitter, Heather Moody, Jim Path, John Pearson, Jan Ricardi, Anna Smith, and Frank Swinehart.

INTRODUCTION

This photographic history of Adrian surveys approximately 100 years of this community located in southeastern Michigan. Beginning in 1825, migration to the Michigan territory became easier with the completion of the Erie Canal, and advertisements placed in newspapers touted inexpensive and bountiful land. Many of the early emigrants were lured from the New England region. This included the Comstock family from Niagara County in New York. Addison, with his father, Darius, came to the territory in 1825 to purchase land on which to settle. Addison purchased 640 acres to plat out a community, retraced his steps back to New York so he could marry Sarah Dean, and returned by the spring of 1826 with his new bride. This timing was extremely important so that they could get their agricultural crops planted. He built a log cabin and sawmill along the Raisin River that same year. Addison was also instrumental in bringing the railroad to Adrian. The Erie and Kalamazoo Railroad was quite a feat of engineering coming through the Black Swamp from Toledo and was completed in 1836.

Adrian grew more rapidly with this improvement in transportation and had continuing emigration from back east. In the 1840s, Adrian also had the immigration of Irish escaping the potato famine, Germans escaping civil unrest, and African Americans escaping slavery. Adrian became a major stop on the Underground Railroad in the 1830s, partially due to the influence of citizens such as Darius Comstock and Laura Haviland. Many of these former slaves stayed, so Adrian had a noticeable African American population that was integrated into the community.

With the growth in population, there was a natural increase in city services. Adrian became the county seat in 1836 and had certain standards to uphold as such. Public safety was a top priority of the local government, so quite early on Adrian had police, corrections officers, and a fire department. Municipal services by the 1870s included postal delivery, clean water, a public library, and street improvements, much sooner than many other cities of similar size in Michigan. The downtown area had a wide variety of businesses in handsome brick Italianate buildings so that any item needed could be found there, with hardware stores, dry goods and groceries, clothing shops, and furniture.

This progressive nature of Adrian is also evident in the realm of education, which was viewed as extremely important in the community. The first schools were subscription in the 1820s, but many reformers brought the idea of the common school with them. The first public schools supported by tax dollars opened in the 1830s. Lenawee County had a variety of other firsts in education: it had the first integrated school in the state with the Raisin Institute; the first integrated training school begun by an African American with the Woodstock Manual Labor Institute; a school open to children of all religious backgrounds with the Raisin Valley Seminary; and the first state school headed by a woman with the Michigan Industrial Home for Girls. The importance of education is still apparent, with a variety of parochial schools, public schools, a college, and a university located in Adrian.

Adrian had great diversity in the realm of both social organizations and religious congregations. Whether residents were interested in abolition, temperance, missions, or sports, Adrian had a group for them. There were also many thriving fraternal organizations, such as the Freemasons and the International Order of Odd Fellows, and groups for hobbies, like photography or bicycling. Early Adrian had several religious communities, as faith was viewed as being as important to development as education. Groups such as Baptists, Baha'i, Catholics, Congregationalists, Dominicans, Lutherans, Methodists, Presbyterians, and Quakers all have a long tradition here. The oldest community of Quakers in the state exists just north of Adrian in Raisin Township. Although there were schisms over issues like slavery and authority like in many regions of the United States, there also often existed an ecumenical tolerance and respect of diversity. Many of the schools were supported by religious institutions, such as St. Joseph's Academy and Adrian College. Quite a few denomination-sponsored social groups and musical groups existed as well. In addition, Adrian was well suited to provide recreational outlets for its citizens. Since 1839, the Lenawee County Fair has been held in Adrian, making it one of the oldest in the state. The Croswell Opera House has hosted numerous concerts, plays, films, and speakers since its opening in 1866, making it the oldest continuously operating theater in Michigan. Many parks were created in the city, and to enjoy a beach picnic at one of the area lakes was just a short trip. If a person was not particularly outdoorsy, he or she could go to the nickelodeon, attend a lecture or art exhibit, watch a baseball game, or listen to an orchestral suite. I am still impressed by the number of activities sponsored in town and often wonder what it would have been like during the Gilded Age when the pace almost seemed frantic.

Much of Adrian's industry, even into the early 20th century, was directly related to the railroads, especially with the Lake Shore and Michigan Central, which had its business offices and machine shops in the city. Although considered a railroad town, it was not the only industry here. For example, factories manufactured furniture, pianos, underwear, beer, and fences. As Michigan began to become closely identified with the automobile industry, firms such as Lion Motor Car and Church Company began to encourage this diversification in Adrian. Unfortunately, some factories were not able to survive the Great Depression, while others did not survive changes in fashion, like the Nu-Way Stretch Company, which made suspenders.

It has been a great joy to collect and research these photographs of a community that means so much to me. I must admit as I walk down the streets now, the past more strikingly interrupts the present. I hope that by discovering these images from the first 100 years, you will experience a bit of this wonderful community steeped in both progress and tradition.

One

Growth of the City

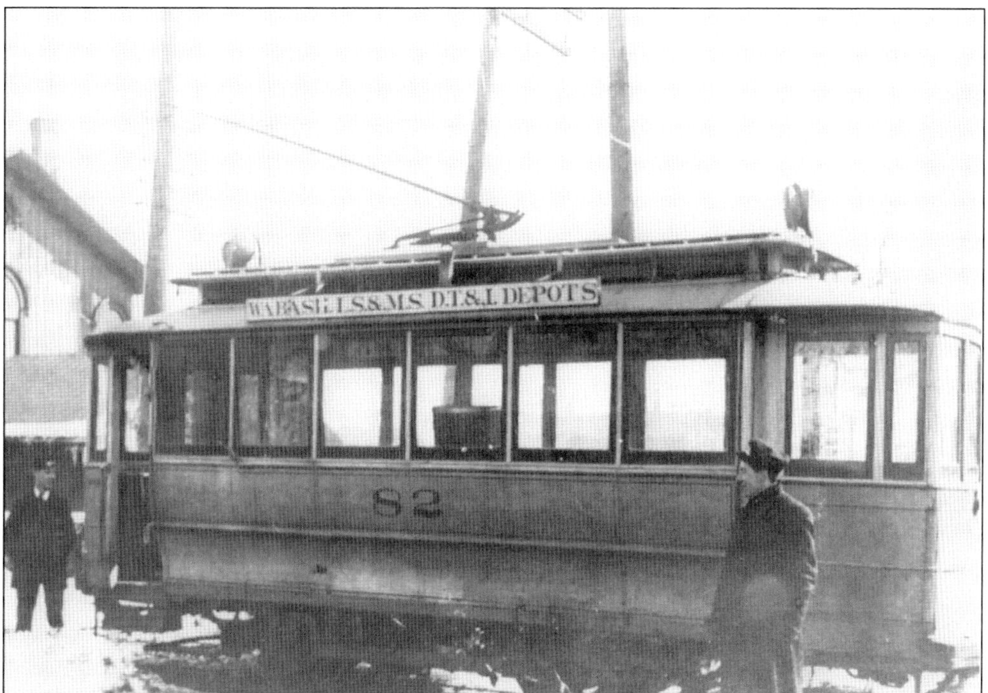

Lake Shore and Michigan Southern Train. Perhaps more than any other event, the coming of the railroad to Adrian created the rapid growth of this city. It generated employment for hundreds, influenced the shift of the county seat, and provided affordable transportation to the city for future residents and visitors alike. The first line was the Erie and Kalamazoo, which eventually merged into the Lake Shore and Michigan Southern.

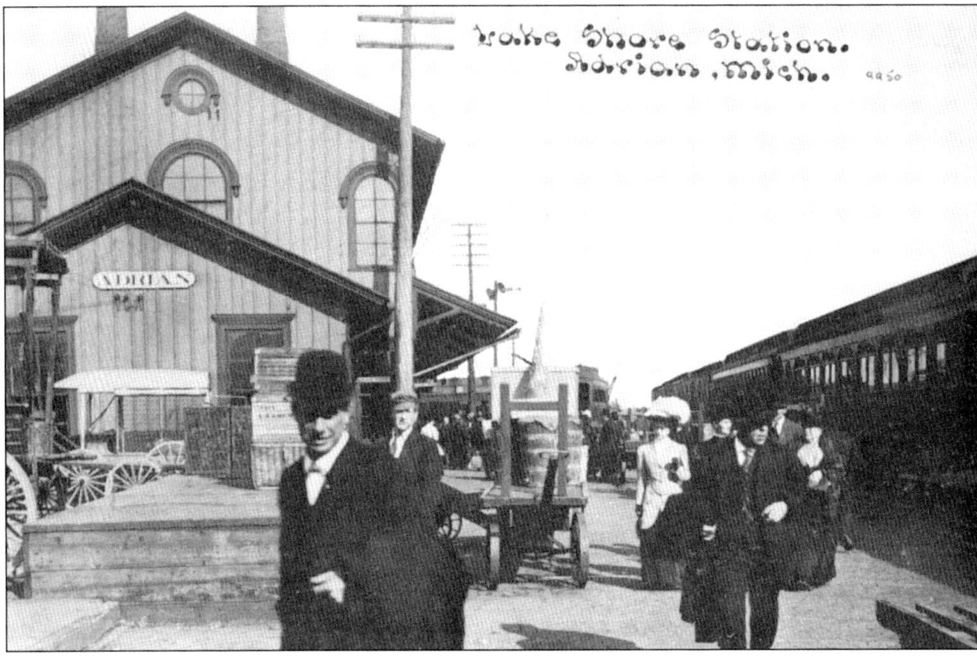

Lake Shore and Michigan Southern Depot. Train stations served as the departure and arrival points for people and freight. Ticket sales, waiting rooms, and lunch counters were typical sights in these buildings. The Adrian depot was two stories high and is shown in these two images. One wonders in the image below if the young lady's train is perhaps late due to the expression on her face.

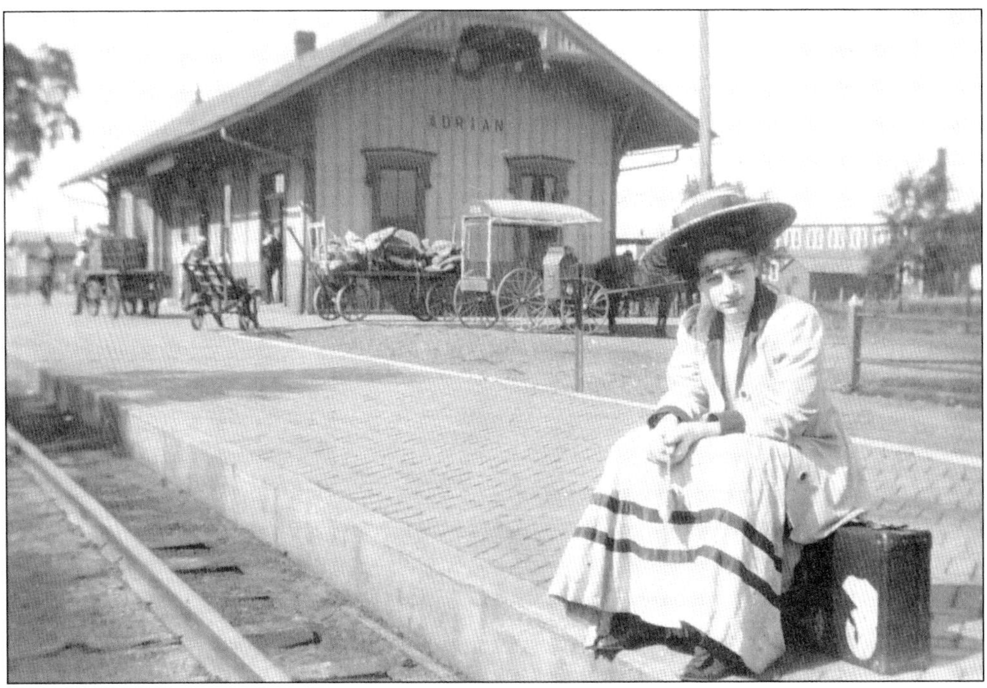

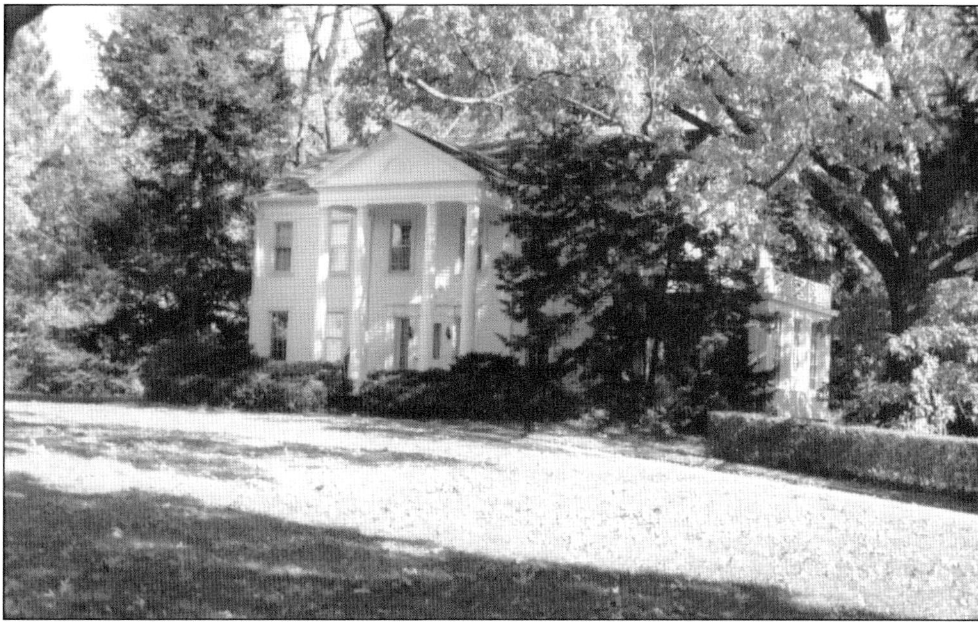

Greek Revival and Italianate Architecture. As the city grew, the increase in wealth became apparent with the many stately homes built near the downtown area. A wide variety of styles are still visible in Adrian. In the early years, Greek Revival and Italianate were extremely popular in the residential areas; Italianate dominated the downtown business district. Above is an example of Greek Revival, and below is an example of Italianate architecture.

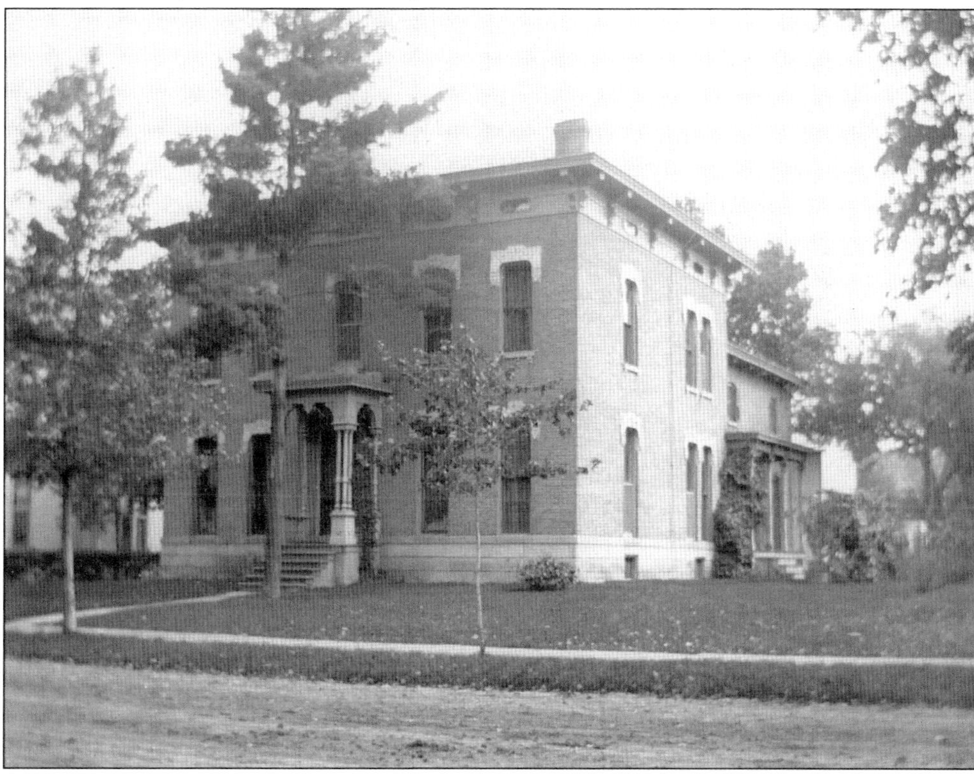

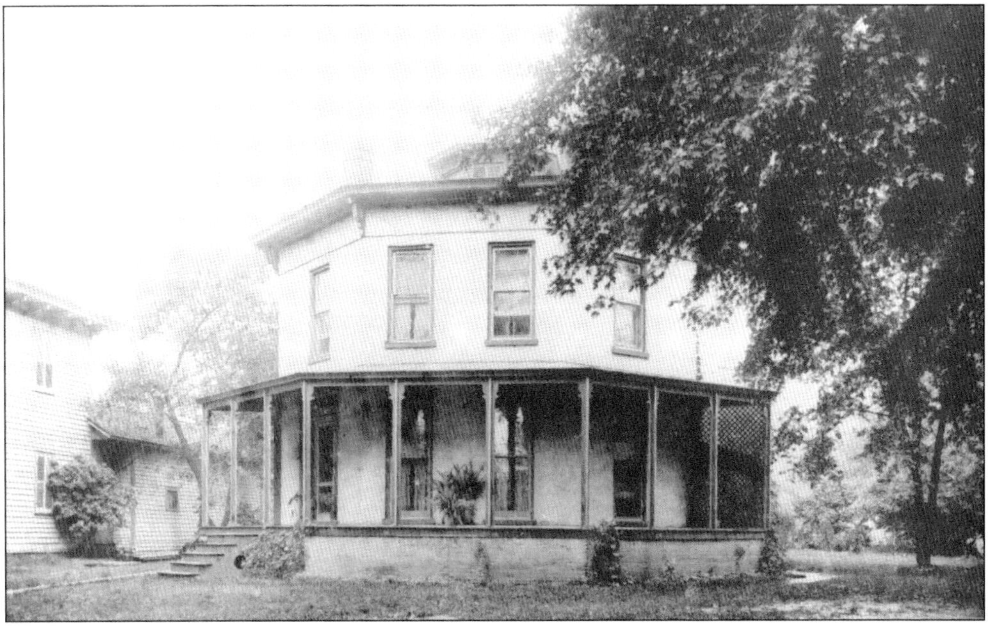

Octagon-Style and Shingle-Style Architecture. Within Adrian, there are also existing homes of architectural styles not as commonly seen. The Octagon style, seen above, could be considered a brief fad in housing construction, lasting for only about 10 years. Proponents of this type of home believed that space would be better utilized and that these homes would be cheaper to build. Below is an example of the Shingle style, which existed from the 1870s until about 1910 as a rustic protest to elaborate Victorian architecture.

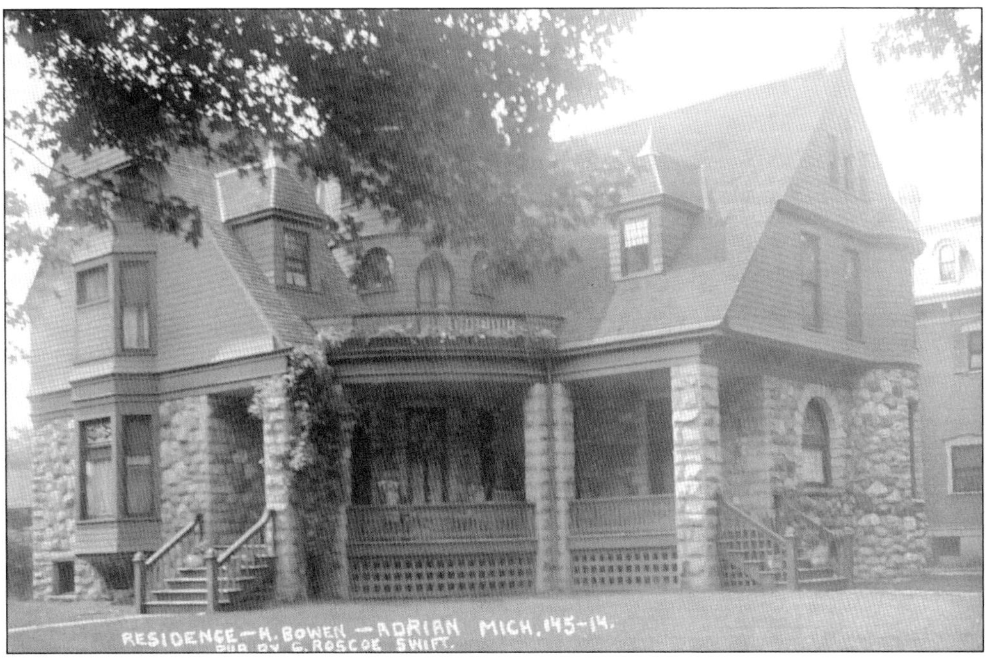

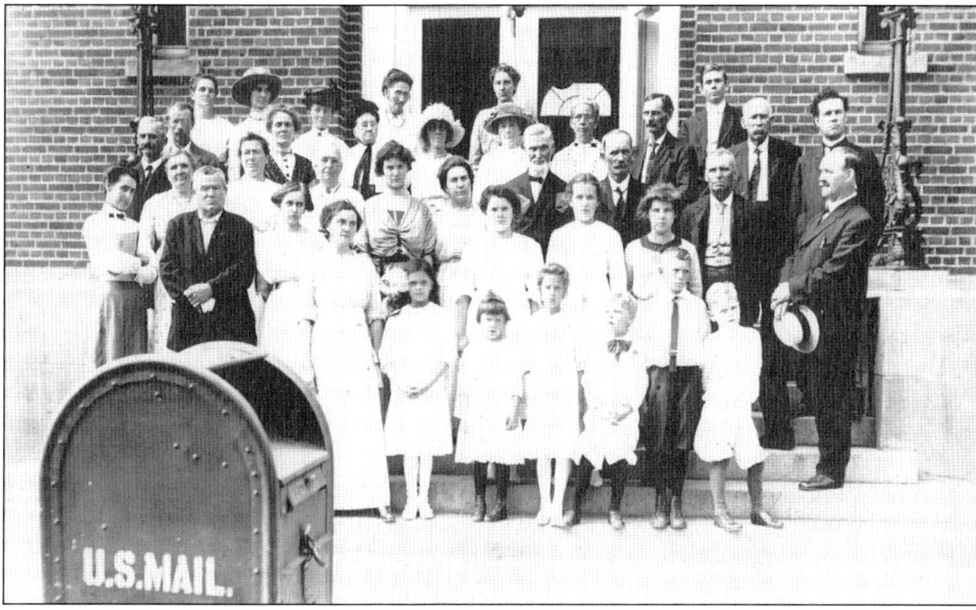

POST OFFICE. The first postmaster of Adrian was Addison Comstock, and the rate of mailing a single sheet of paper within 80 miles was 10¢. With better transportation by the 1840s, a dime would send a one-page letter over 300 miles. In 1863, delivery within the city was free, although those that lived outside the limits would have to come into town to pick up their mail until rural free delivery was implemented in 1899. Bids were taken by the federal government in 1905 in order to build the new post office shown here.

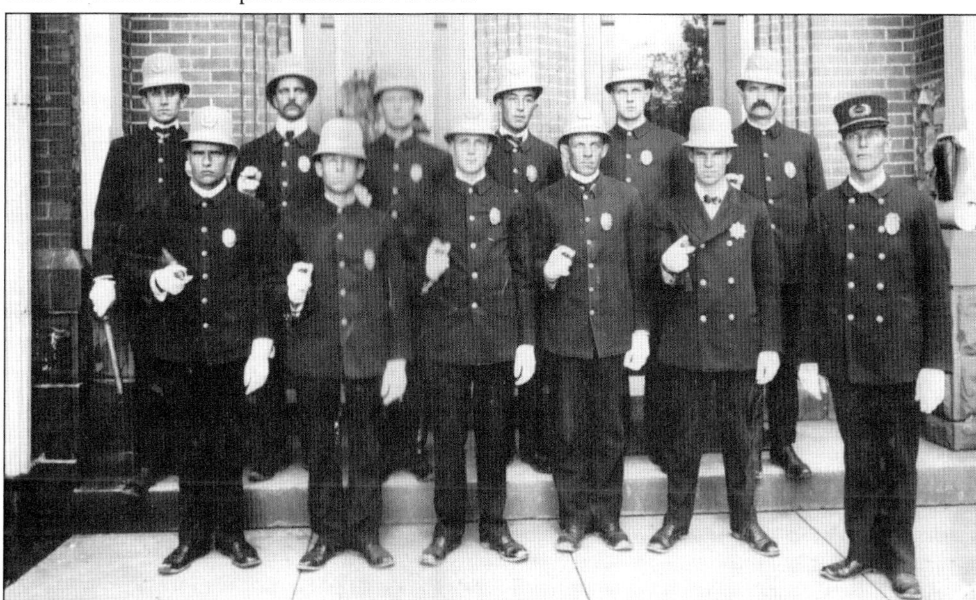

CITY POLICE DEPARTMENT. The original city charter broke Adrian into four wards, each with its own constable appointed by the mayor. With the growth of the city, there were six wards by 1900 with one police chief, three deputy sheriffs, four constables, four officers, and six night watchmen. Men on the force were paid $1.65 per day with no time off. Included here is a photograph of the force in 1903.

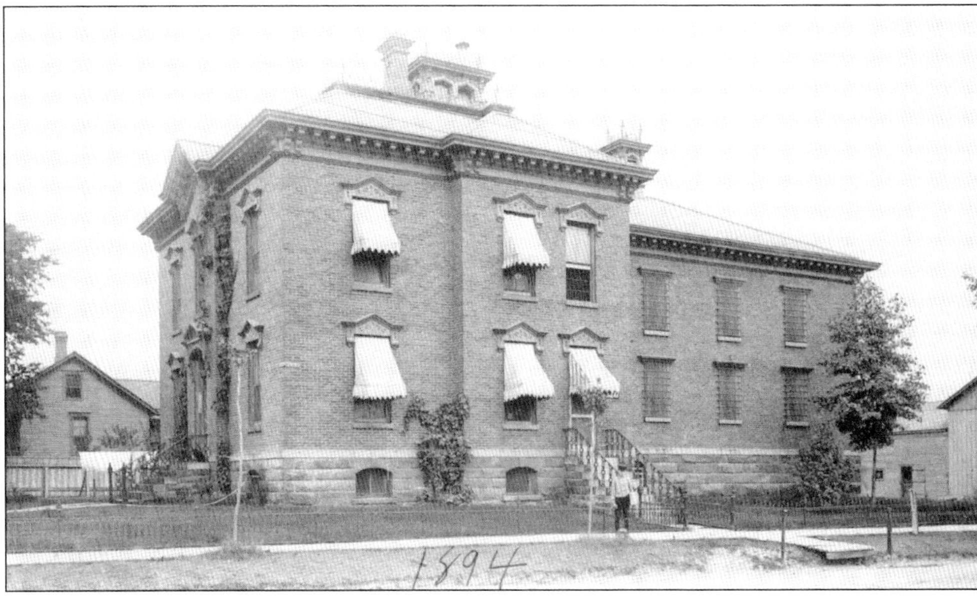

LENAWEE COUNTY JAIL. A county jail existed in Adrian since the time of the first courthouse in 1836. A new jail, unfortunately, was necessary when the old jail fell into disarray. James Donough oversaw the construction of the new building, completed in 1877 at a cost of just under $20,000. It had 12 stone cells with a bathroom on each floor. Women were confined in cells located in the sheriff's residence instead of in the jail.

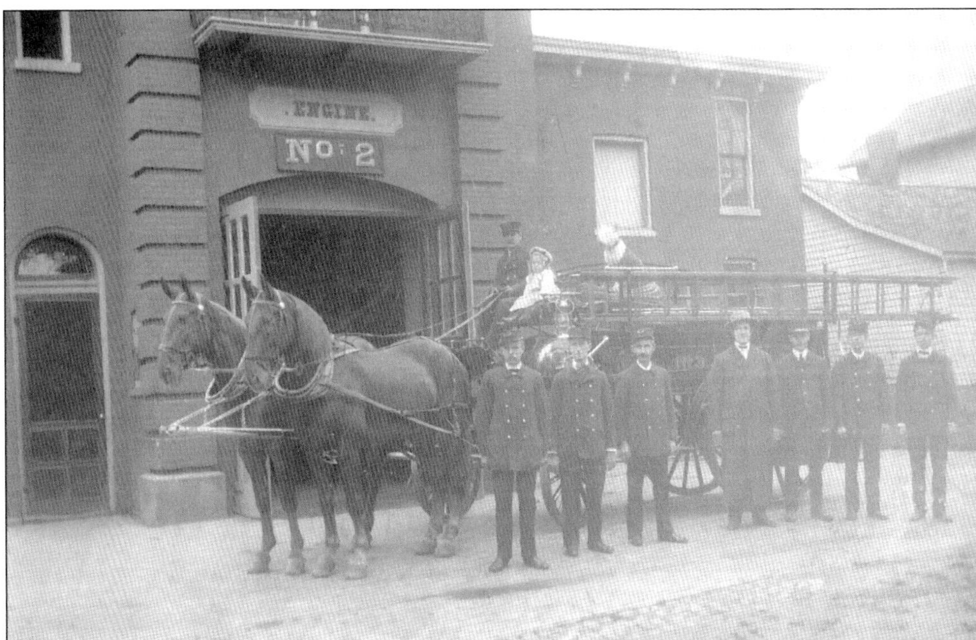

ADRIAN FIRE DEPARTMENT. By 1841, the city council decided to create a centralized fire department. Adrian was ahead of its time, as this was not typical until the late 19th century; many US cities relied on private firefighting companies instead. Carlisle Norwood served as the first chief engineer. Adrian also utilized horse-drawn steam pumpers in the 1870s, one of the few cities to utilize such technology outside of Detroit.

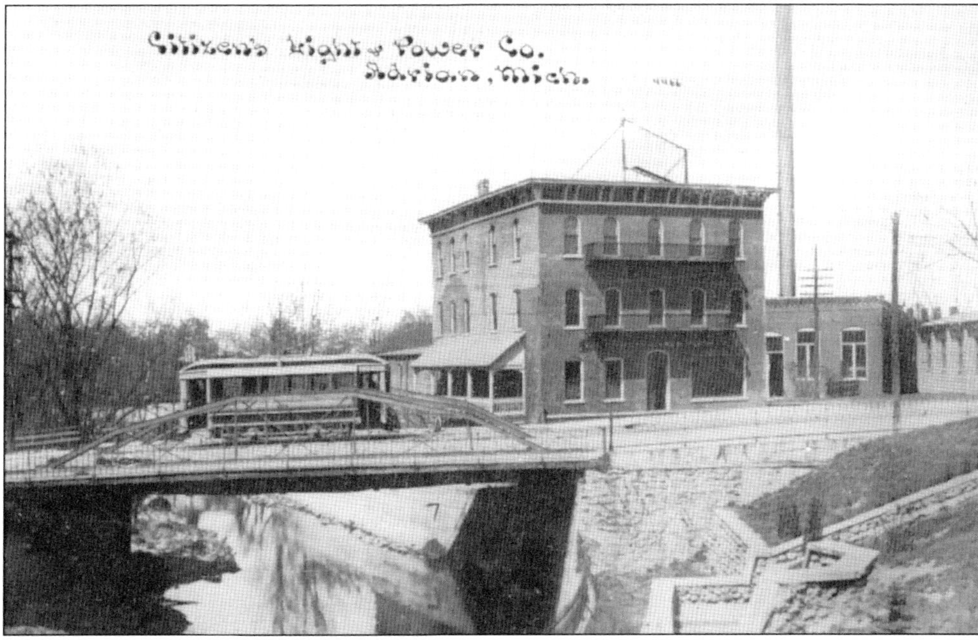

CITIZENS LIGHT AND POWER COMPANY. Founded in 1856, originally the illumination this company provided was by gaslight. By 1903, the company branched out to generate electricity for southeastern Michigan with a coal-fired plant along the Raisin River, and Harry Fee served as the president. In the 1920s, the company was purchased by the New York company seen below, Doherty Gas & Light. With the stock market crash and the resulting Great Depression, this business was not able to survive intact. Detroit Edison and Consumers Power bought out the electric properties, and the gas properties were purchased by R.A. Burger to form Citizens Gas Fuel Company.

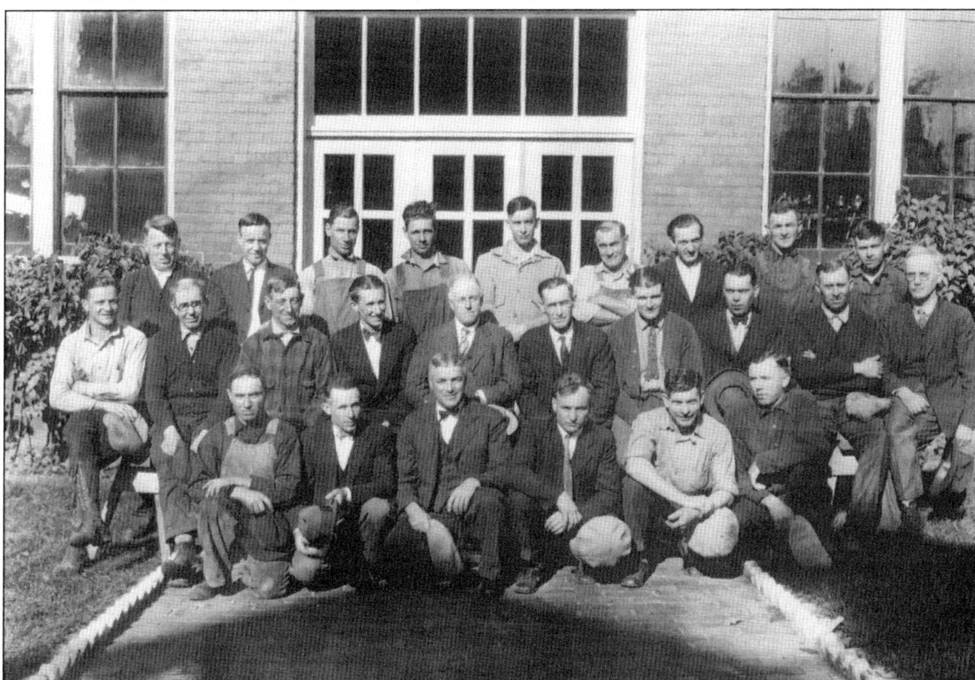

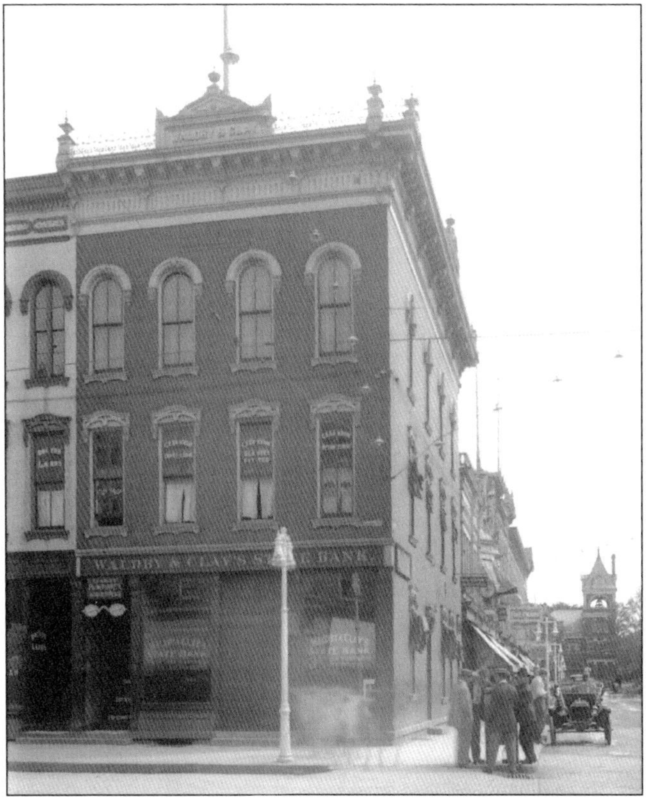

Waldby & Clay Bank. The first banks date from the 1830s in Lenawee County, but they failed due to unsound business practices and, in some instances, outright fraud. It was not until 1850 that bankers had recovered their reputations sufficiently to attempt to start another bank, which was opened by William Waldby and Ira Bidwell. In 1878, E.I. Waldby and Frank Clay purchased this bank located on Maumee and Main Streets and renamed it after themselves. By 1908, the bank had $800,000 in resources.

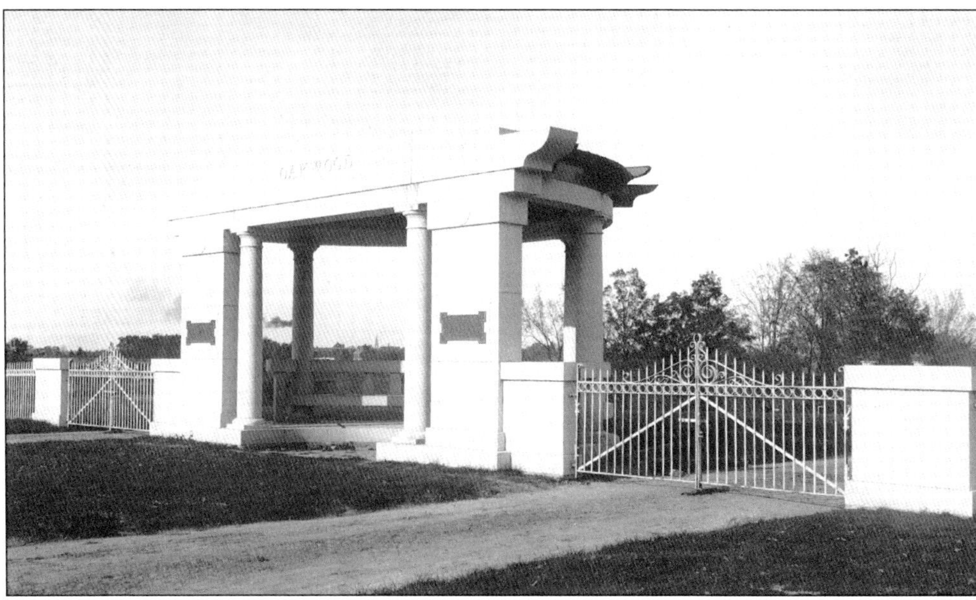

Oakwood Cemetery. This burial ground on the outskirts of town is an excellent example of the US garden cemetery movement, with its park-like landscaping and classical memorial statuary. Many prominent citizens have been interred here since it was initiated in 1848. The cemetery archway shown here was dedicated to the memory of businessman William Wilcox in 1897 by his widow, Josephine.

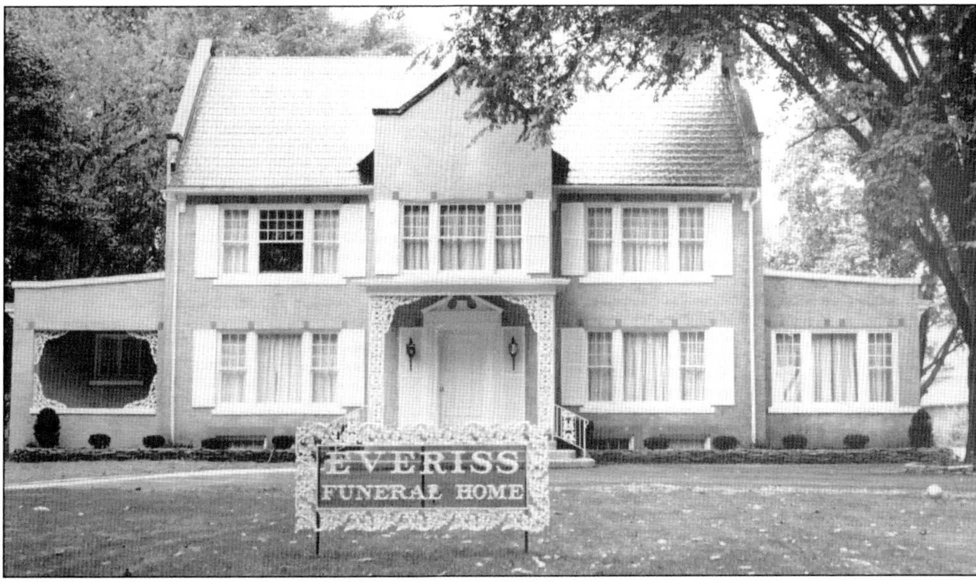

J.E. Everiss & Sons. In 1854, Joseph Everiss immigrated to Adrian from England after a brief interlude in New York. A trained cabinet maker, in 1867 he opened the first funerary business in the county, offering embalming, hearses, burial, or if one was lucky, only ambulance service. After the Civil War, there was a shift in the United States to the use of professional undertakers to care for the dead, especially after great improvements in embalming techniques.

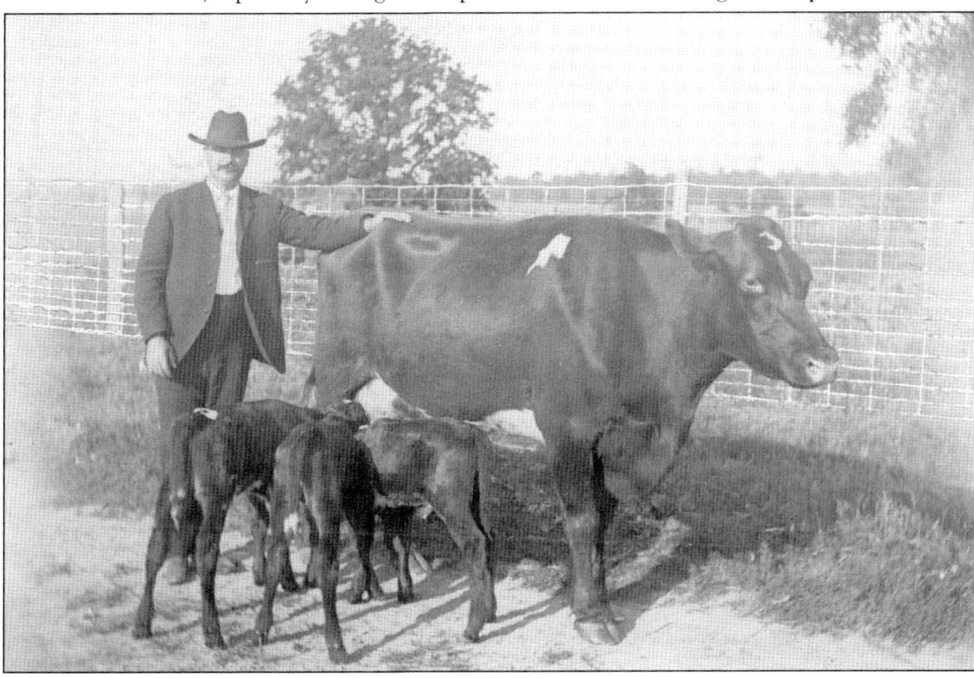

Dairy. By the 1850s, cows had replaced sheep as the preferred livestock in the county. Dairy cows were especially popular, increasing approximately 50 percent by the turn of the century. Because of the abundant supply of milk, Lenawee County became one of the top counties in the state for both butter and cheese production. Later, other dairy products would be manufactured in Adrian, like ice cream and evaporated milk.

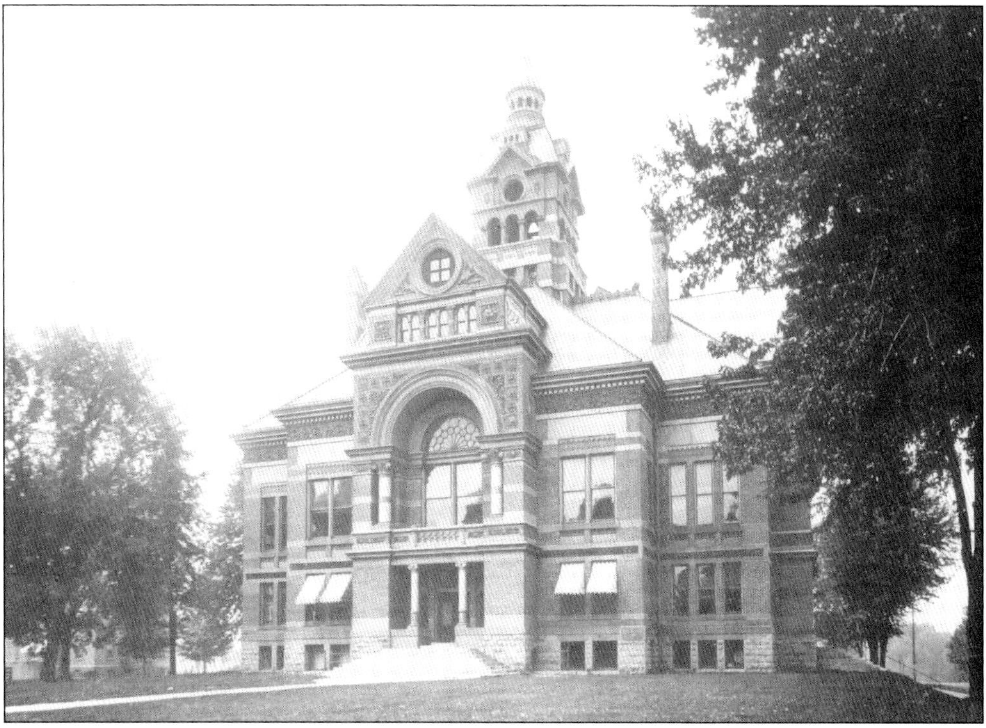

Lenawee County Courthouse. The first county courthouse had been located in Tecumseh, but this changed when the county seat moved to Adrian in 1837. Erected at the former location of the Erie and Kalamazoo Railroad terminal, this 1885 Romanesque-style building replaced the original courthouse in Adrian that burned down in 1852. Several terra-cotta figures adorn the building, such as the historical figure Tecumseh and the goddess of agriculture Demeter. The beautiful building seen above still serves as the county courthouse today. Below is an early pool of jurors that seems to be racially integrated.

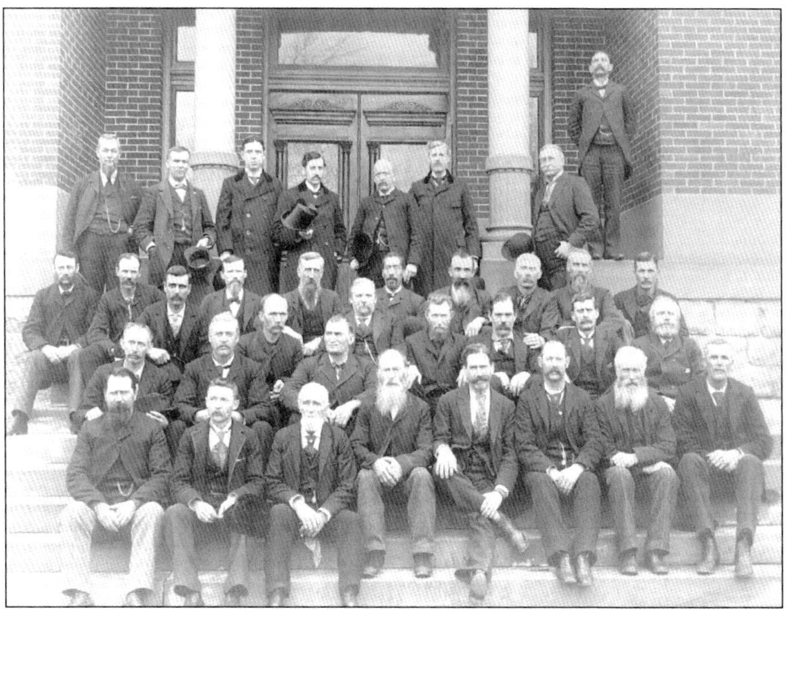

ADRIAN CITY HALL. Adrian's city hall building opened in 1885 and served the community until 1970, when it was replaced by a more modern structure. A statue of Laura Haviland stands at the front of the building. This was dedicated by the Women's Christian Temperance Union, and the statue also served as a water fountain, quite appropriate considering Haviland's stance regarding temperance.

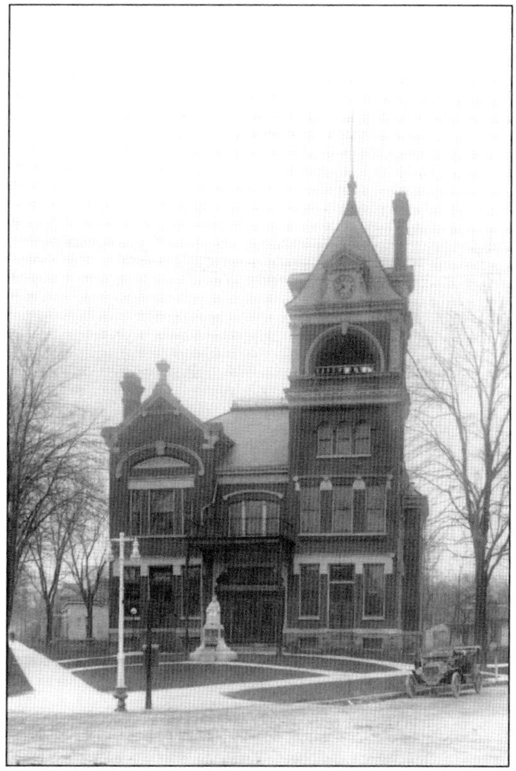

THE 4TH MICHIGAN INFANTRY. During the Civil War, the 4th Michigan Infantry was the only regiment organized and trained in Lenawee County. This regiment left the state in 1861 with 1,025 men to defend the Union. The 4th saw action in Pennsylvania, Maryland, and Virginia. The Grand Army of the Republic post in Adrian was named in the honor of Col. Dwight Woodbury, the commander of the 4th. Here is a rare photograph of the boys in blue marching through Adrian.

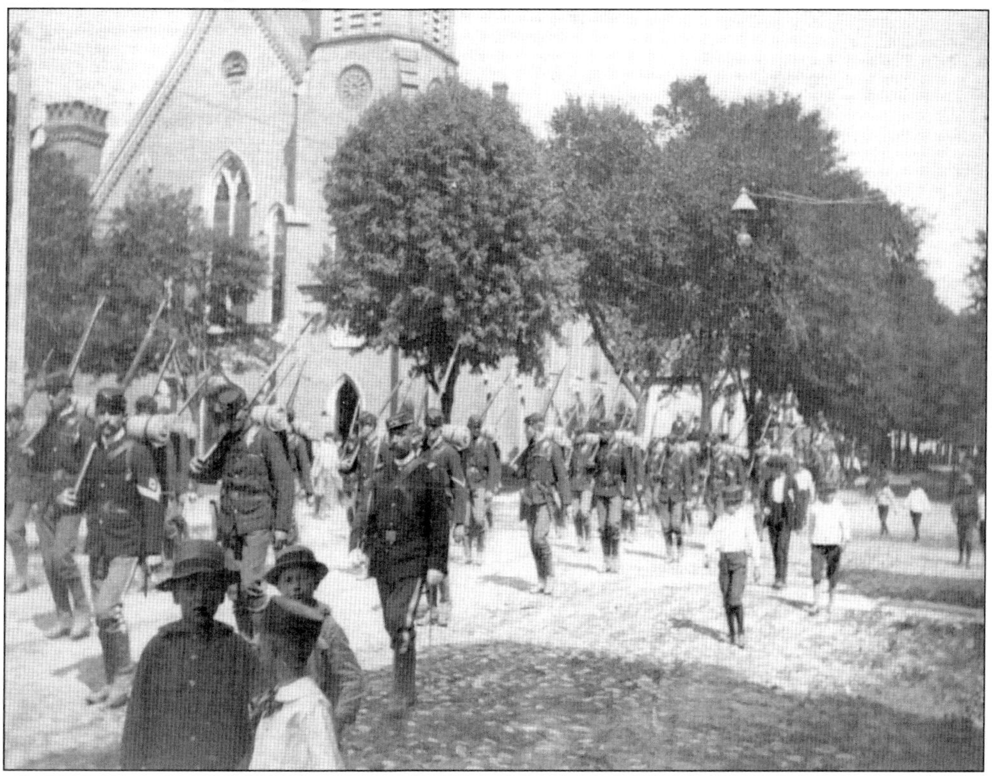

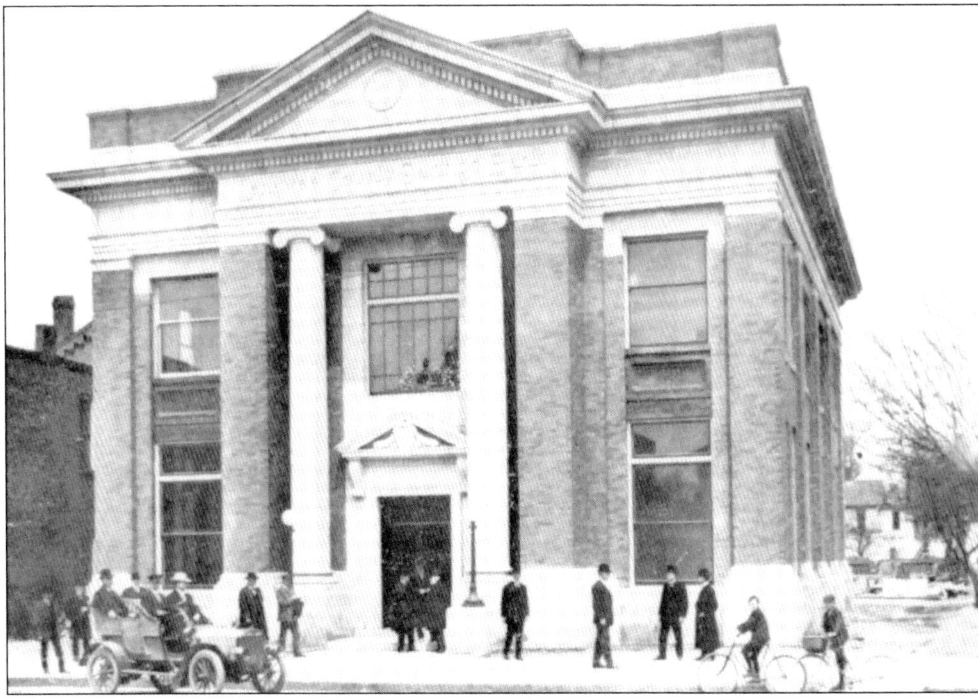

LENAWEE COUNTY SAVINGS BANK. With capital of $50,000, this bank opened to serve Adrian in 1870. By 1872, the bank relocated to the corner of West Maumee and Winter Streets and stayed in this location for approximately 34 years. This image is of the new bank they built in 1906, located on East Maumee Street. The architecture, with its symmetry and columns, hearkens back to the beginnings of Adrian and its love of the Greek Revival style.

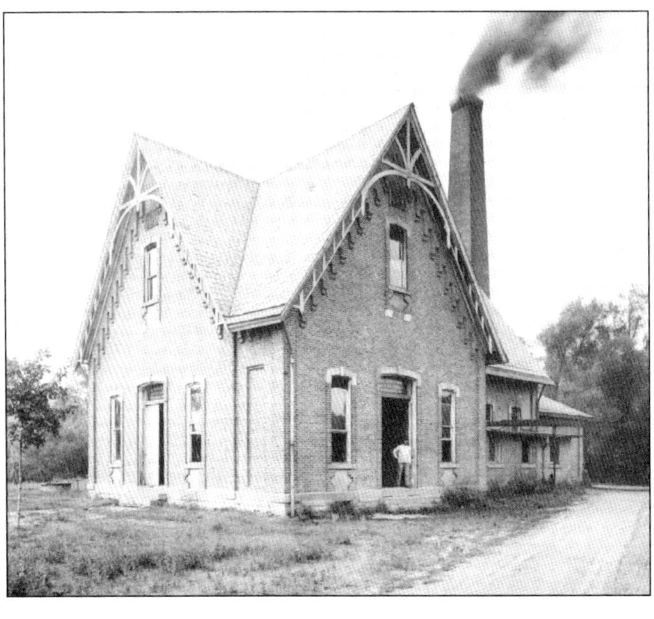

ADRIAN WATERWORKS. In 1883, the Adrian Council passed a proposal to put into place the infrastructure for a municipal water system. Solon Wiley received the contract to organize Adrian Waterworks but soon entered into conflict with the city, especially regarding rates and failure to deliver services. The City of Adrian brought a suit against the waterworks that was eventually heard by the Michigan Supreme Court in 1887. In 1888, a New York company purchased the foreclosed waterworks, which had a debt of $145,000.

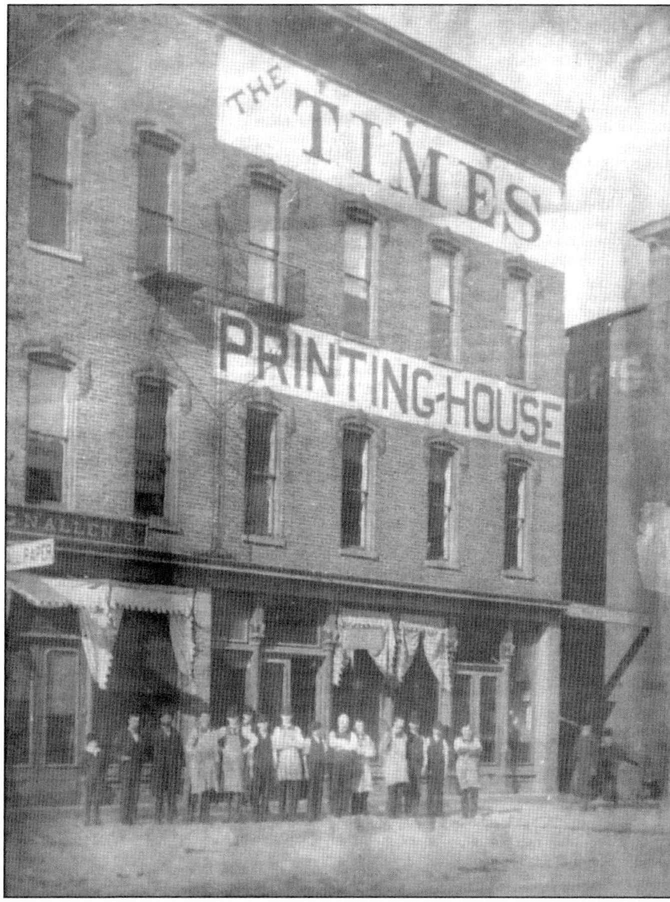

ADRIAN GAZETTE. The first weekly newspaper in Adrian went to press in 1834, initially called the *Adrian Gazette*, and it was a staunchly Democratic publication. In 1865, William Humphrey bought it, renamed it the *Adrian Daily and Weekly Times*, and switched the party affiliation to Republican. This paper existed until the early 20th century, when it was purchased by the *Daily Telegram*. In 1907, Stuart Perry was the owner of the *Telegram*, and his experience was vital to the increase in readership throughout Lenawee County. At right is an exterior shot of the Times Building, and below is a picture of the presses at the *Telegram*.

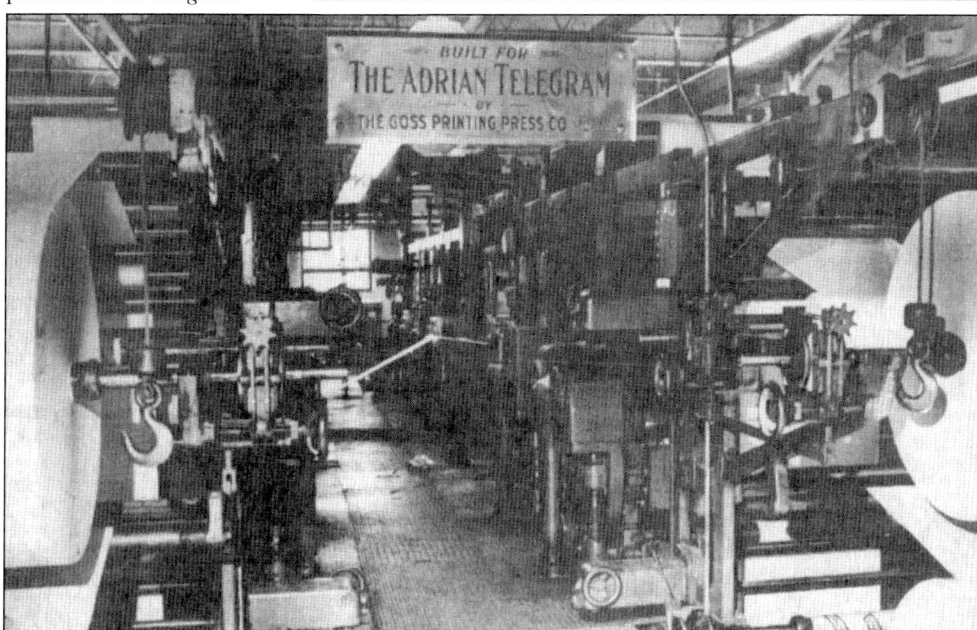

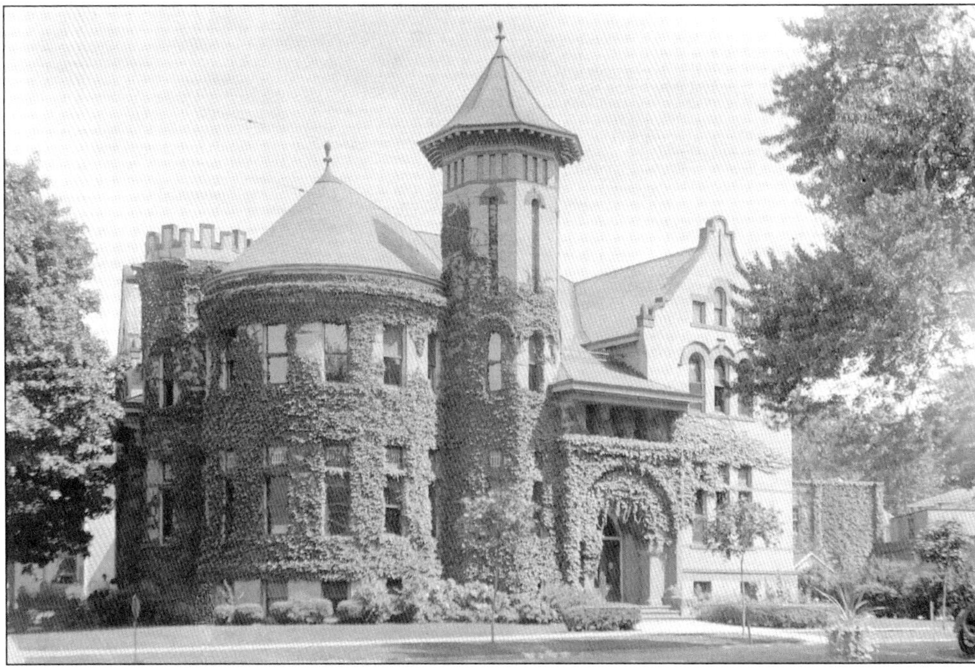

ADRIAN CARNEGIE LIBRARY. Industrialist Andrew Carnegie used some of his wealth philanthropically, and as a result in 1904 Adrian received a Carnegie grant for $20,000 to build a library. The library, which is a mix of Romanesque, Mission, and Spanish Colonial styles, opened in 1909. The city sold the building for $10 in 1978 to the Lenawee County Historical Society for its collections and archives, and it reopened in 1980 after renovation.

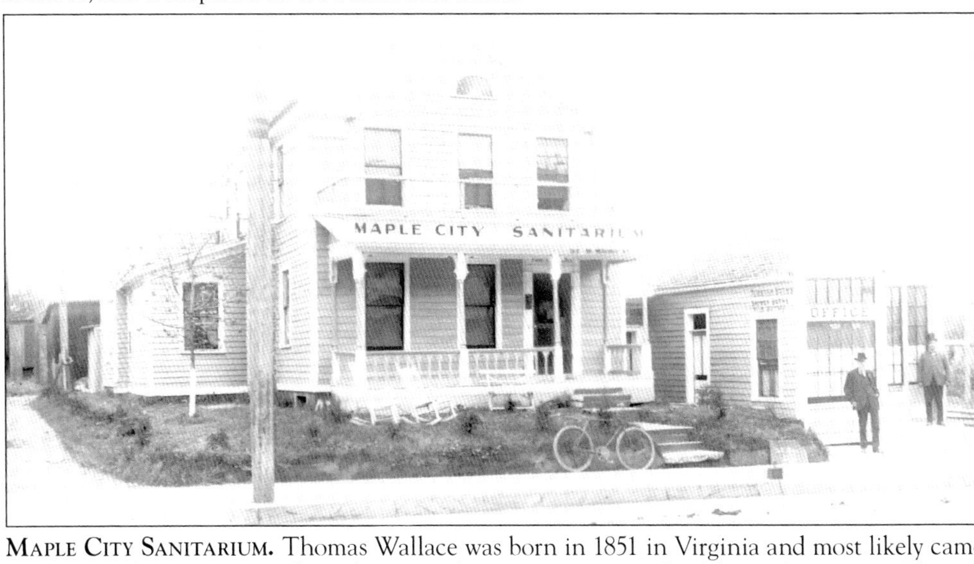

MAPLE CITY SANITARIUM. Thomas Wallace was born in 1851 in Virginia and most likely came north to Michigan in 1877, where there were better opportunities for African Americans. Thomas Wallace had no formal education, but he discovered a talent for healing and opened a successful practice on West Maumee Street in 1898, taking the title of professor. He called his science "myopathy" and specialized in treating neuromuscular disorders like rheumatism, crooked limbs, and paralysis. In 1911, he also opened a restaurant at the sanitarium to provide healthful, healing fare to the city.

ADRIAN CITY ELECTRIC BELT RAILWAY COMPANY. During the 1870s, M.E. Chittenden sold wholesale tobacco and oil, but in 1888 he decided to shift into the business of mass transportation. He opened shop at 25 South Main Street to construct and operate an interurban electric streetcar line. Approximately eight miles of line were laid, and overhead wires were placed to provide electricity to his four streetcars. The streetcars were a welcome attempt to provide cleaner and cheaper transportation than horse-drawn vehicles.

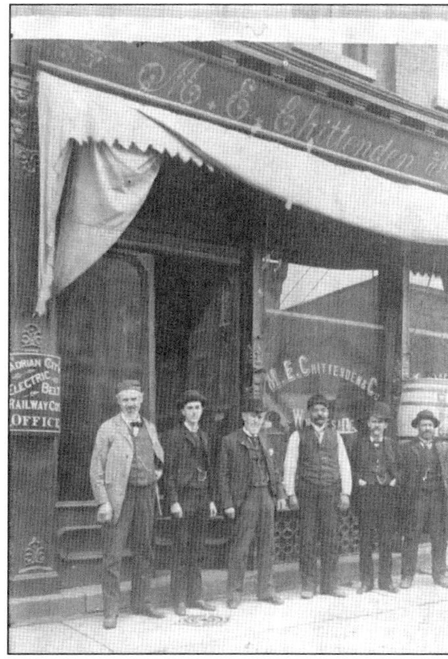

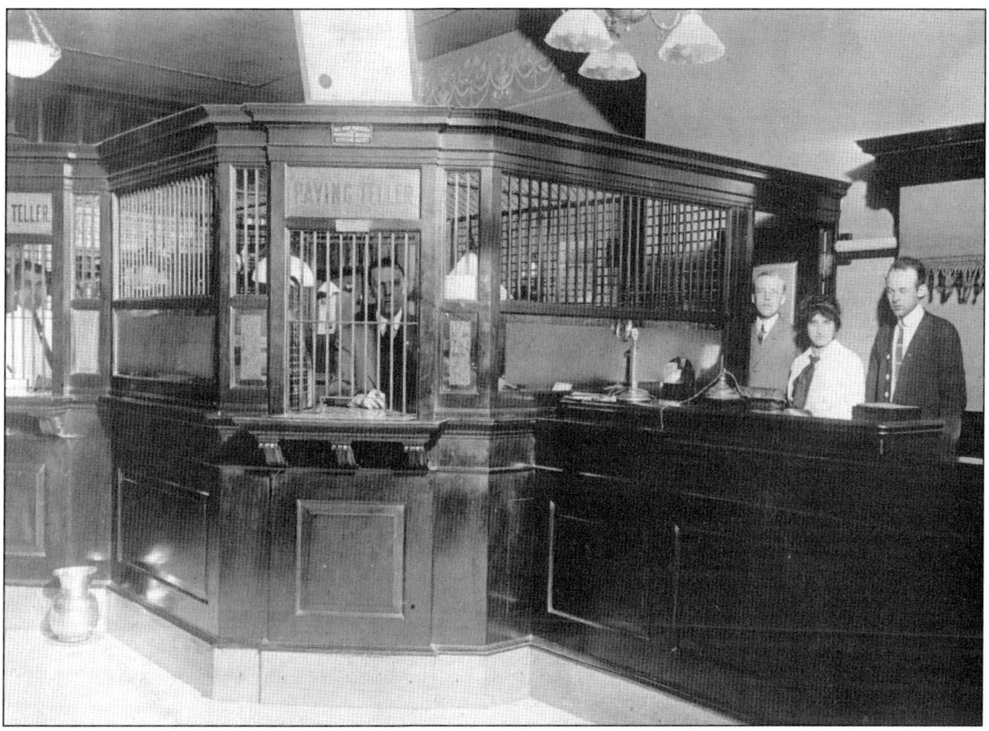

COMMERCIAL SAVINGS BANK. In 1888, a bank begun by Berry & Stone in 1849 became reorganized under new management to provide financial services to both individual and commercial accounts. The Commercial Savings Bank continued to expand and relocated to South Main Street in 1894. Assets were valued at $1.7 million by the 1920s, and the bank was able to weather the Great Depression. It was the first bank in Adrian granted permission to reopen after the bank holiday of 1933 and continued to prosper over the next 50 years.

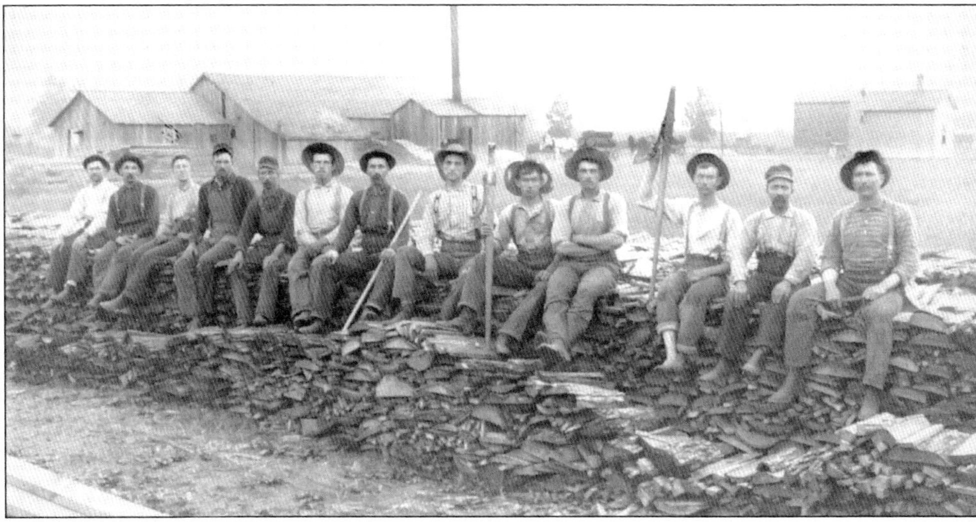

THE 31ST MICHIGAN INFANTRY, COMPANY B. Upon President McKinley's plea for enlistees in the Spanish American War of 1898, four regiments of Michiganders responded to the call. All were mustered at Island Lake before deployment. The 31st Regiment volunteers served as a security detail in Santa Clara province in Cuba. The 20 casualties suffered by the outfit were due to disease, as was characteristic from this so-called "splendid, little war."

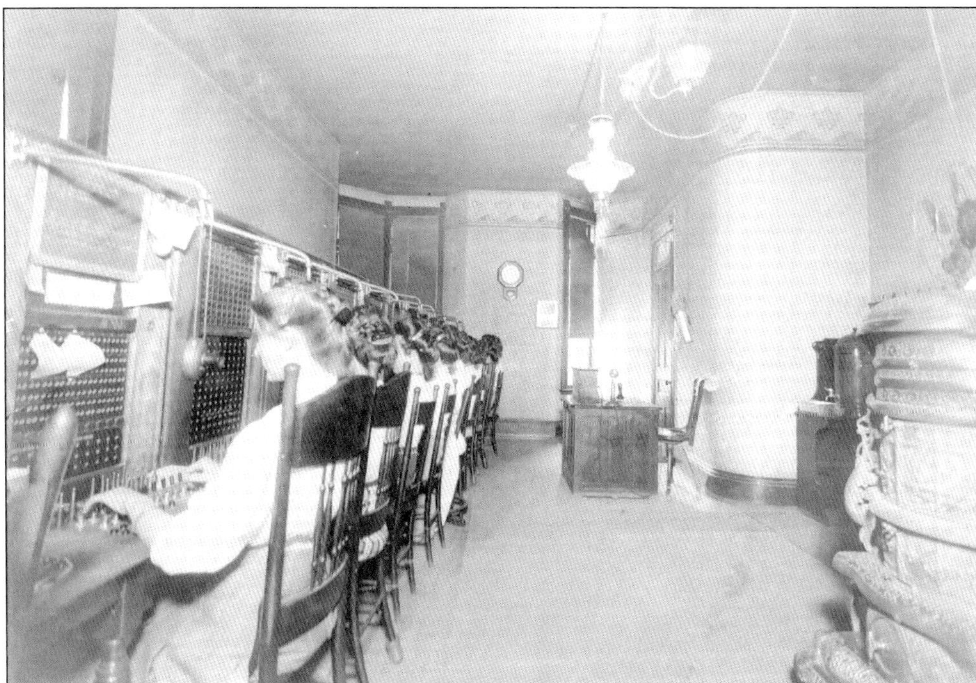

LENAWEE COUNTY TELEPHONE COMPANY. The oldest telephone exchange, the Adrian Telephone Company, dated back to 1896 and by 1910 merged with the Michigan State Telephone Company and the Lenawee County Telephone Company into one entity. There were over 350 miles of telephone lines in the county, and 2,664 phones existed in Adrian by 1922, which was higher than average for the state. Women were the preferred telephone operators at this time because the companies believed they had better voices, patience, and would work for less than men.

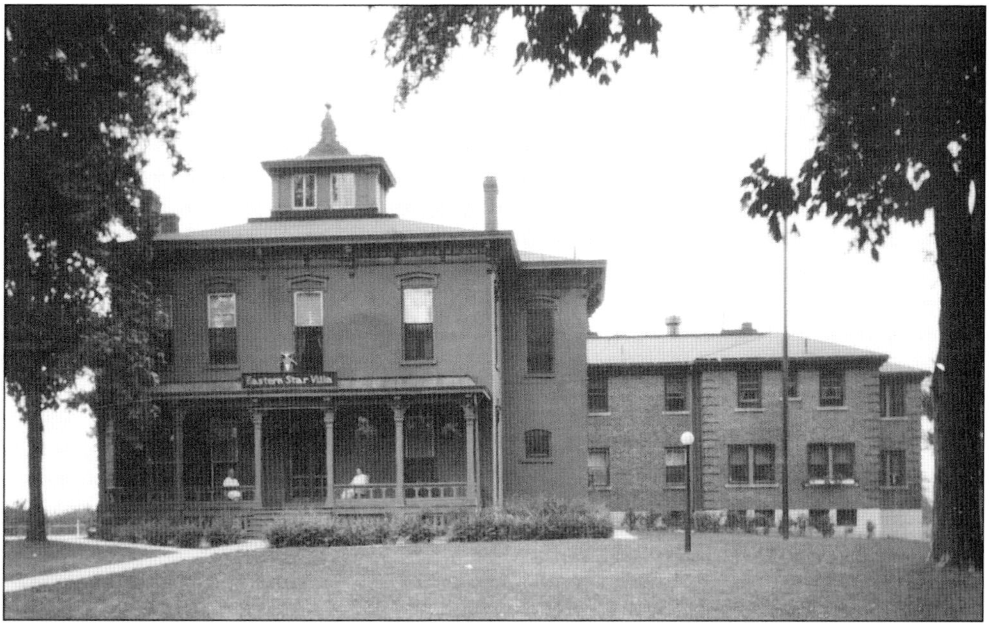

EASTERN STAR ORPHANAGE OF MICHIGAN. As a fraternal organization, the Order of the Eastern Star was also involved in charity work. For example, the order sponsored homes for the aged, widows, and orphanages nationwide. In 1919, the Order of the Eastern Star purchased the old Wilcox home in Adrian for $2,634.59 to serve as an orphanage, the Eastern Star Villa. This orphanage was selective in that only orphaned children whose parents had been either members of Eastern Star or Masonic lodges were housed here. Above is the villa, and below are some orphans with their matron.

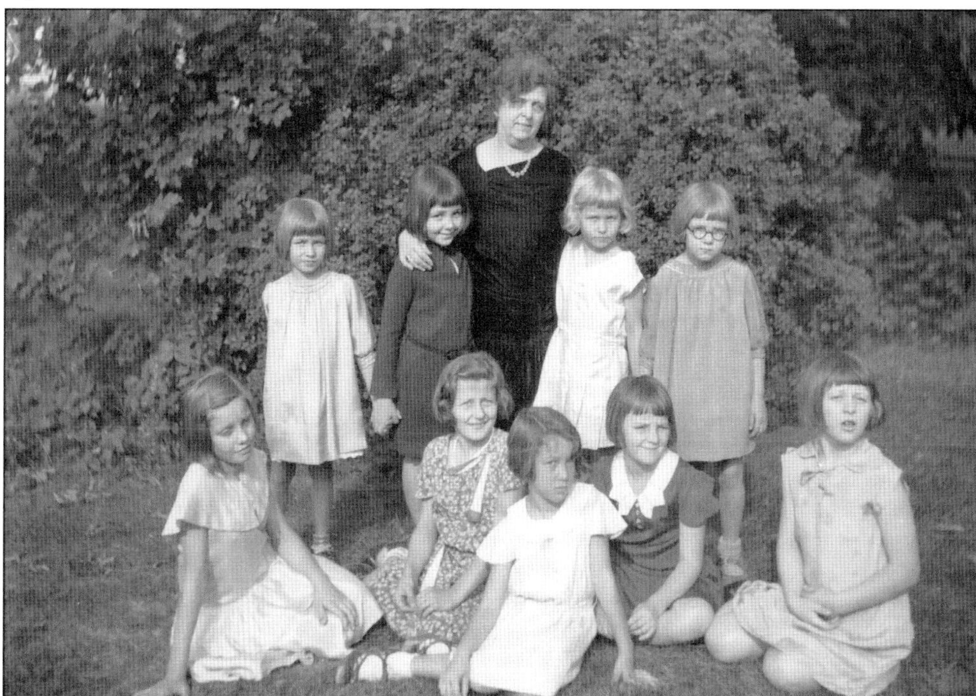

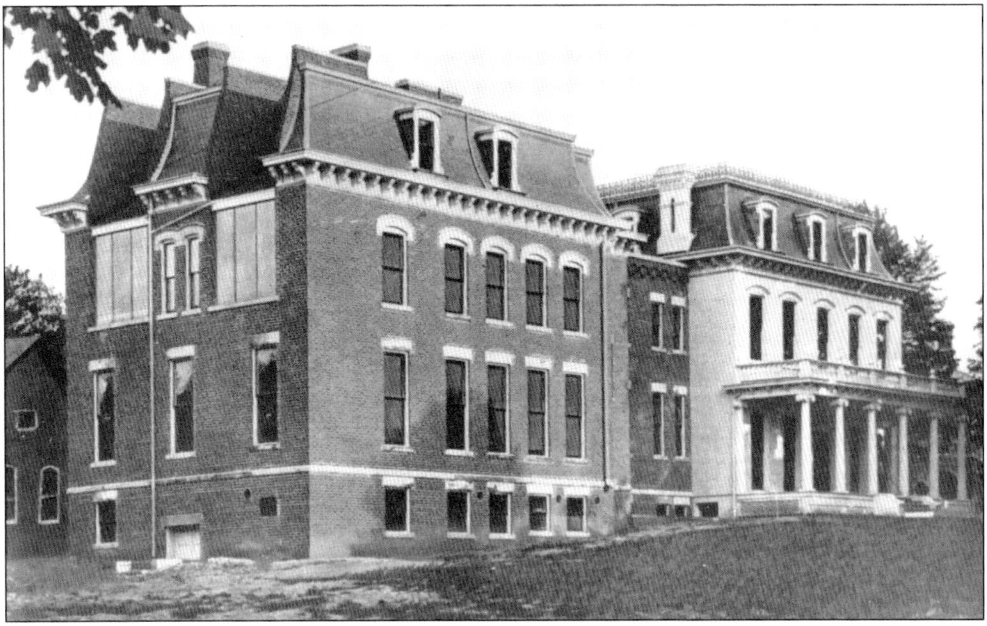

Emma L. Bixby Hospital. Emma Keeney was a teacher who married attorney Alonzo Bixby of Adrian. After her death, her son William Bixby donated funds in his mother's name to establish a hospital after his son died due to a lack of medical care in Adrian. This hospital opened in 1911 at East Maumee Street and North Locust Street. Though it moved locations in 1957, the Bixby Medical Center still serves the community with an 88-bed acute care facility.

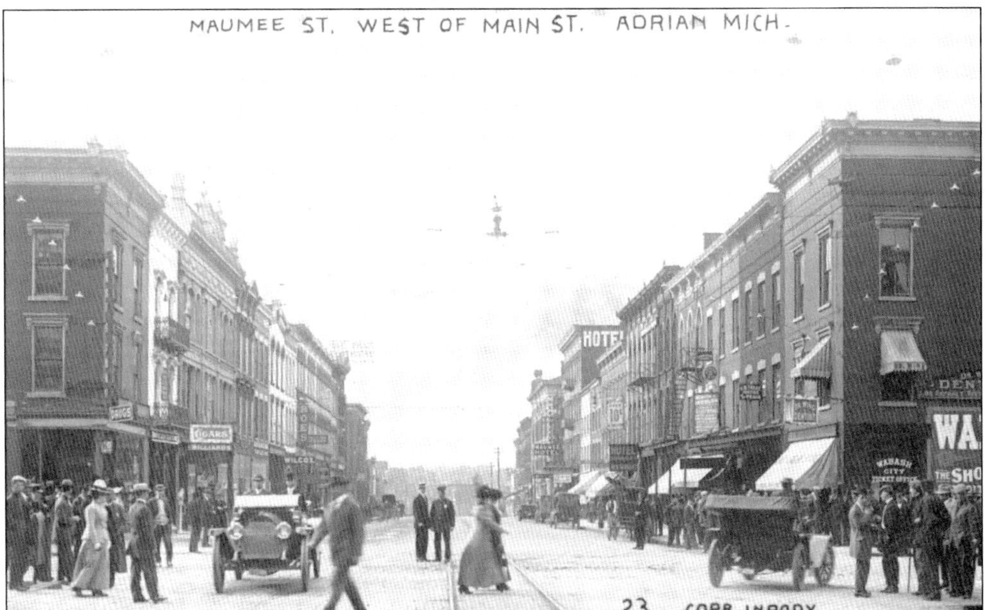

Main Street. This view of downtown dates from 1916. Hoag and Smith Real Estate is located on the right and King's Jewelry store on the left. At this time, the population began to slowly decline in Lenawee County from the apex of 48,000 people reached in 1880. A police officer is being used to direct traffic, as the first practical (first four-way, three-color) traffic light was not invented until 1920 in Detroit.

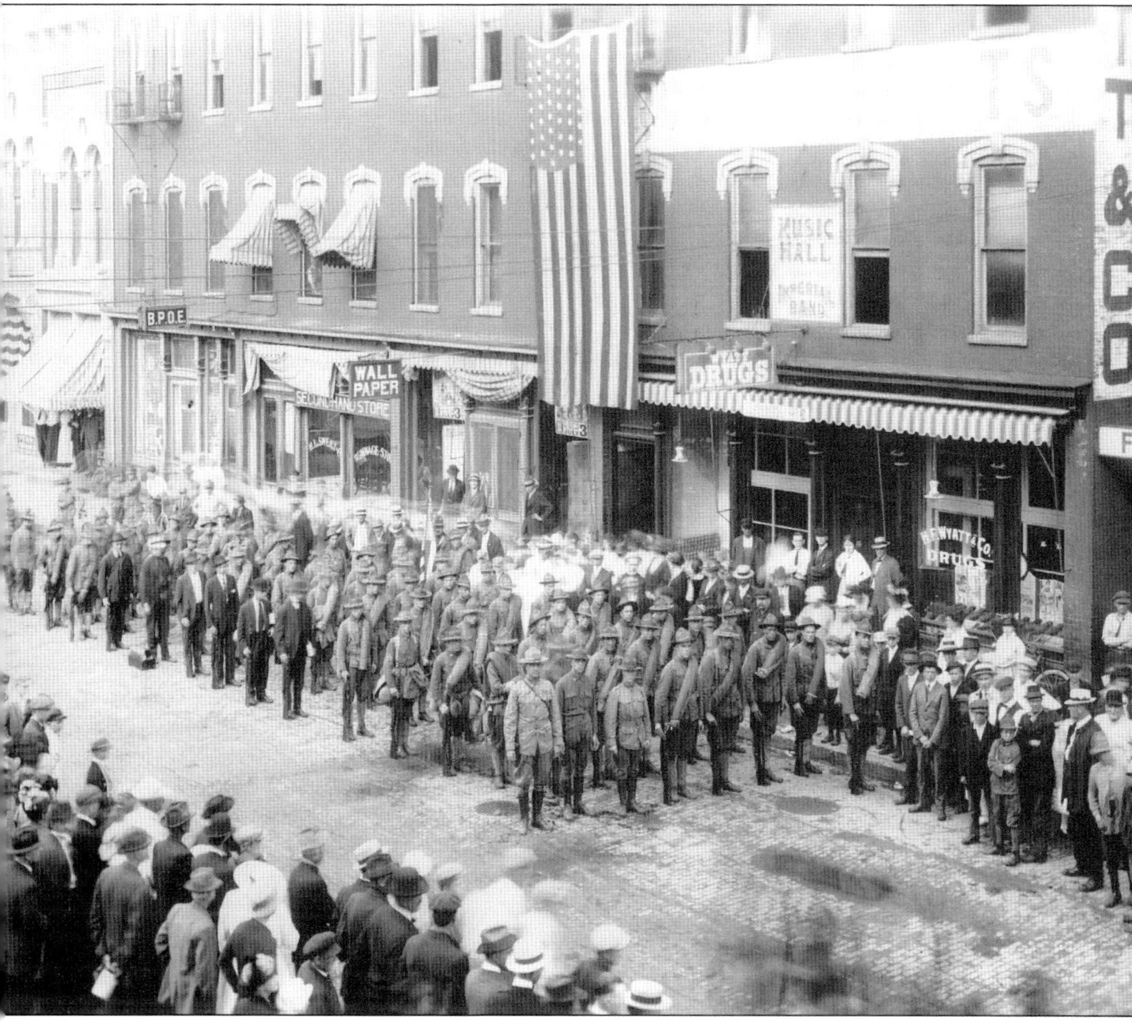

Punitive Expedition of 1916. Angered by President Wilson's support for Venustiano Carranza, Pancho Villa and his men made raids into New Mexico and Texas in 1916. US troops and national guardsmen, including these men from Adrian, were sent to the border to restore order and capture Villa. Capt. John Pershing and his men spent nine months in pursuit without any success. The mission was cancelled with the advent of World War I.

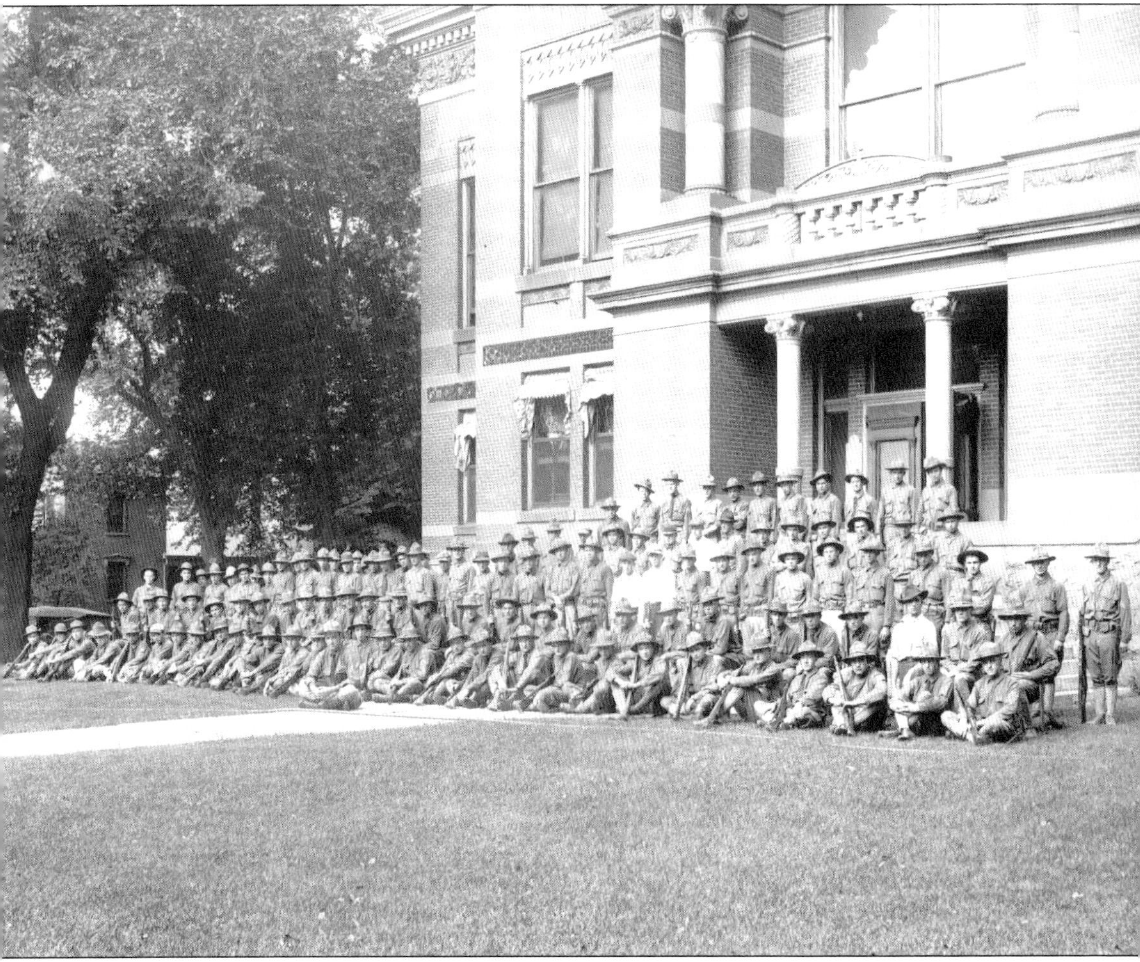

World War I. Although the United States attempted desperately to stay out of this conflict, on April 6, 1917, war was declared upon the axis powers. Of those who served the US cause, 175,000 were Michiganders, and they made up significant numbers in units such as the 32nd Infantry Division, 63rd Infantry Brigade, 119th Field Artillery, and 107th Field Signal Battalion. Twenty-one service people from Adrian died in this war.

Two

BUSINESS

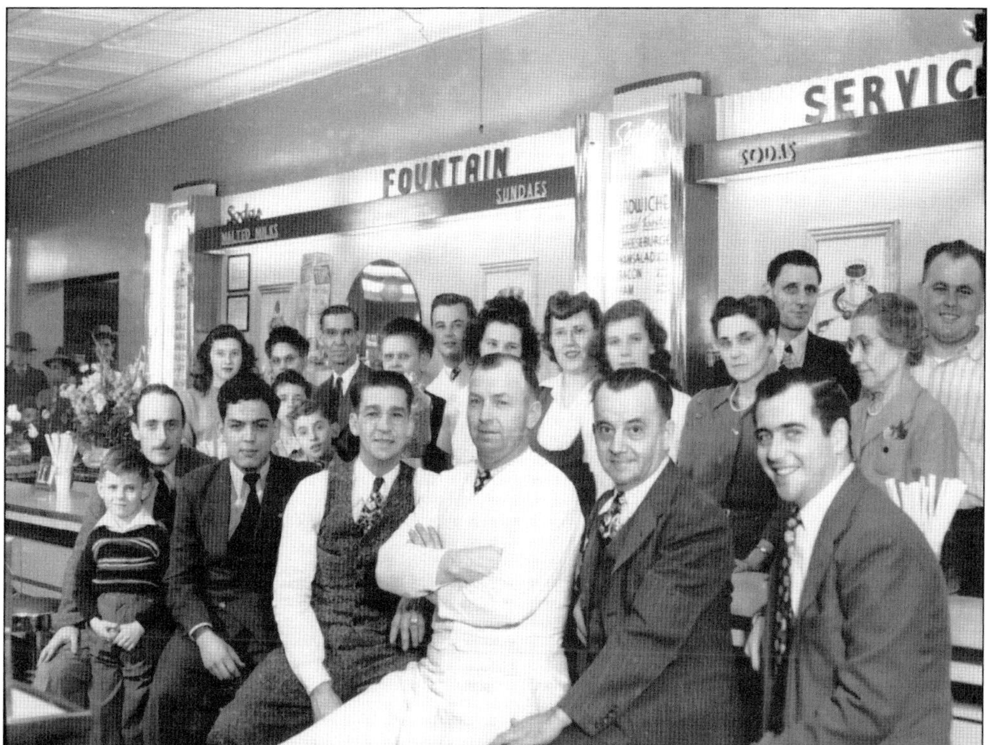

SEALTEST SODA FOUNTAIN. One way that Sealtest Dairy products reached the consumer was through its franchised soda fountains across the Northeast and Midwest. Often these soda fountains were located in drugstores and served such treats as milk shakes, egg creams, malts, sundaes, and sodas. By the mid-20th century, such establishments were also lunch counters, cooking up traditional American fare like a cheeseburger with French fries.

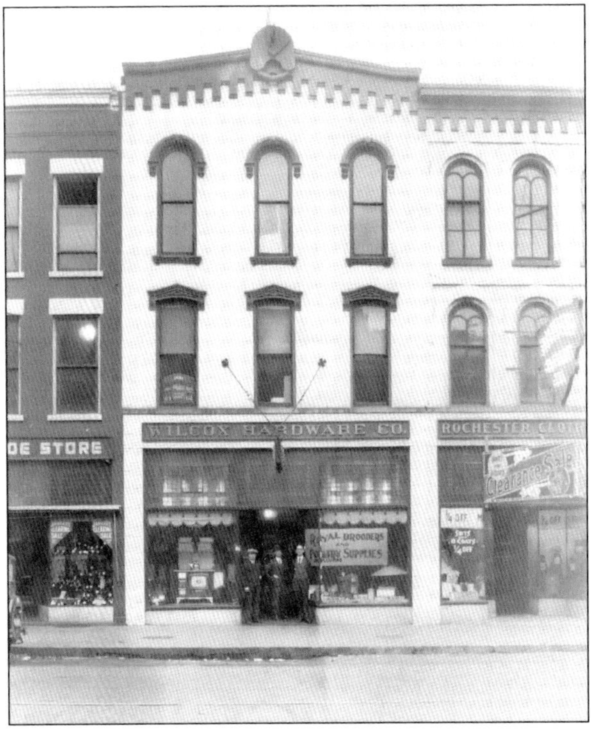

Wilcox Hardware. In 1855, William Wilcox shifted from the dry goods business to selling hardware on West Maumee Street and would begin one of the longest lasting and most successful companies in Adrian. This well-stocked store carried tools, farm implements, tinwork, plumbing supplies, and heating supplies. He had various partners over the years, with his son George joining him in the business in 1865. At left and below are two images of this company that continued to operate at the same location through the 1940s.

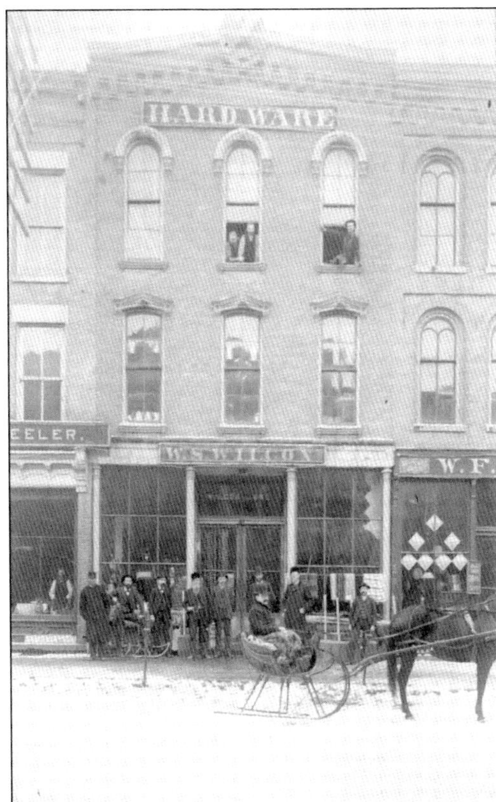

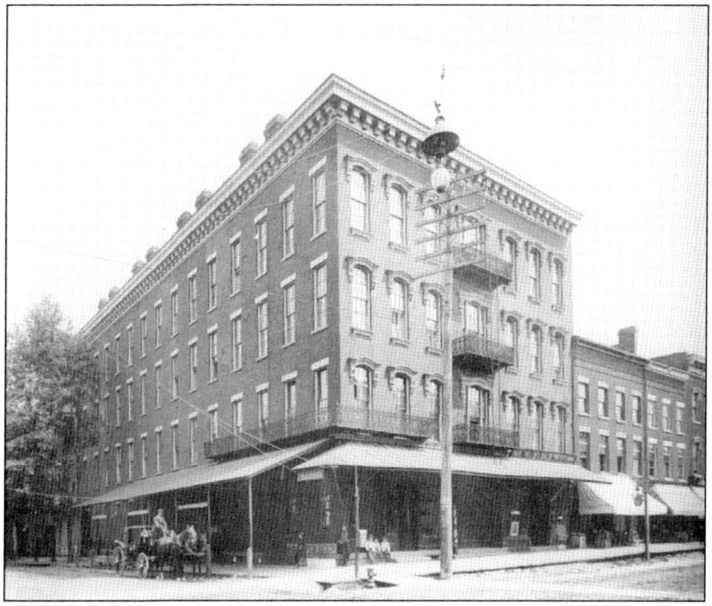

W.F. King Store. William King emigrated from Scotland after he had learned the watch-making trade. He arrived in Adrian and found employment in the Newell jewelry store; he became a junior partner in 1861. He left this employment to open up his own shop in 1863 with James Thomson on South Main Street. They carried gold and silver watches, jewelry, clocks, silverware, and eyeglasses.

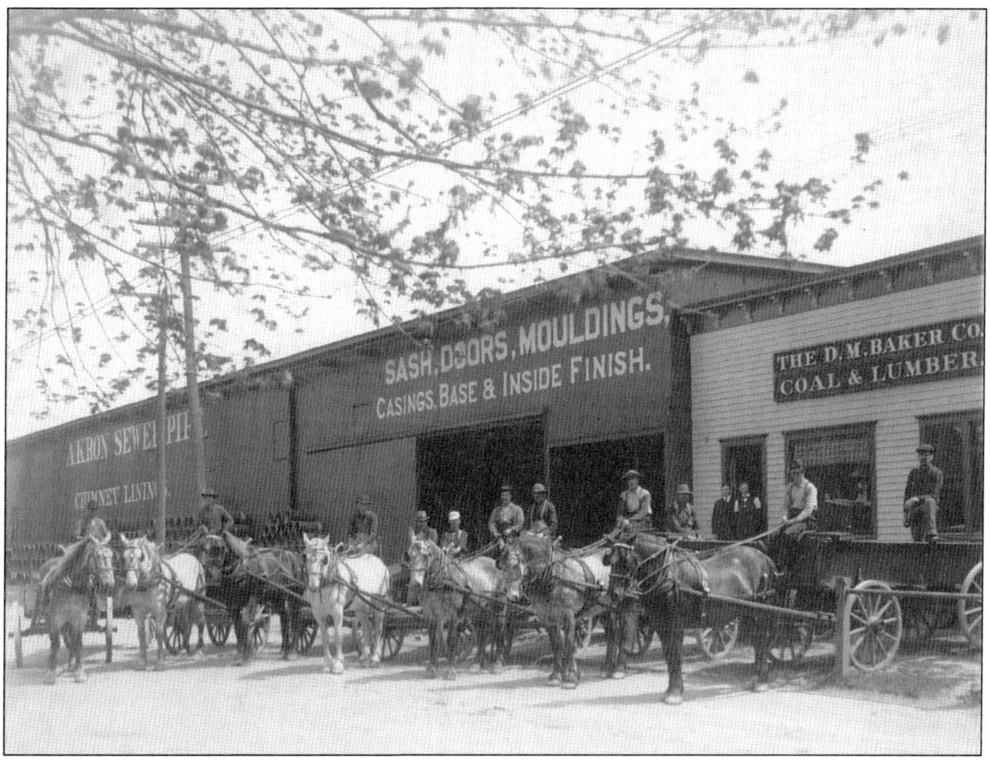

D.M. Baker Company. In 1872, Delos Baker bought out his partner to solely control this company, which sold both lumber and coal. His business was located on the corner of Michigan and Division Streets. He was also active in the Michigan & Indiana Retail Coal Association, delivering a paper at their 8th annual convention entitled, "Can the Sale of Coal by Manufacturers be Controlled?"

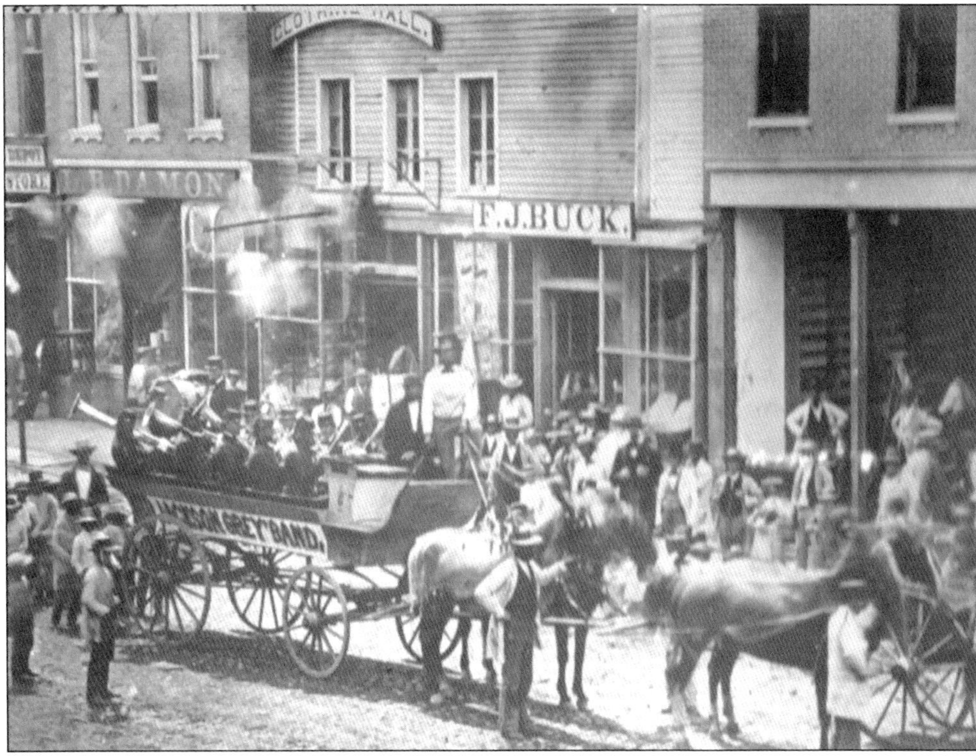

F.J. Buck & Company. Prior to starting his hot air furnace manufacturing company, Francis Buck owned and operated a general hardware store. He arrived in Adrian in 1838 with only 50¢ to his name, working at various jobs until he saved enough to open this hardware store around 1846. He operated this business with various partners until he sold to Smith and Jewell in 1873.

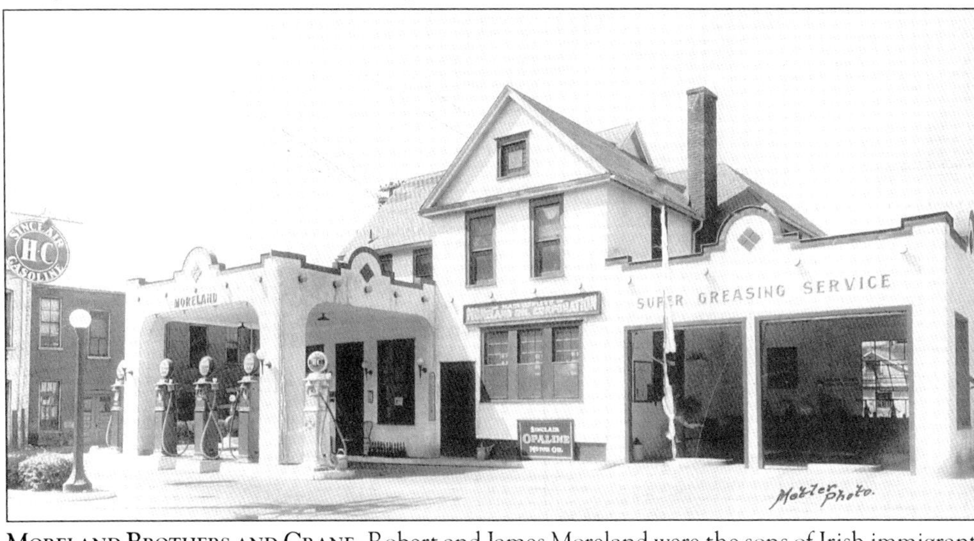

Moreland Brothers and Crane. Robert and James Moreland were the sons of Irish immigrants who had come to Adrian to make a better life. Around the year 1880, the two brothers formed a partnership with Eugene Crane as wholesale dealers of tobacco and oil. Their business grew to serve the tristate area and relocated from Main Street to Winter Street by 1916. This company promoted Diamond M Motor Oil as "life insurance for your automobile."

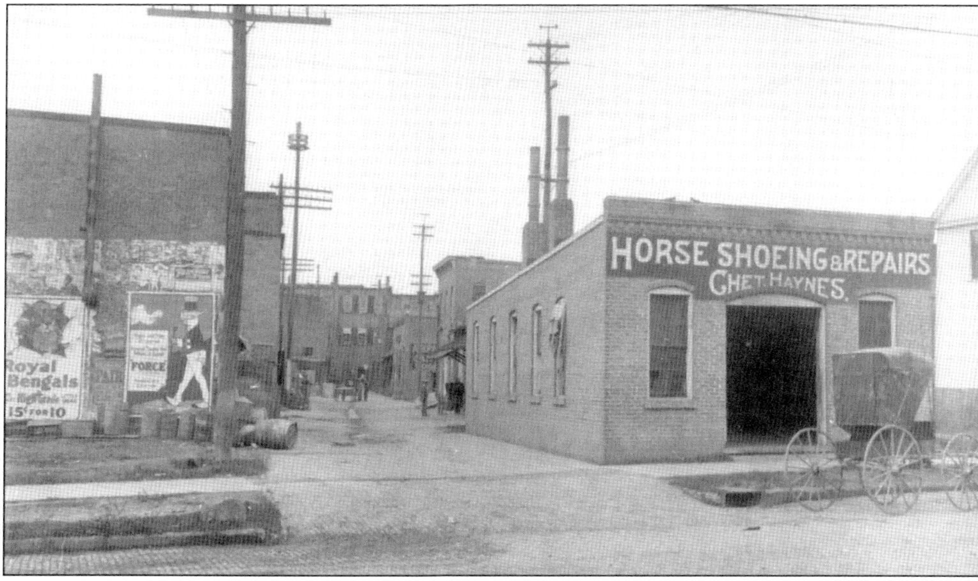

CARLTON & HAYNES. J.B. Carlton and C.A. Haynes opened a blacksmith shop together on Front Street by the 1890s. Blacksmithing was learned through an apprenticeship system to teach how to properly forge, weld, and finish iron and steel. With the growth of mass production, blacksmiths had less demand for their services. Many, such as this shop, began to supplement their income by shoeing horses.

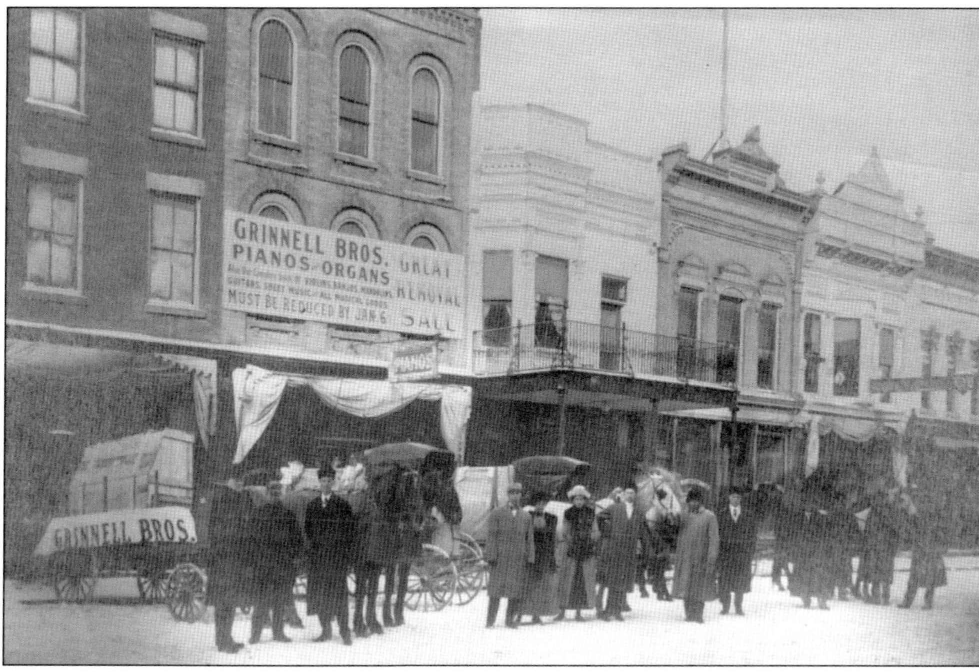

GRINNELL BROTHERS MUSIC HOUSE. Clayton and Ira Grinnell started their first business as salespeople for Singer sewing machines in Ann Arbor. They relocated to Detroit in 1882, still selling sewing machines but also some musical instruments as well. In 1886, they decide to only sell instruments, and in 1901 they began to manufacture their own line of pianos. By 1922, the Grinnell Brothers Music House had 20 branch stores throughout Michigan, including Adrian.

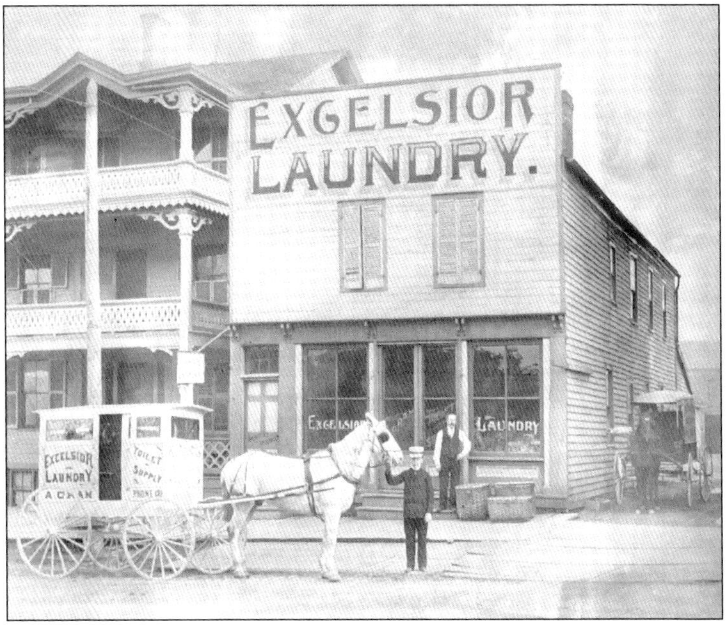

Excelsior Laundry. Arthur Oram began his career selling sewing machines before opening his steam laundry on West Maumee Street in the late 1890s. In the beginning, he also sold toilet supplies, which at that time would have included items such as bowls, traps, and powdered lime or lye. With the spread of indoor plumbing, the business focused only on laundry service. On average, 12 people were employed at Excelsior.

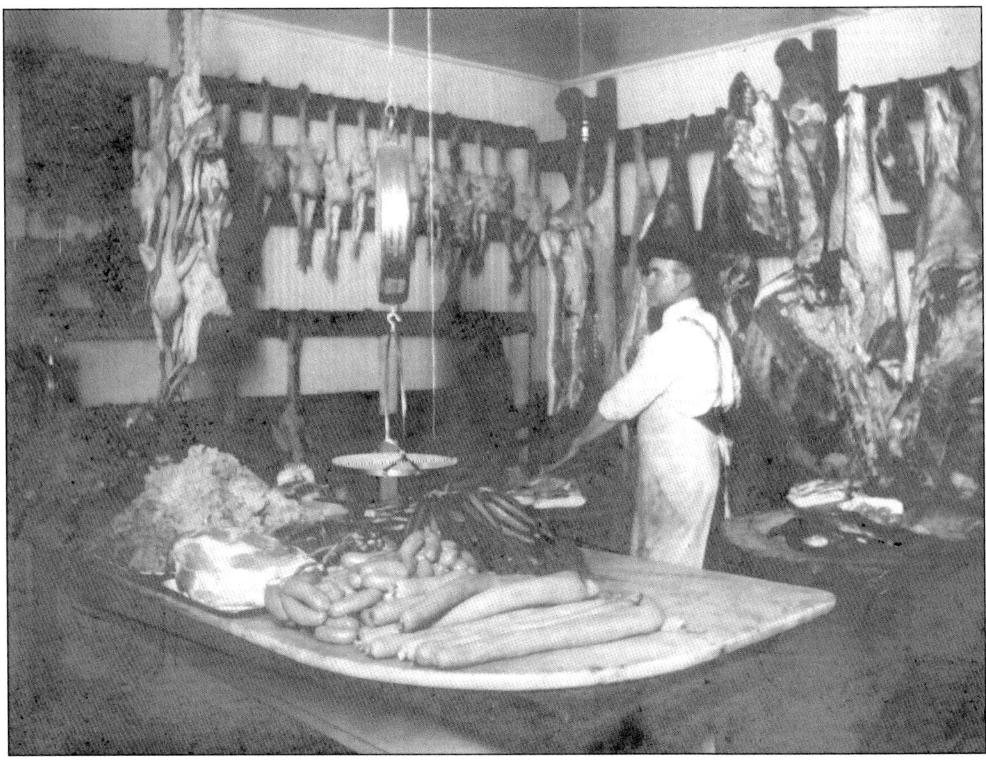

Boyd Meat Market. Butchers not only dressed meat but also prepared special cuts for sale. Robert Boyd's Meat Market thrived for many decades at its location on Main Street. His butcher shop was opened by 1870. Eventually, his son joined him in the business, and by 1897 they were also selling groceries at this store. In 1904, the business had an estimated value of between $5,000 and $10,000.

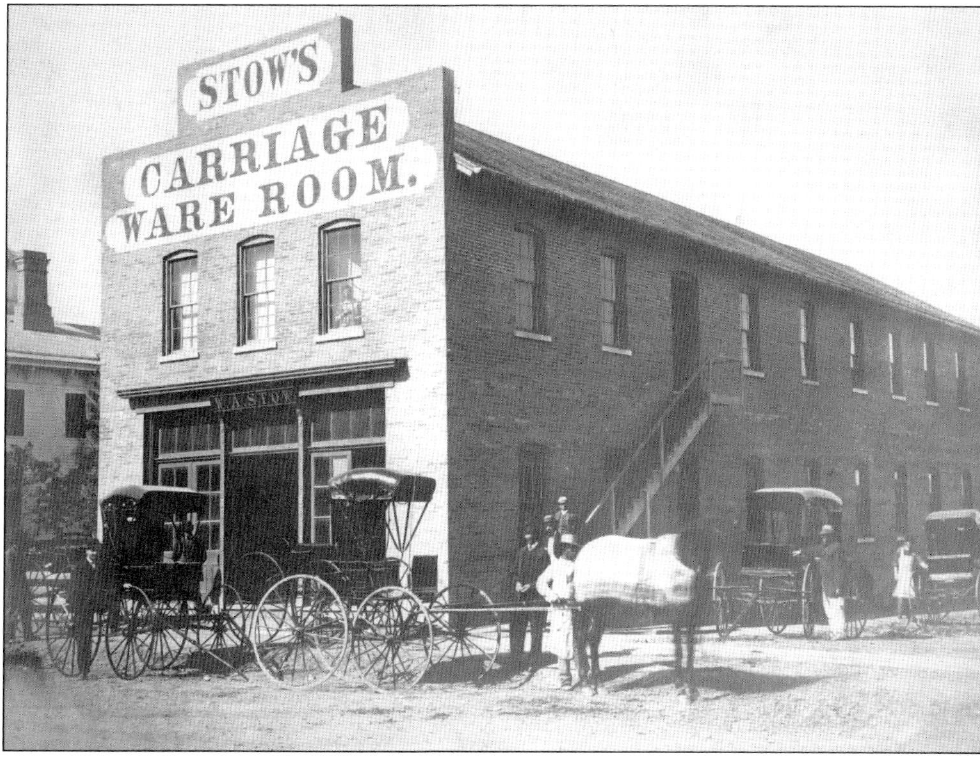

Stow Carriage Shop. During the 1870s, William Stow's carriage shop was located on the corner of Winter and Pearl Streets. Although Stow's trade included manufacturing carriages, customizing coaches, and selling top-of-the-line vehicles, his specialty was in repair work. As transportation by railroad became more popular, there was a natural decline in the carriage and coach trade.

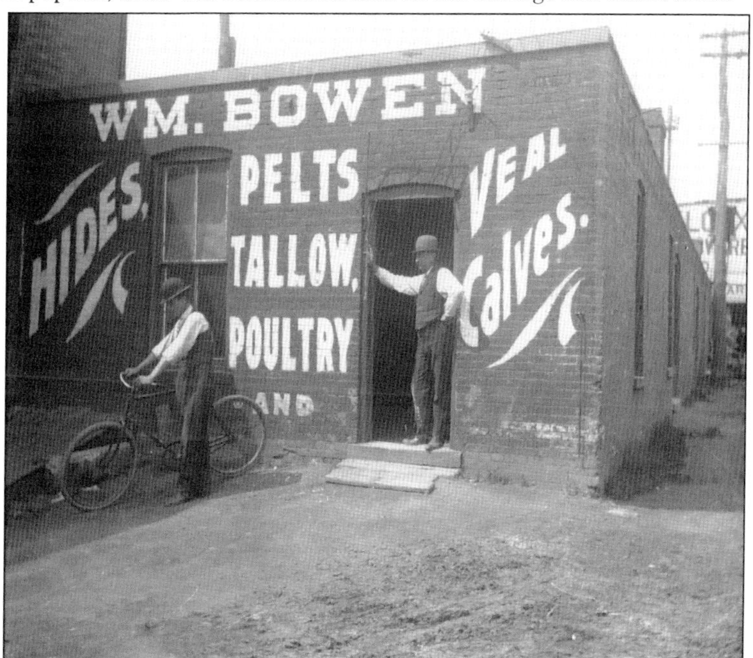

William Bowen & Son. Industrial rendering businesses focused on using up by-products of meat production, such as feathers, fur, and tallow. The Bowen pelt processing and rendering plant was in operation in 1916; the small building was located behind the YMCA. This region of downtown would not have been the most pleasant smelling, as dry batch processing did not develop until the 1920s.

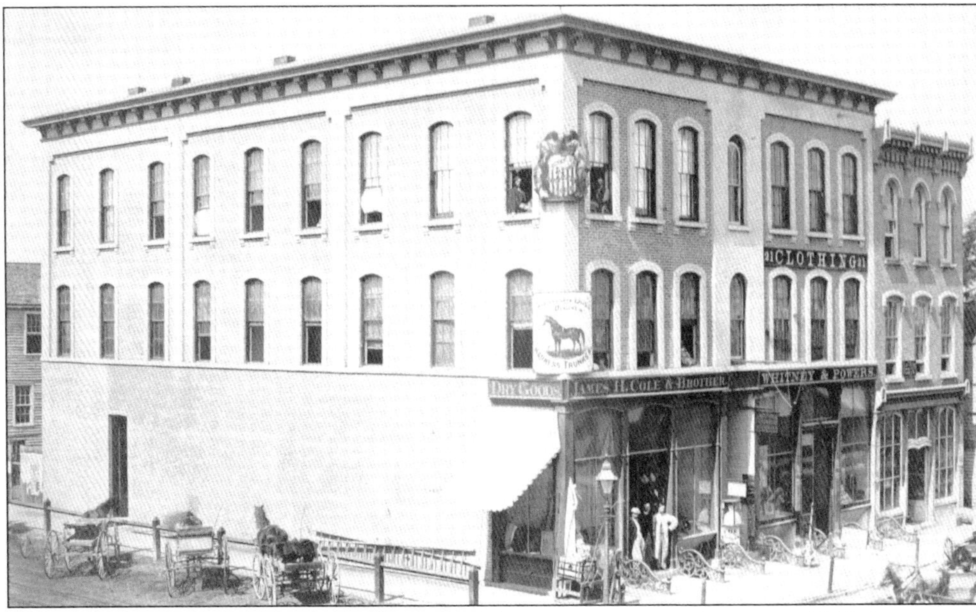

COLE CLOTHING STORE. James Cole purchased an existing apparel store in 1860 that catered to men. Cole sold both readymade clothing products—such as collars, suits, gloves, shirts, and drawers—as well as manufactured menswear to order. His business was interrupted for a time, as he served as a captain in the Adrian Volunteers during the Civil War. He saw action at Gettysburg and was lucky enough to be able to return to his business after the war.

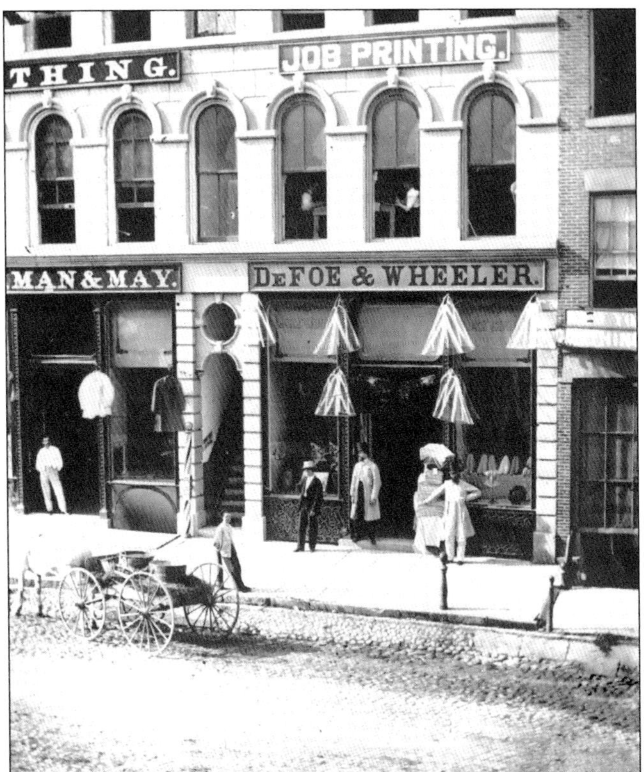

DEFOE AND WHEELER. Adolf Wheeler started out as a clerk in a general store before entering into a partnership with James Defoe around 1864 to operate a dry goods store on West Maumee Street. These stores typically carried cloth, readymade apparel, carpets, and toiletries. This local collaboration existed until 1874, when Wheeler sold out to Defoe and entered into the shoe business. Afterwards, Defoe carried on this business with his son William.

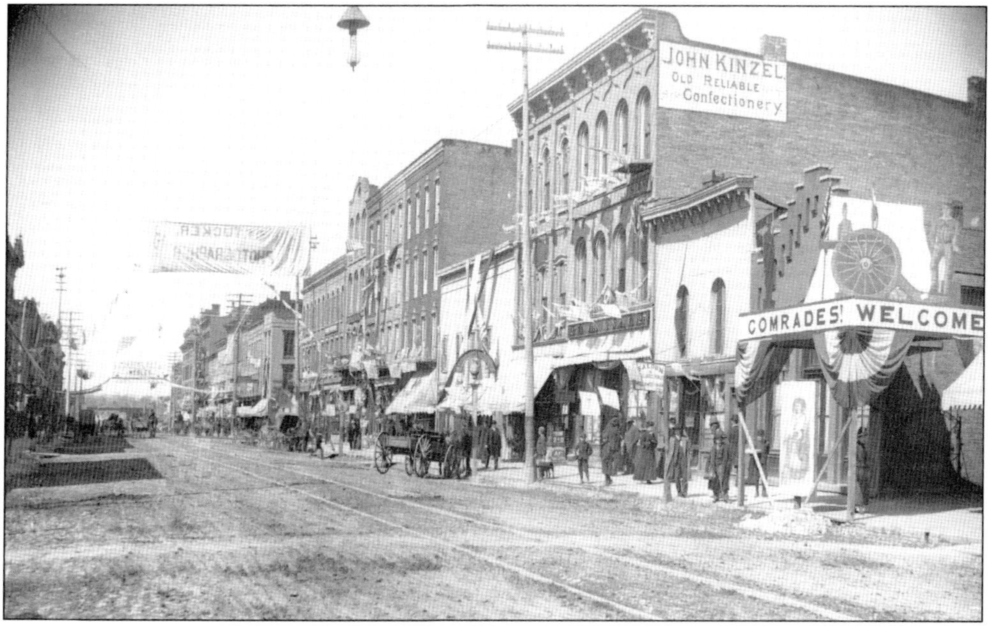

KINZEL CONFECTIONERY. Initially formed as Smith and Kinzel and located on East Maumee Street, in 1874 John Kinzel became the sole proprietor of this popular store when Smith retired. Kinzel's sold fruit wholesale but also ice cream and candies. Popular treats from this period would have included peanut brittle, chocolate, candy sticks, and lozenges. John died in 1896, but the sweet legacy was carried on by the next generation.

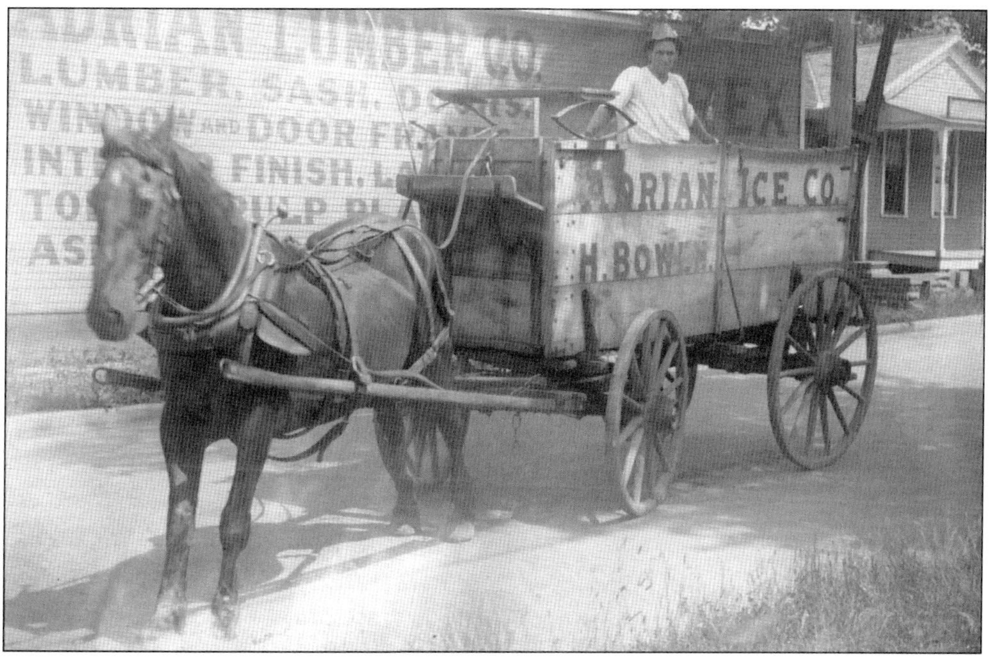

ADRIAN ICE COMPANY. Like their father before them, the Bowen brothers were ice dealers. Their company, Adrian Ice, was incorporated in 1883. The business had two large wagons in order to deliver harvested ice to customers, which helped the company become the largest ice dealer in town. Later, Henry Bowen would be one of the key investors in the Lion Motor Car Company.

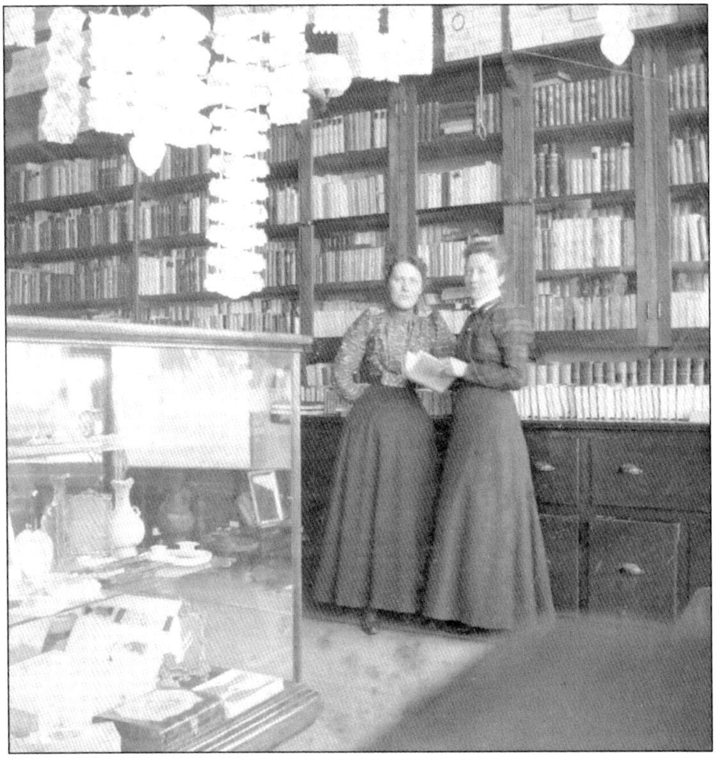

Swift Bookstore. In 1889, G. Roscoe Swift bought a bookstore from Charles Humphrey that dated from 1862. This business was located on West Maumee Street and, in addition to books, also sold paper, stationery, and postcards. Swift published numerous postcards of local scenes and also the book *Railway Employees' Book of Ready Reference and General Information* in 1899.

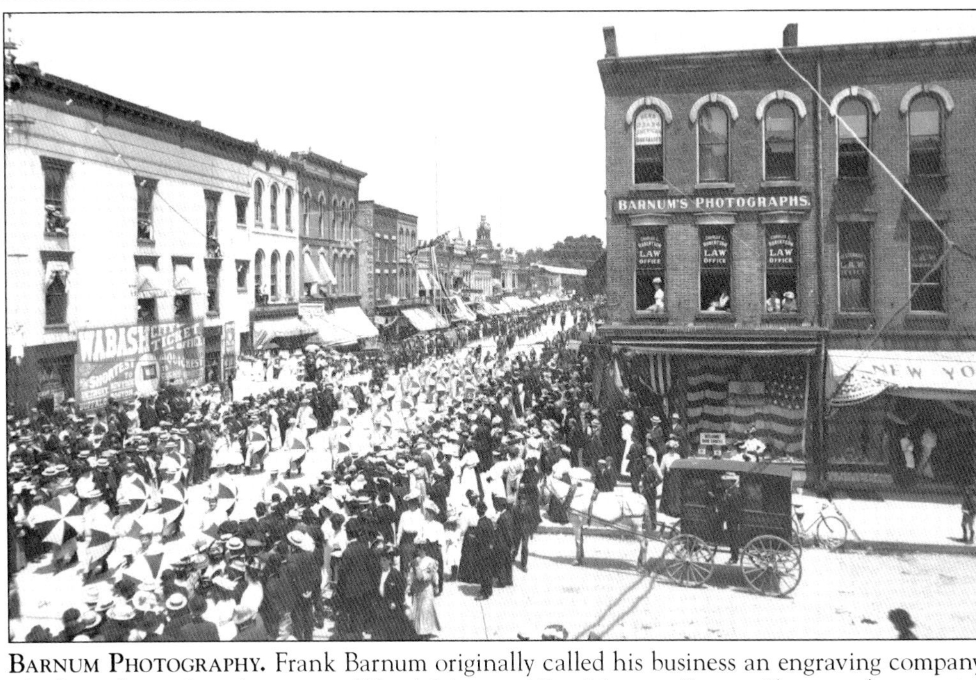

Barnum Photography. Frank Barnum originally called his business an engraving company, which was located on the corner of North Main and East Maumee Streets. Photograph engraving over time was done on glass, tin, paper, and finally film. Barnum was very active in the local community and this extended to the political realm. In 1906, he was elected mayor of Adrian. In this photograph, his photography studio is to the right of center.

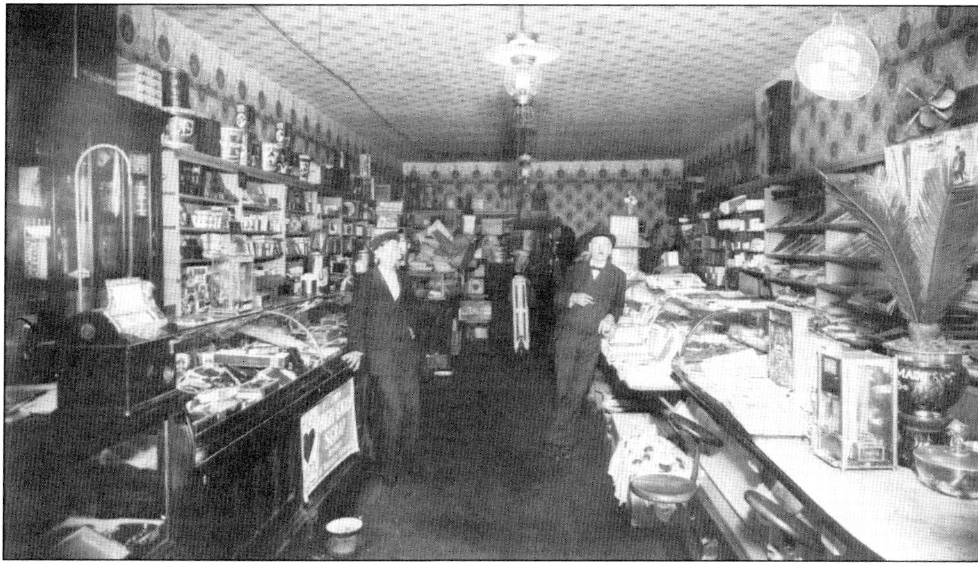

CHALONER AND COMPANY. Charles Chaloner was born in London, England, and immigrated to the United States as a young man. He eventually arrived in Adrian and opened a cigar and newspaper shop. He was a leading citizen of the town, active in both the Republican Party and the Episcopal Church. He also served as chief of the fire department. His store relocated to 108 West Maumee Street in 1880, where one can still buy a cigar to this day.

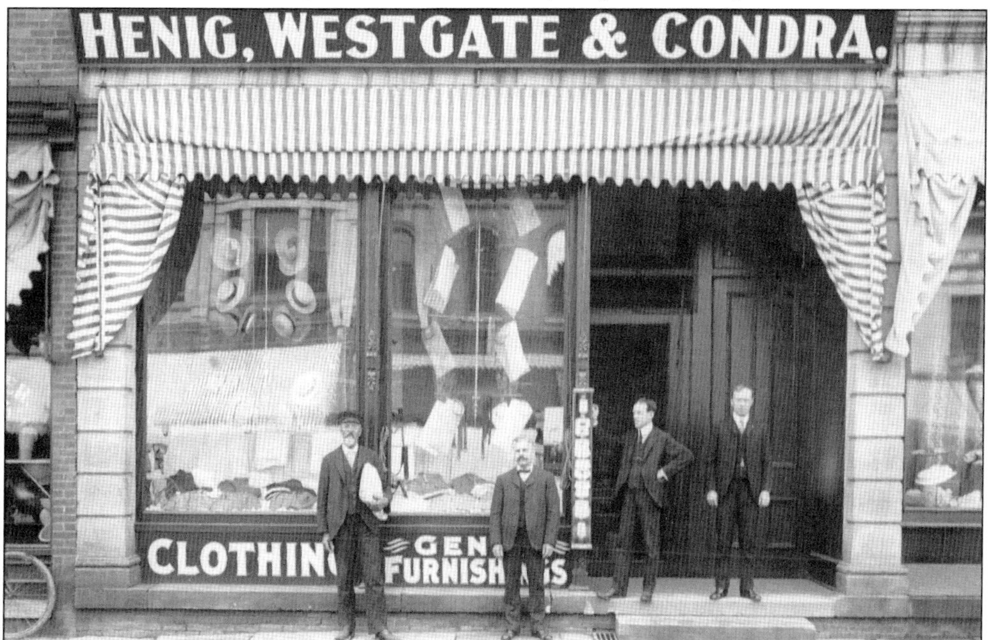

HENIG, WESTGATE & CONDRA. Three local men joined together in 1903 to create the leading clothing store for men in the city. From its central location on Main Street, attire, hats, and furniture were sold to the public. This image appears to have been taken in the late spring due to the hats in the front display window. These straw formal hats with a ribbon around the crown were called boaters and were worn in the hot summer months by men. Much like the robin, when these hats appeared it indicated that the long Michigan winter was finally over.

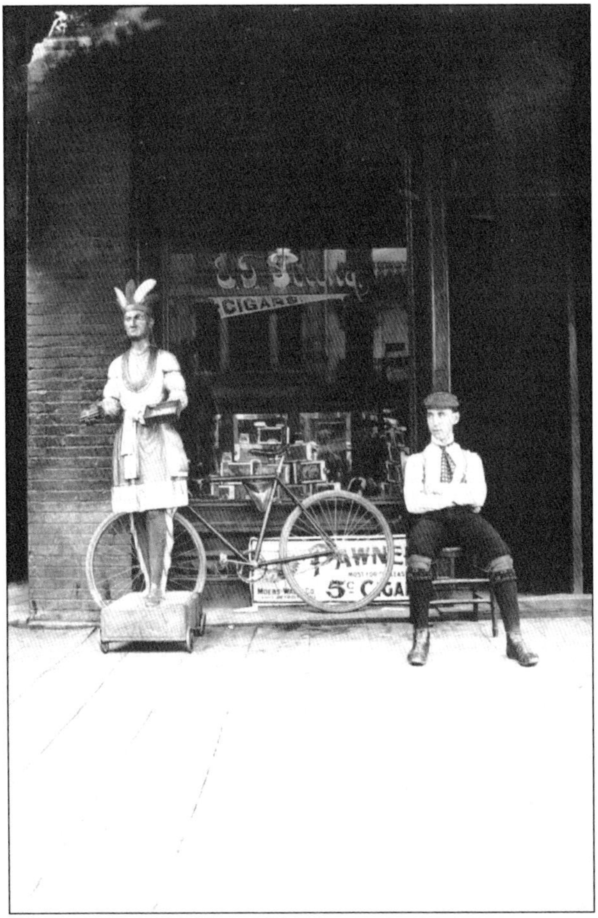

E.T. STRONG CIGARS. In 1899, Michigan had 1,355 cigar-making factories, and this industry had a loyal customer base. By 1916, Adrian had 11 cigar and tobacco retail stores. Earl T. Strong's place on West Maumee Street also offered billiards at the back of his shop. This is an image of the exterior of the store. Cigar store Indians were a common advertising image dating back to the 17th century and still in evidence in the 20th century.

A.E. LINDVALL SHOP. Although the tailoring trade was negatively impacted with the increasing availability of readymade clothing, middle-class and upper-class men continued to have their fine attire made by tailors. Originally, this firm was Karloff and Lindvall and had a small shop on Maumee Street over the Whitney & Wilcox Bank. By the 1880s, Lindvall had relocated to South Main Street and employed seven people in his store.

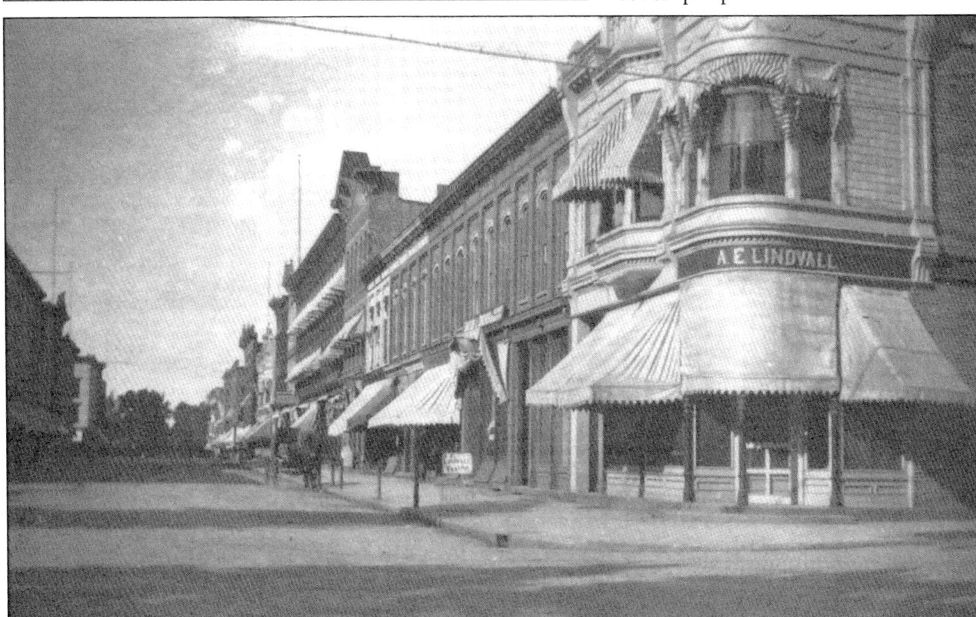

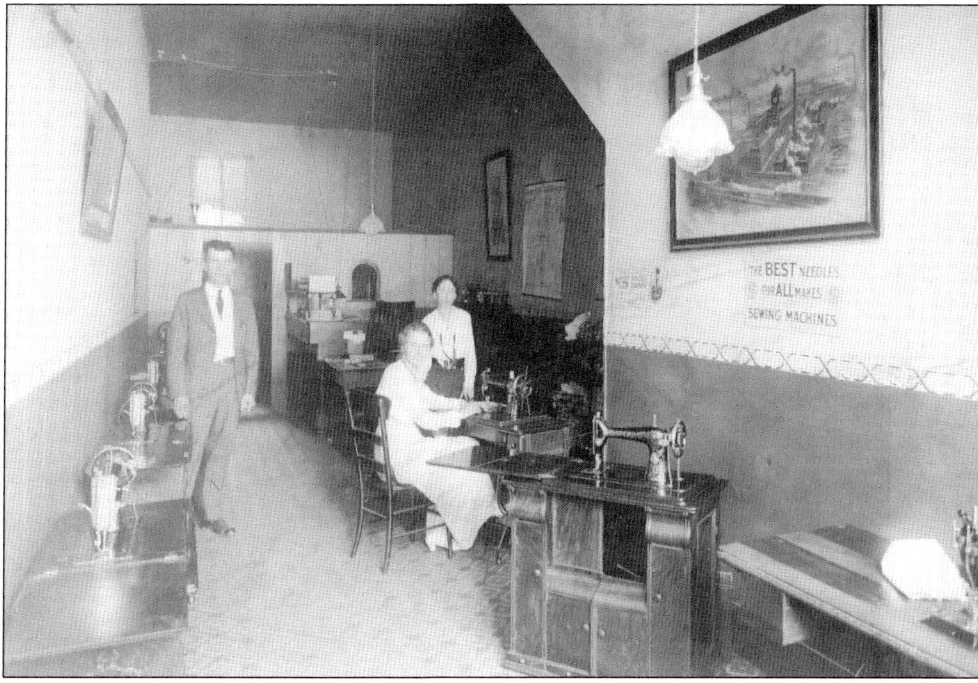

Avery's Machine Office. The Singer Manufacturing Company was incorporated in 1865, with roots back to 1851 with the invention of the Singer Sewing Machine. Innovations in machine design made Singer extremely popular with consumers. Headquartered at this time in New York City, its machines were sold through recognized dealers, such as O.J. Avery of Adrian. His office on East Maumee Street sold these machines by 1873.

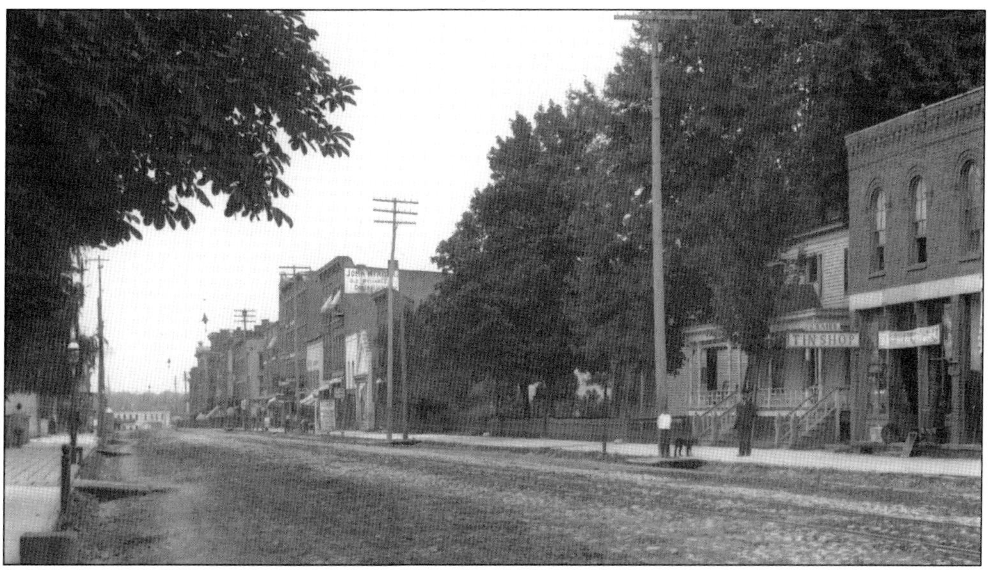

Baier Tin Shop. This business sold fans, registers, plumbing, steam and gas fittings, and tin. This establishment, which dated from 1885, also manufactured the Maple City Hot Air Furnace. Born in Monroe, Joseph Baier was the proprietor and an accomplished tinsmith. Tinplate was available in the United States from the early 19th century, and tinsmiths would typically serve an apprenticeship between four and six years.

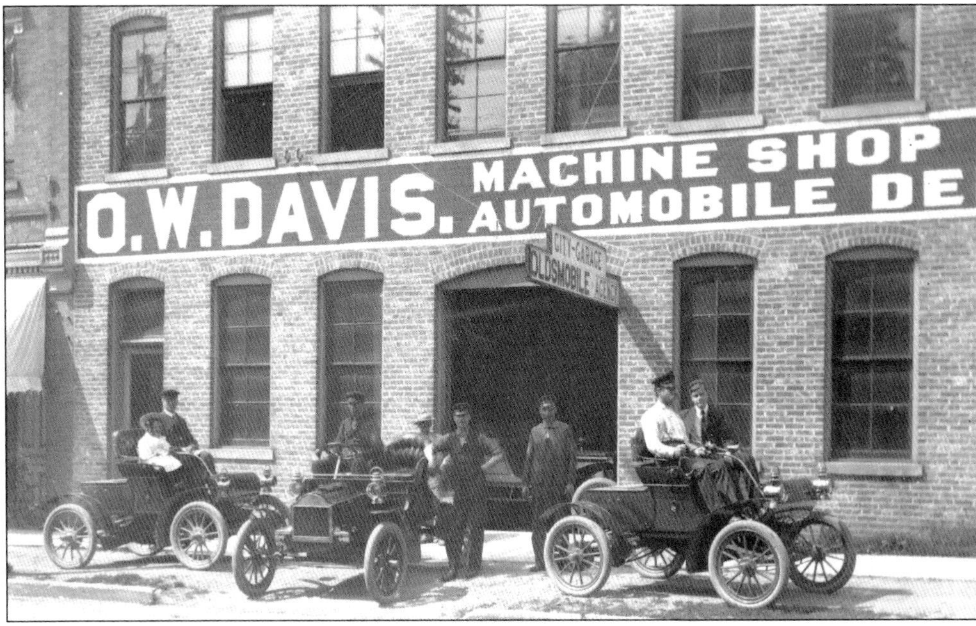

O.W. Davis Oldsmobile Dealership. Ransom Olds began his automobile company in 1897, centered in Lansing, Michigan. Although other prototypes were created, only the Curved Dash was produced during the time when Olds was affiliated with the company. General Motors purchased this business in 1908 and increased the number of Oldsmobile models. This photograph highlights the O.W. Davis dealership showing off the Dash, which sat two comfortably and sold for $650.

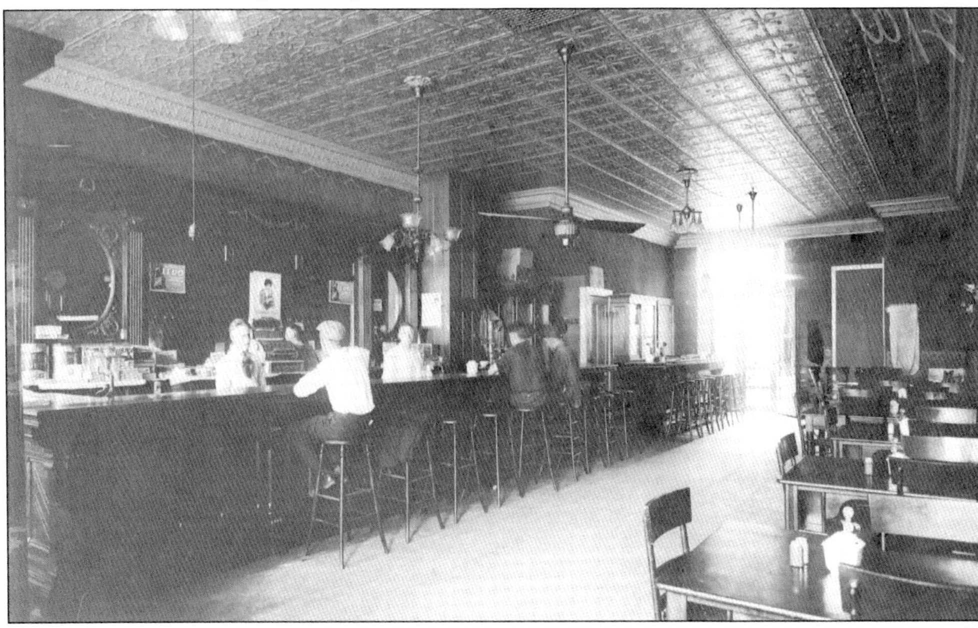

Schwartz & Emmer Saloon. The Schwartz name was connected to various saloons since the 1860s in Adrian. Saloons during this period catered to men, as respectable women would not be seen in such establishments. George Schwartz and Frank Emmer together had the saloon located on North Main Street since 1897. The Schwartz family continued on in the bartending trade, and by 1942 the business had expanded into a full restaurant.

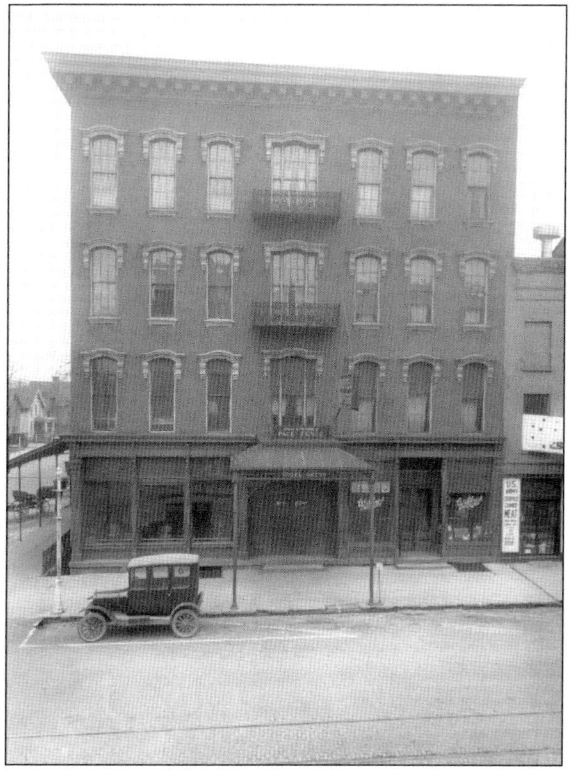

HOTEL GREGG. Charles Gregg came to Adrian in 1901 after owning hotels in Jackson and Ionia. He purchased the former Lawrence Hotel located on the corner of Winter and Maumee Streets. Gregg renovated the building, which dated to 1860, adding modern conveniences to the 100-room hotel such as electricity and steam heat as well as updating the decor. Rooms rented from 75¢ to $1.50 per night.

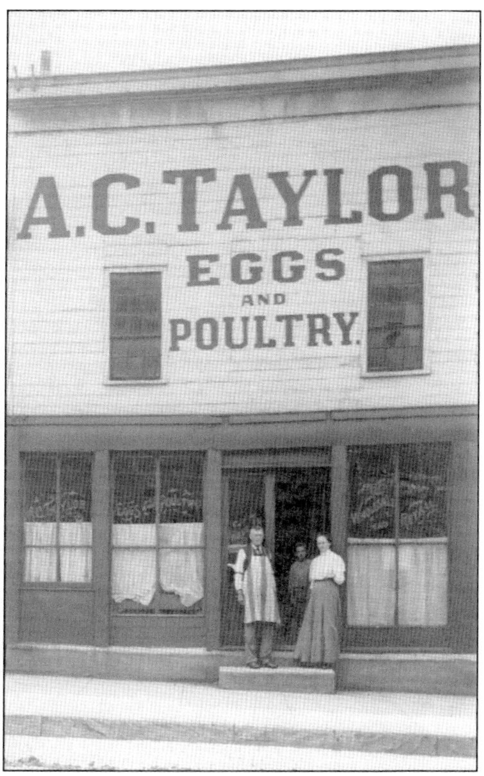

A.C. TAYLOR STORE. Aaron C. Taylor sold not only eggs, but also chicken in his store located on West Maumee Street in 1911. Although the egg carton was also invented that year, it is more likely customers of Taylor would have still brought their wire egg baskets in when they purchased this product. Adrian had poultry farms such as Rose Lodge and Sunnyside, with Leghorns and Buff Cochins as popular breeds.

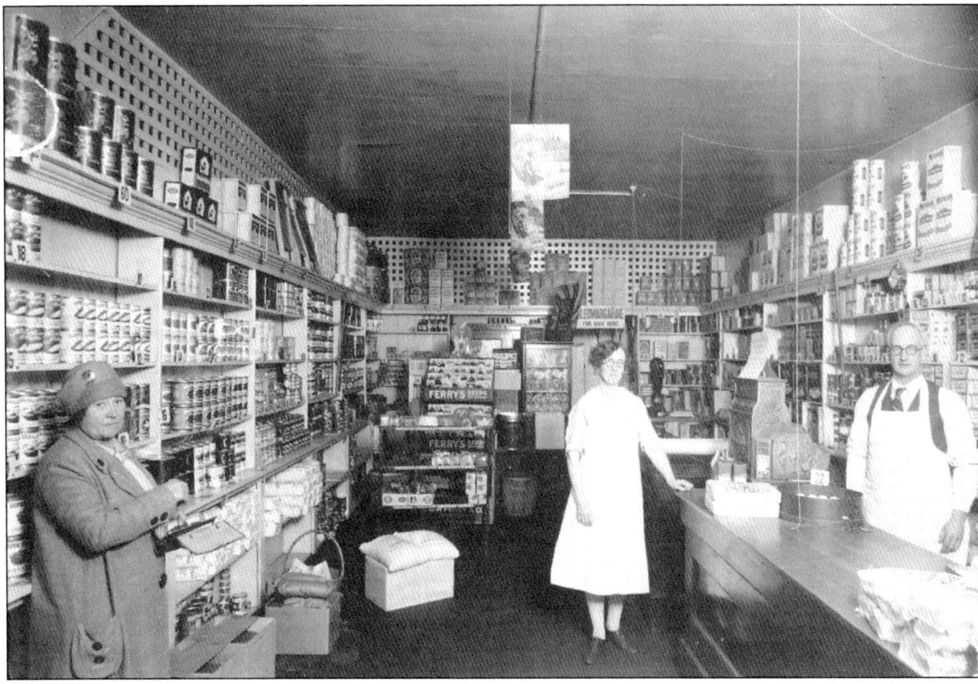

FAMILY GROCERY STORES. Grocery stores were a 20th-century innovation that combined products typically sold in a dry goods store with perishable goods that could previously only be found in specialty shops all under one roof for the consumer. Shoppers would give their list to the clerk behind the counter to fill the order. It was not until the advent of the supermarket in the 1910s that customers would fill their own baskets. The early grocery shops were often family owned and operated, such as the C.L. Smith grocery above or the A.J. Kaiser store below.

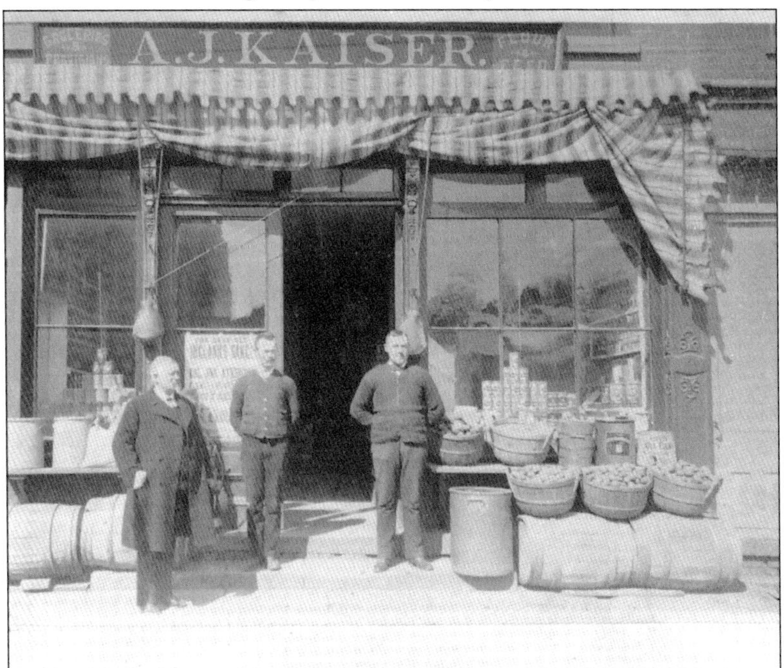

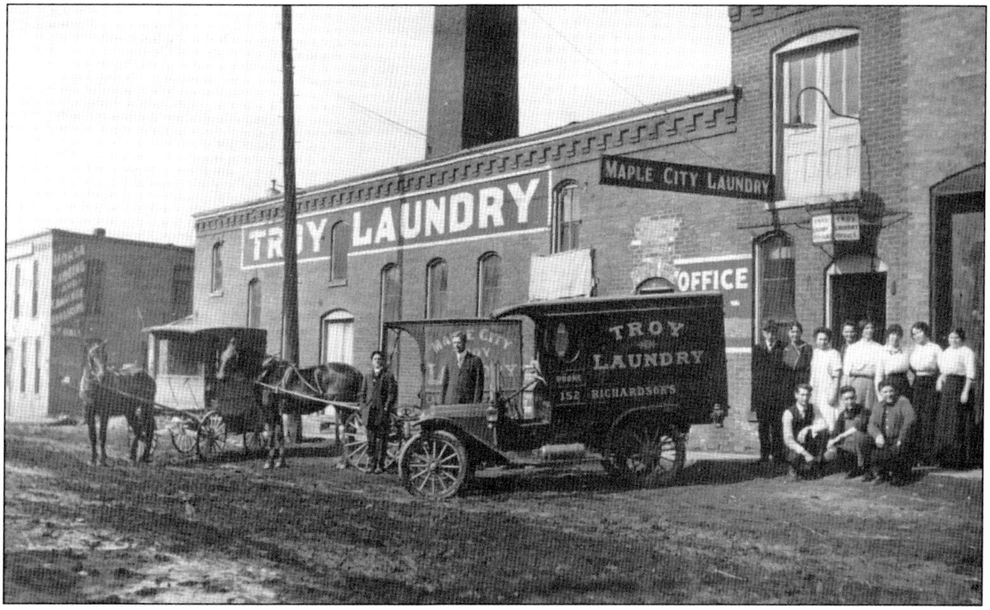

Troy Laundry Company. By 1911, Adrian could boast of five steam laundries. The Troy Laundry Company on Pearl Street had many owners over the years and typically employed equal numbers of men and women: men repaired the machines and drove the delivery vehicles, while women ran the hand-operated washing machines and irons. Work in such establishments was backbreaking, and long hours were common.

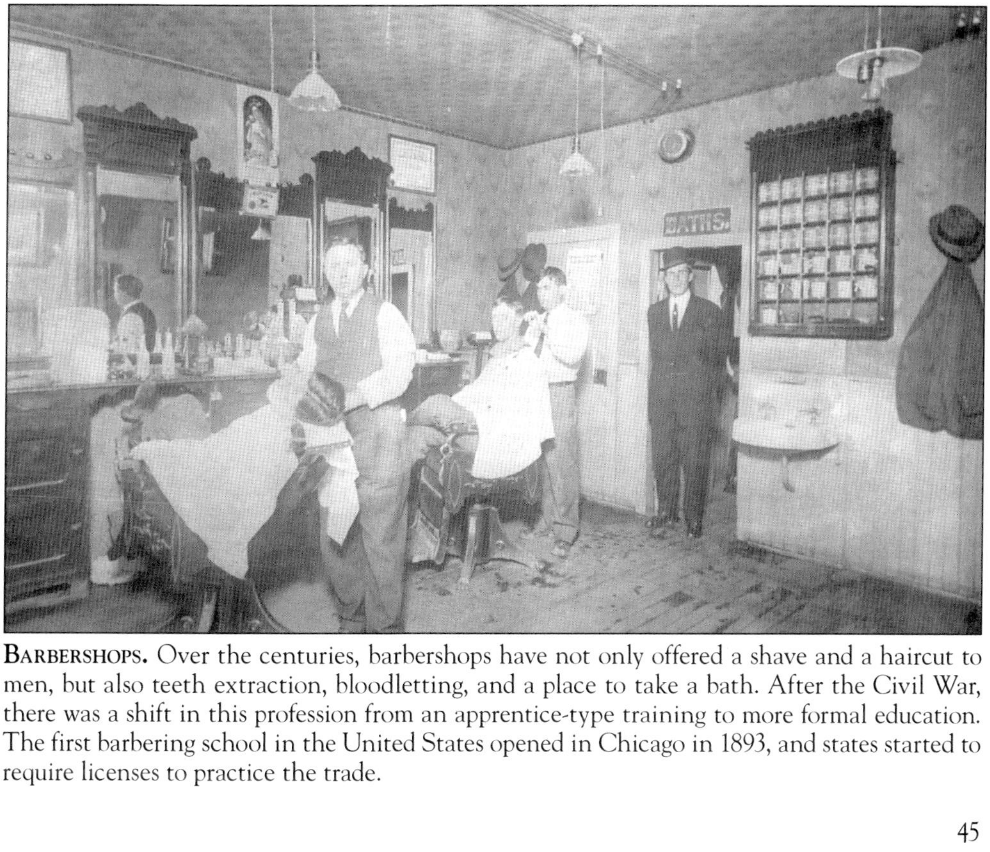

Barbershops. Over the centuries, barbershops have not only offered a shave and a haircut to men, but also teeth extraction, bloodletting, and a place to take a bath. After the Civil War, there was a shift in this profession from an apprentice-type training to more formal education. The first barbering school in the United States opened in Chicago in 1893, and states started to require licenses to practice the trade.

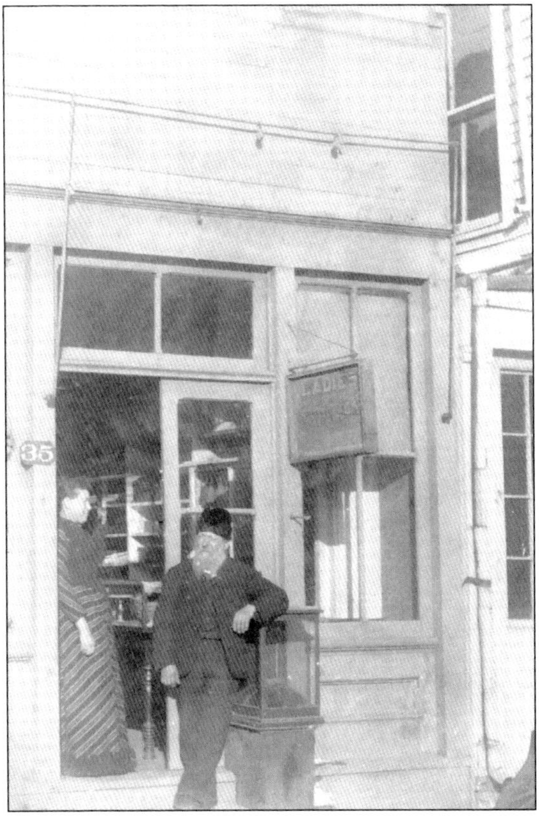

The Misses Holzworth. Like men with their barbershops, women had their hair parlors. Both Kate and Carrie Holzworth were initially trained as seamstresses in their father's successful tailor shop on North Main Street. However, by 1893, the daughters had opened up their own hairdressing business on South Main Street. Kate was still operating this business in 1916 when she would have been about 63 years old.

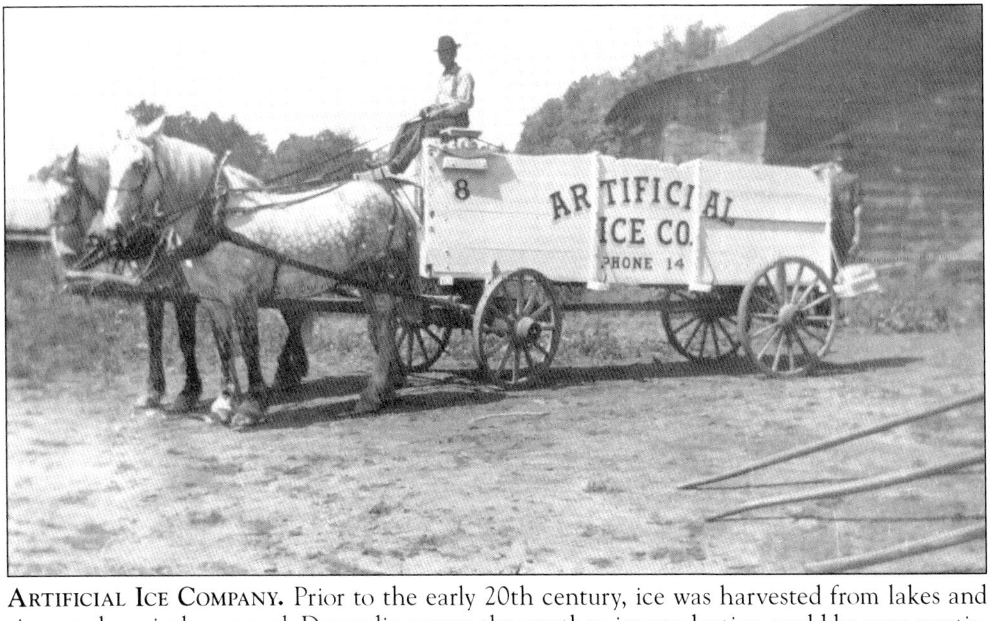

Artificial Ice Company. Prior to the early 20th century, ice was harvested from lakes and rivers to keep iceboxes cool. Depending upon the weather, ice production could be very erratic. By 1914, the Artificial Ice Company opened in Adrian, employing nine people. Water would be placed into different sized molds and frozen to manufacture ice that would then be put into cold storage. Iceboxes were slowly replaced by refrigerators by the 1950s.

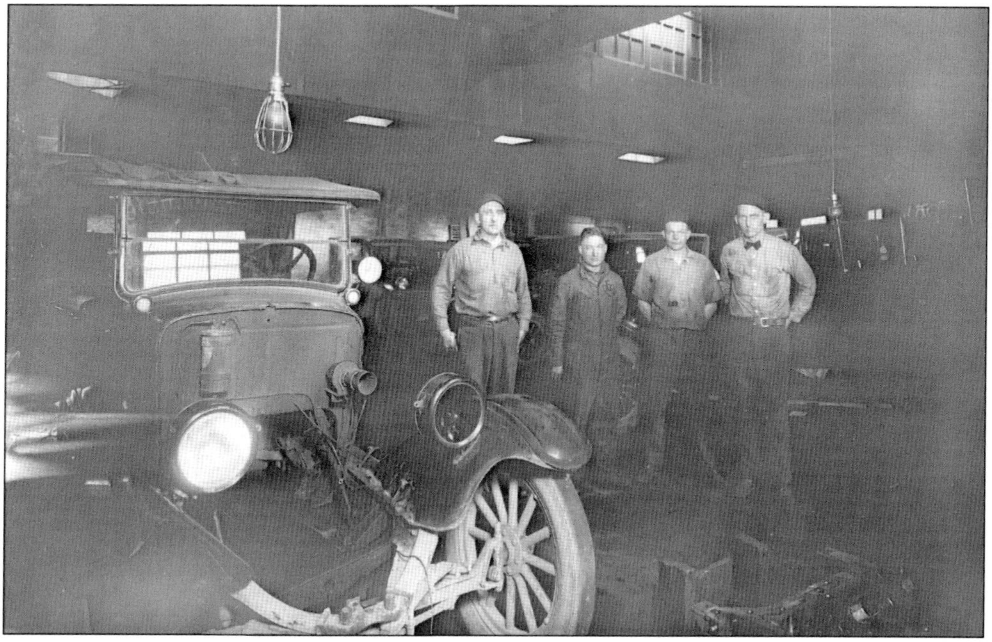

McKinster & Company. This business on Maiden Lane originally sold and repaired bicycles from approximately 1892 to 1916. Bicycles were extremely popular as a low-cost form of conveyance compared to the expense of feeding and boarding a horse. With the transportation revolution of the automobile, by the 1920s Frank McKinster wisely shifted the focus of his garage to car repair.

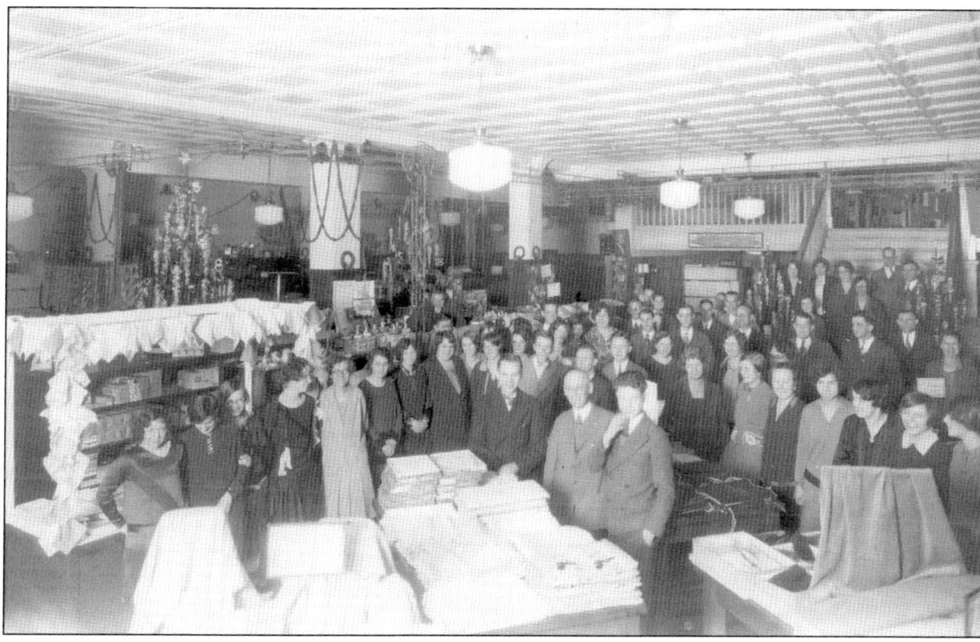

J.C. Penney Department Store. Originally simply a few dry goods stores located in the West, James Cash Penney began working in the business in 1898 and eventually was able to purchase a store in Wyoming. He renamed and expanded the organization to carry clothing, shoes, bedding, jewelry, and furniture. He opened stores east of the Mississippi by 1916, with Adrian's store being opened in 1922 and first managed by Jack Maynard.

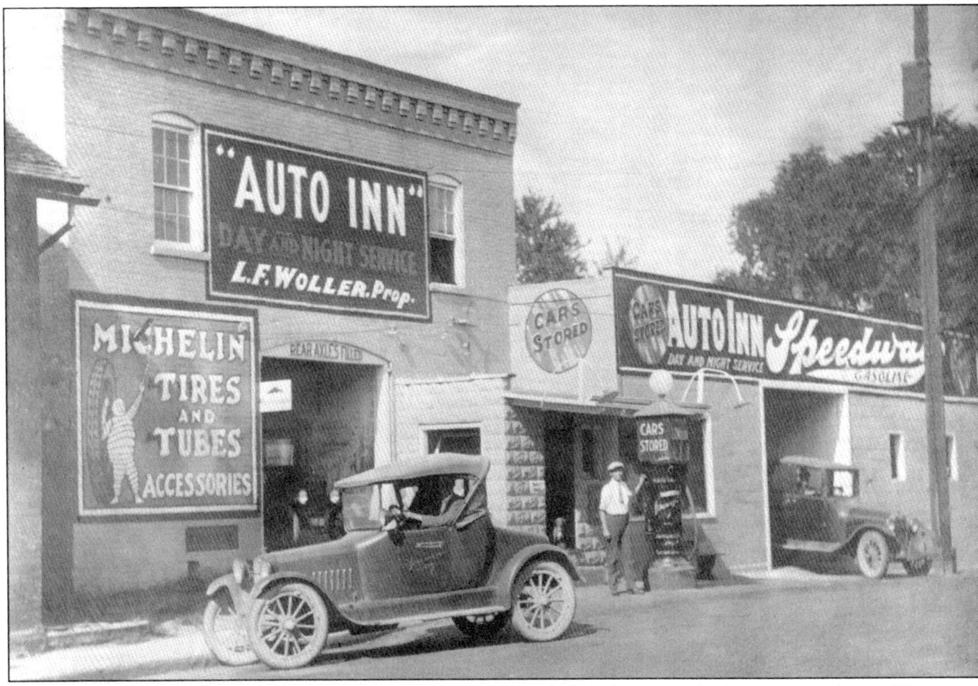

WOLLER AUTO INN AND TAXI. As the cost of automobiles decreased, they were adopted by more and more businesses for a variety of purposes. Louis F. Woller had quite a few transportation-related businesses over the years and all within a relatively short period of time during the 1910s. He was a teamster, milk dealer, taxi driver, and garage/gas station owner. Above is an image from his garage, and below is his taxi service.

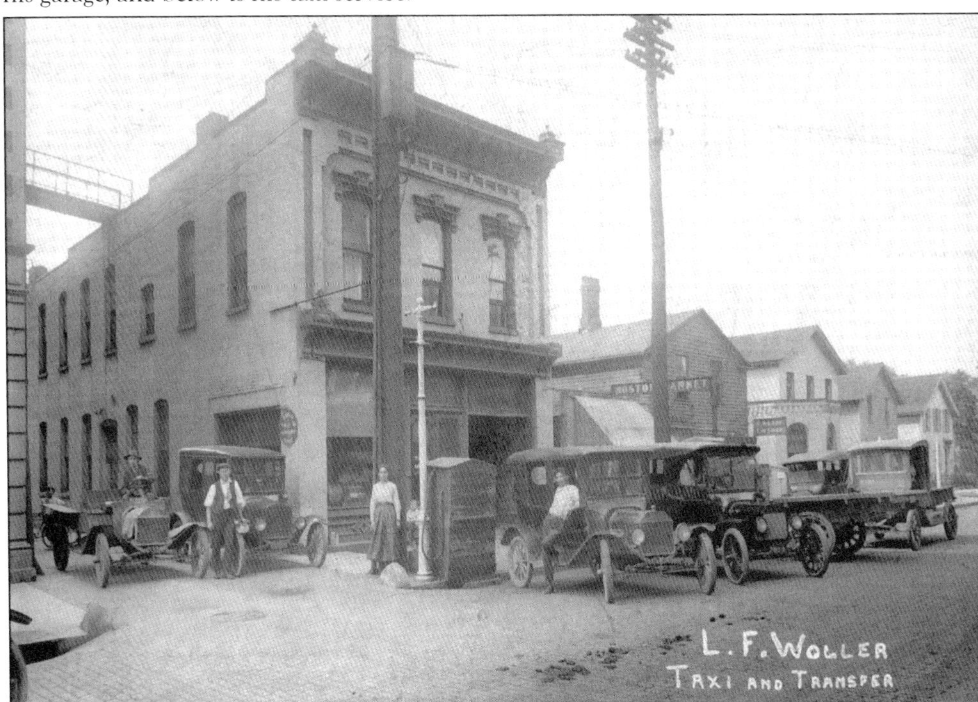

Three

Education

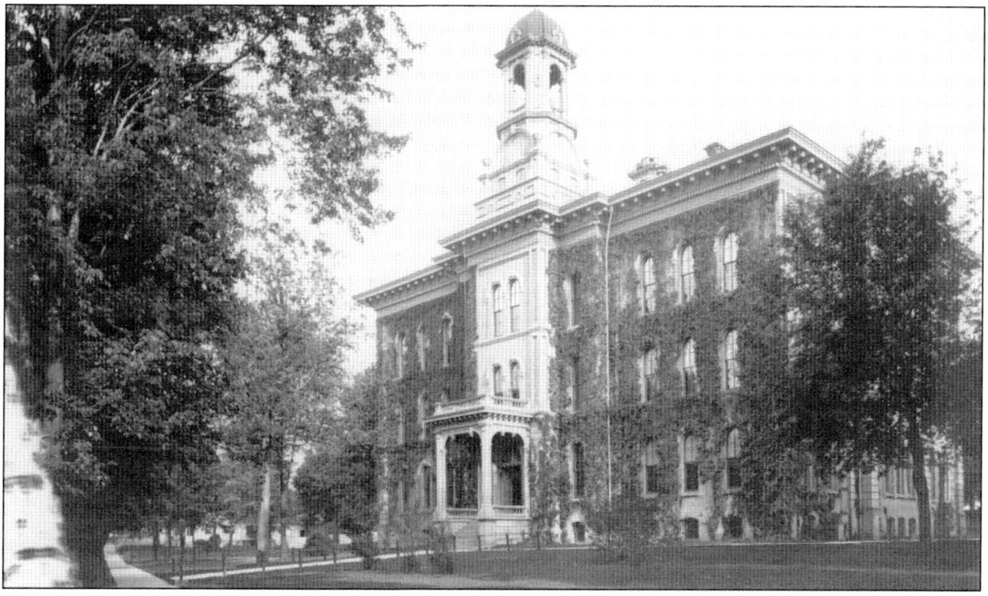

Central School. The first school opened in 1828 as a select (private) institution, as was common during this time period. Over time and with population growth, public schools became established in the city. By 1861, Adrian had five tax-supported public schools for each ward. This image of the second Central School, rebuilt of brick and stone in 1868 after the first one burned down, dates from a time when it had a student body of approximately 500 students.

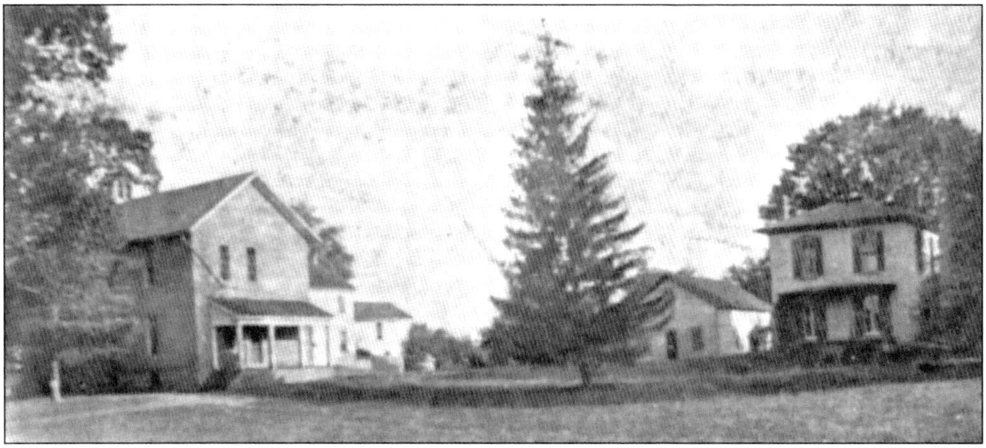

Raisin Valley Seminary. Darius Comstock, father to city founder Addison, started the Raisin Valley Seminary in 1850. This school, supported by Quakers like Darius, was opened to young men and women of all faiths. The curriculum had four courses of study: English, Latin, Latin-Scientific, and Scientific. The school closed in 1908. Seen below is a photograph of a graduating class from the late 19th century.

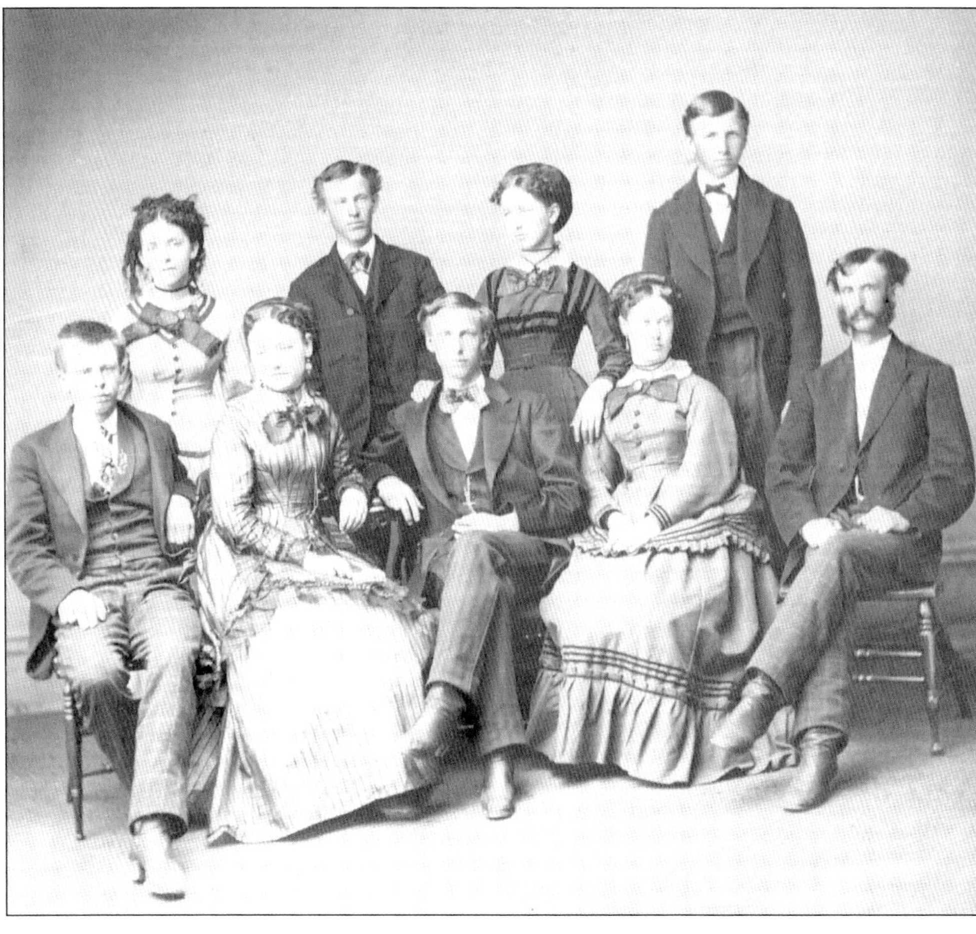

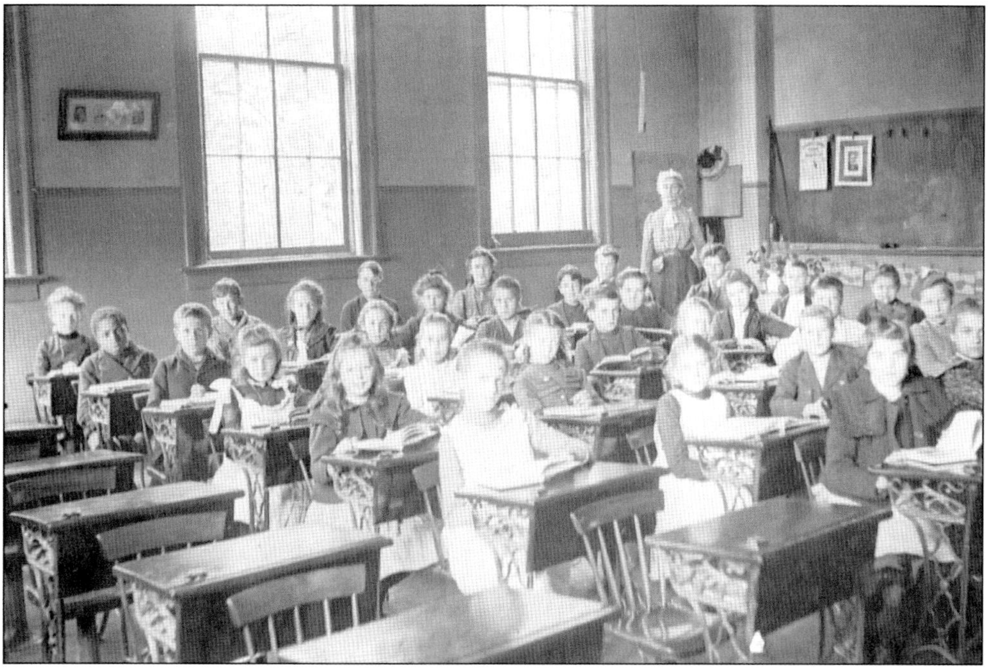

Central School. This is a 1905 image of an interior classroom at the Central School. American education during this era was focused on maintaining social order and proper socialization to create good citizens and workers. However, this scene also indicates that Adrian had an integrated school system, unlike many of its counterparts around the country.

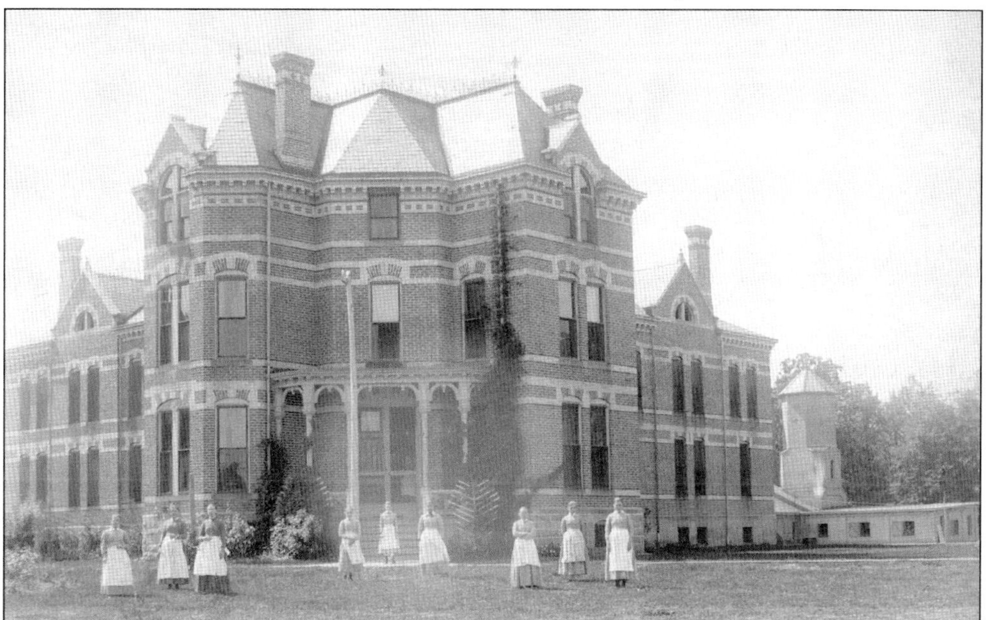

Michigan Industrial Home for Girls. With growing urbanization and crime, the state established an institution of reform for wayward young women. This residential school opened in Adrian in 1881, serving girls from ages 7 to 20. For most of its history, this training school primarily served delinquent girls until its closing in 2009.

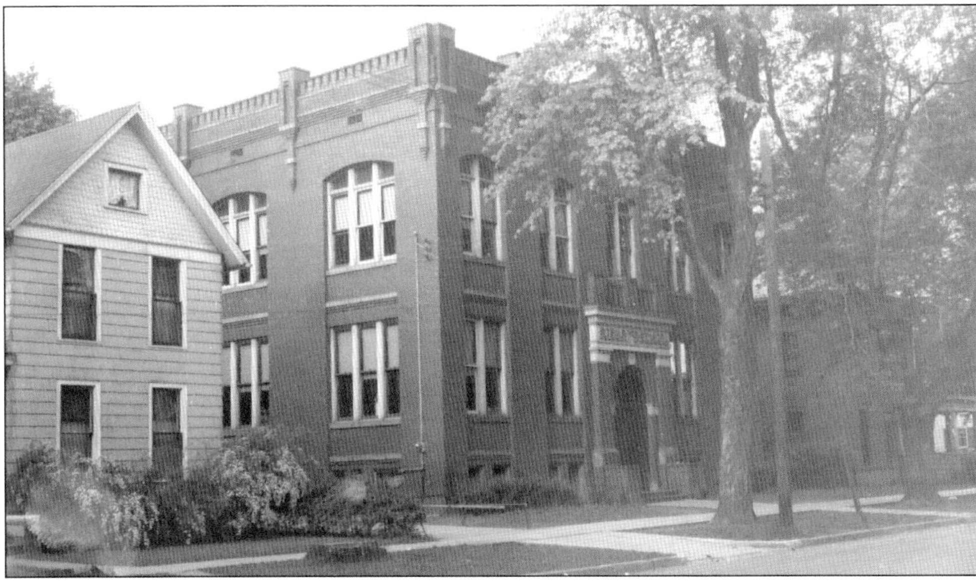

St. Mary's Catholic School. Due to anti-Catholic bias in the public schools, Catholics found it necessary to start their own parochial school systems. Plenary councils ordered that each church must have a parish school, and Catholic parents must send their children to these schools. Religious instruction was thus added to the curriculum. By the late 19th century, Adrian had two Catholic parochial day schools. St. Mary's educated ethnically Irish Catholic pupils, while St. Joseph's educated ethnically German Catholic pupils.

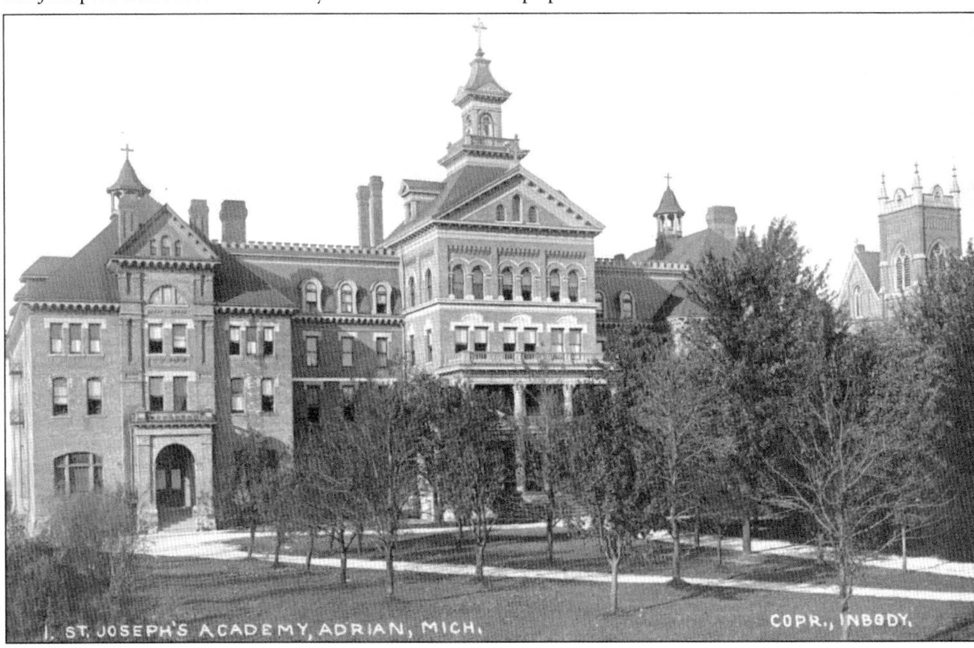

St. Joseph Academy. The establishment of this Catholic boarding school for young women in 1896 was the culmination of a dream of Mother Camilla Madden of the Adrian Dominicans. In 1911, Madden Hall was built to house the academy. Some of the alumni of this institution became Adrian Dominicans themselves and dedicated their lives to service in fields such as parochial education and nursing.

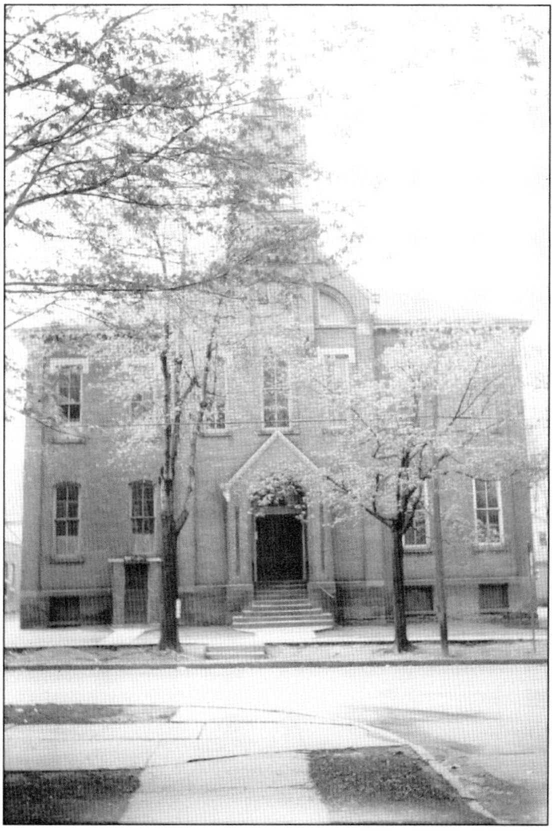

St. John's Lutheran School. Adrian also had two Lutheran parochial day schools. In 1847, one church-supported school, St. John's, opened to educate ethnically German Lutheran pupils of the Missouri Synod. With growth, a new school was constructed on Church Street in 1887. The curriculum focused upon the Bible, doctrine, and the German language as well as reading, writing, and arithmetic. At right is the school, and below are some pupils.

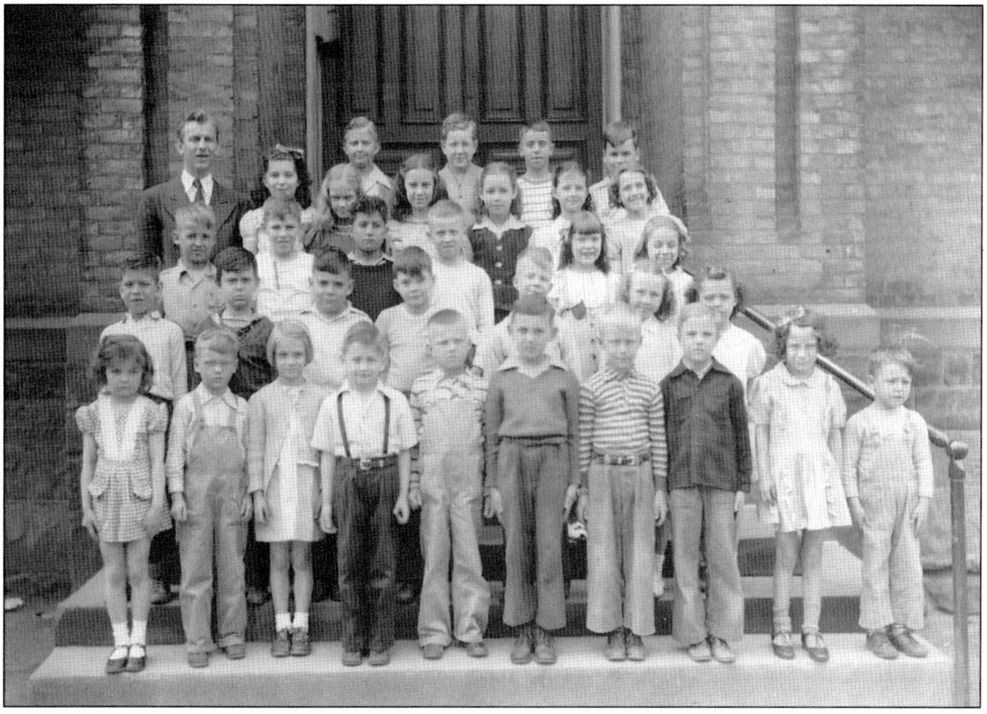

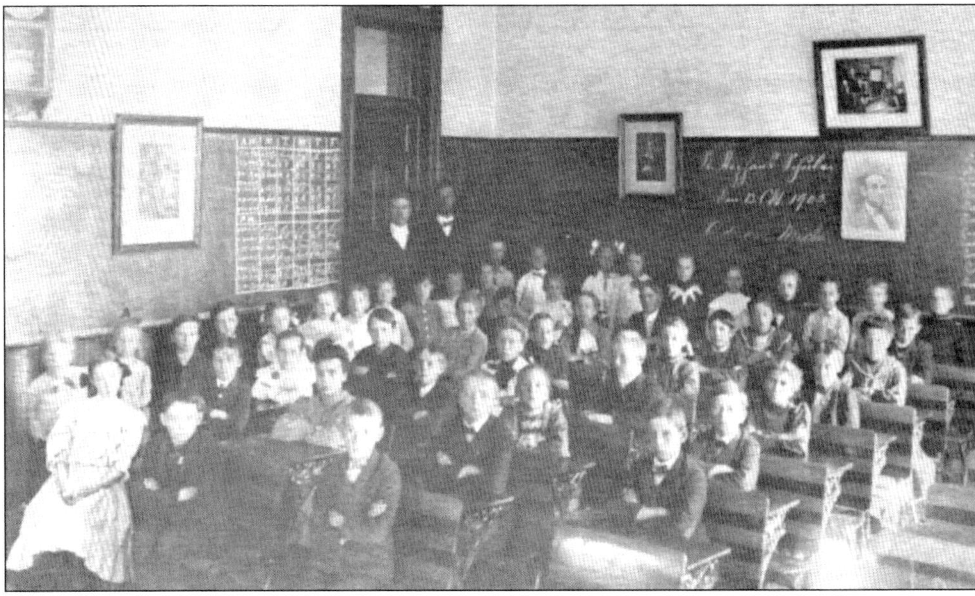

St. Stephen's Lutheran School. When members of St. John's Church left the congregation in 1860 to start their own, they also eventually needed to start their own school in 1864. St. Stephen's educated ethnically German Lutheran pupils of the Michigan Synod. Their school building at Front and Finch Streets was completed by 1899. The curriculum also focused on the Bible and German language, with reading, writing, and arithmetic, but it differed regarding doctrine as compared with St. John's.

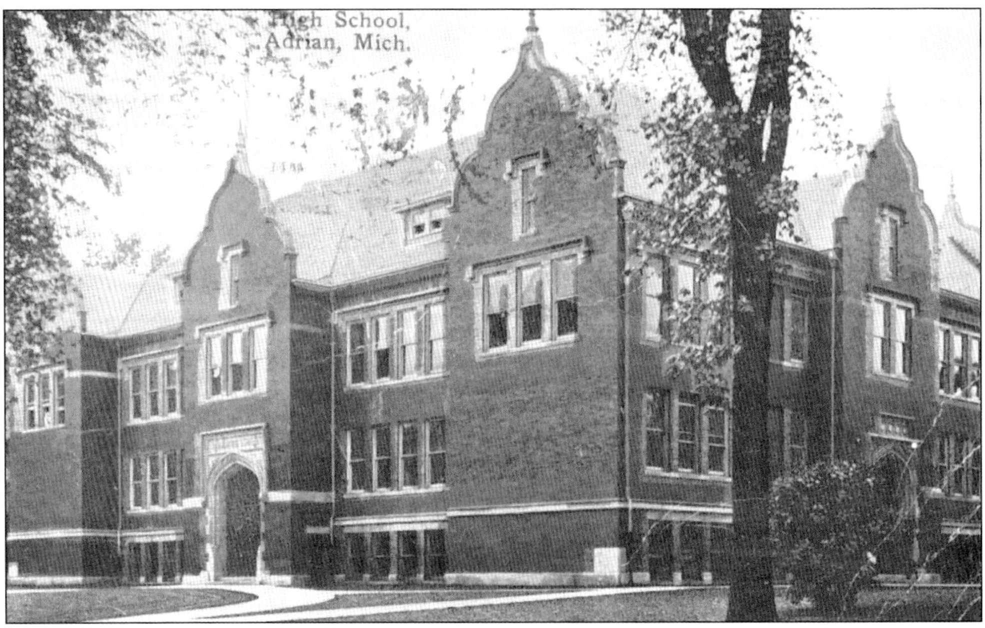

Adrian High School. Near the turn of the 20th century, a high school was built close to the Central School, and the curriculum was expanded to respond to modern concerns. As America shifted away from an agricultural economy to an industrial one, more education was deemed necessary to be successful. Students would need to stay in school past the eighth grade, so the Central School housed the junior high with the senior grades located at the high school.

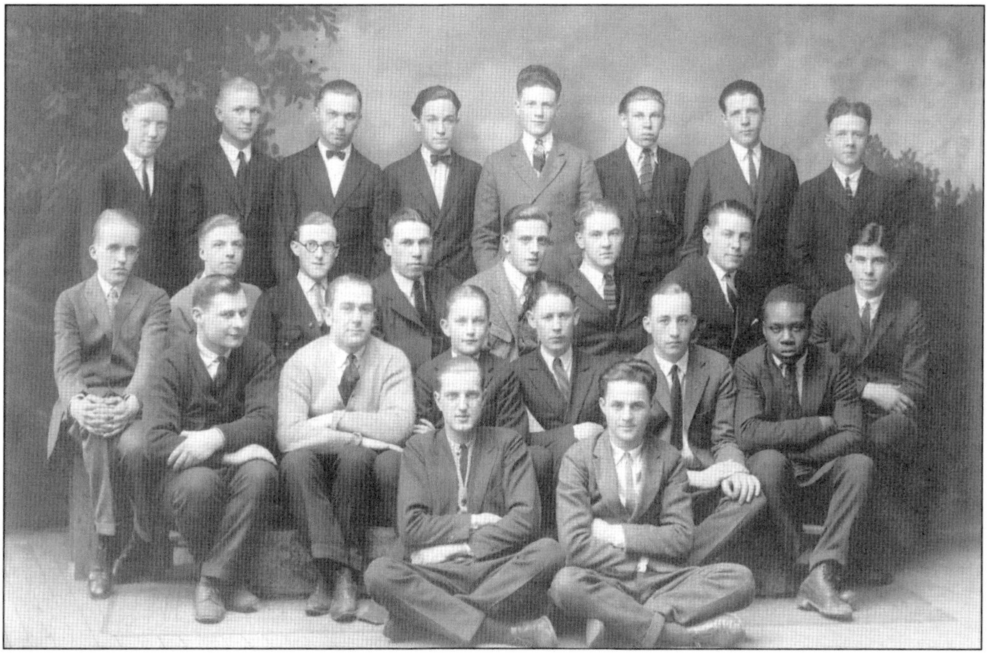

Adrian High School Glee Club. Glee clubs became popular in the United States in the mid-19th century. Traditionally, such groups are made up of males who sing short, unaccompanied songs (also known as glees) that have parts for countertenor, tenor, baritone, and bass voices. This photograph features the 1924 state championship club from Adrian High School.

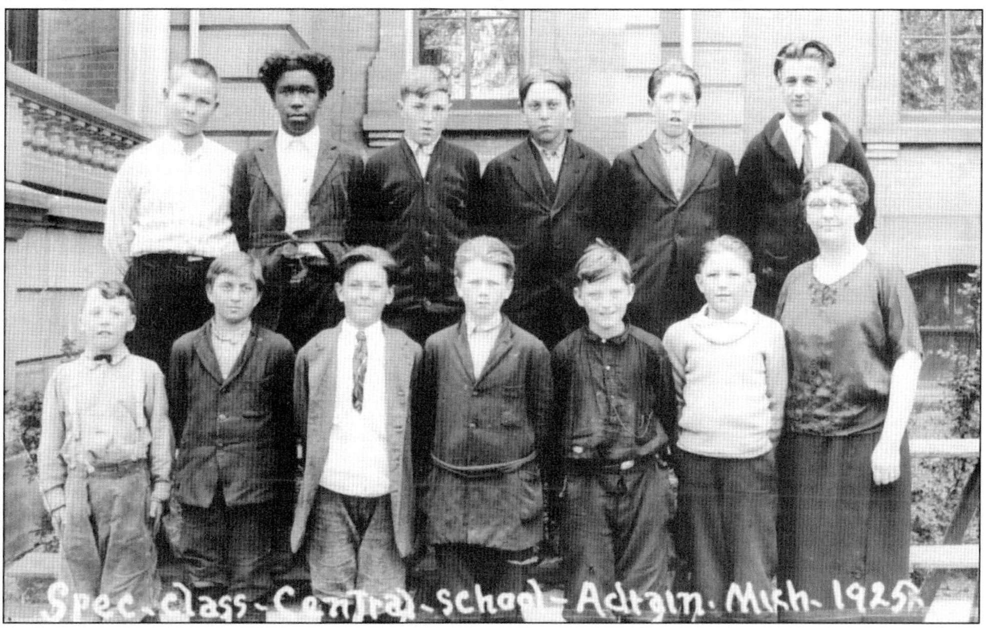

Special Class, Central School. In 1883, Michigan passed a compulsory education law. Children who had previously been excluded from schooling, like those with learning disabilities or behavioral problems, now were expected to attend school. Nationally, in the late 19th and early 20th centuries, special classes were created to manage such children, with the majority of them being male. Adrian reflected the trend, as evidenced by this class picture from 1925.

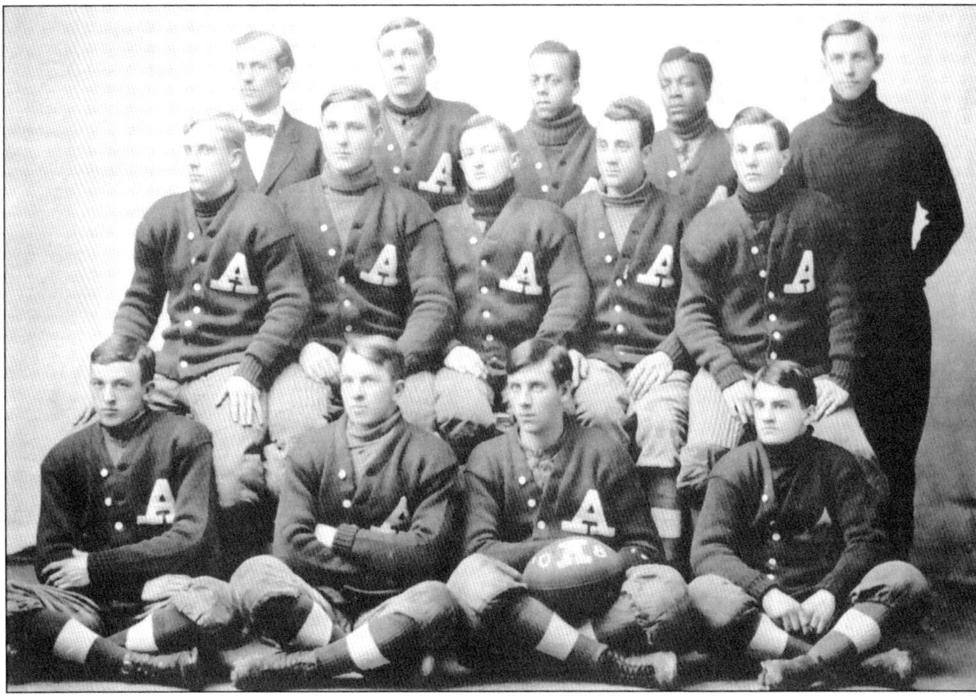

Adrian High School Athletics. In the early 20th century, many public schools added athletics as an extracurricular activity. Such competition was viewed as a way to help encourage a strong, democratic society in the United States. Sports were believed to teach both cooperation and the importance of good health to young men and women. High schools organized teams, especially in football and basketball, to also foster school spirit and as a way to gain positive goodwill in the community. The image below is of the 1918 women's basketball team from Adrian High School, and above is the 1908 football team, also from Adrian High School.

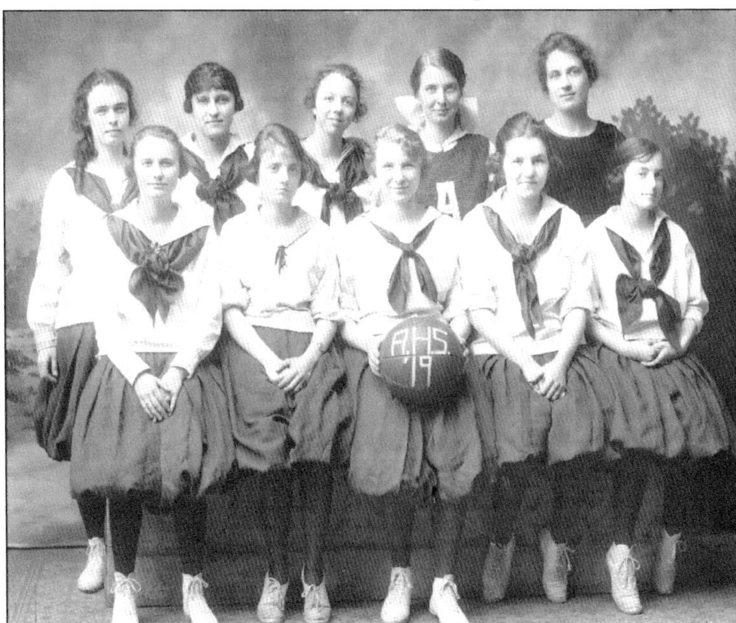

ADRIAN HIGH SCHOOL PLAY. Theatrical Arts offered yet another venue to highlight talent from the schools. The annual high school play in Adrian, instead of being performed in a modest school auditorium, was often showcased at the Croswell Opera House downtown. The costumed students in this photograph performed the comedy *A Scrap of Paper* by French dramatist Victorien Sardou in 1907 for the enjoyment of the community.

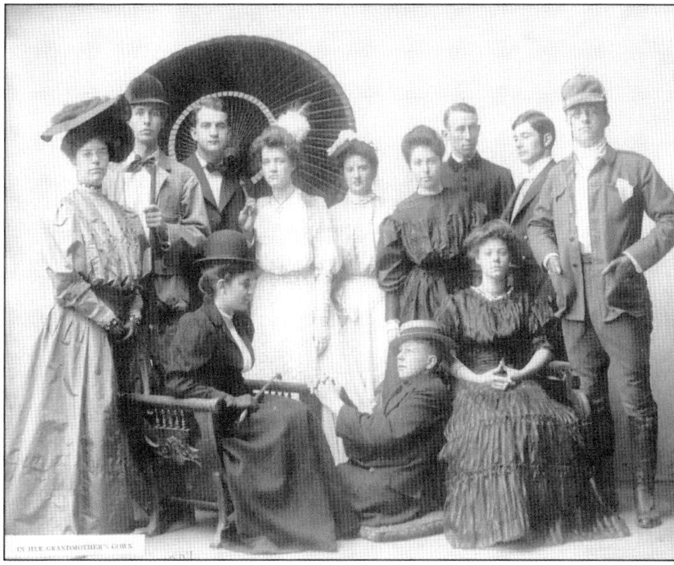

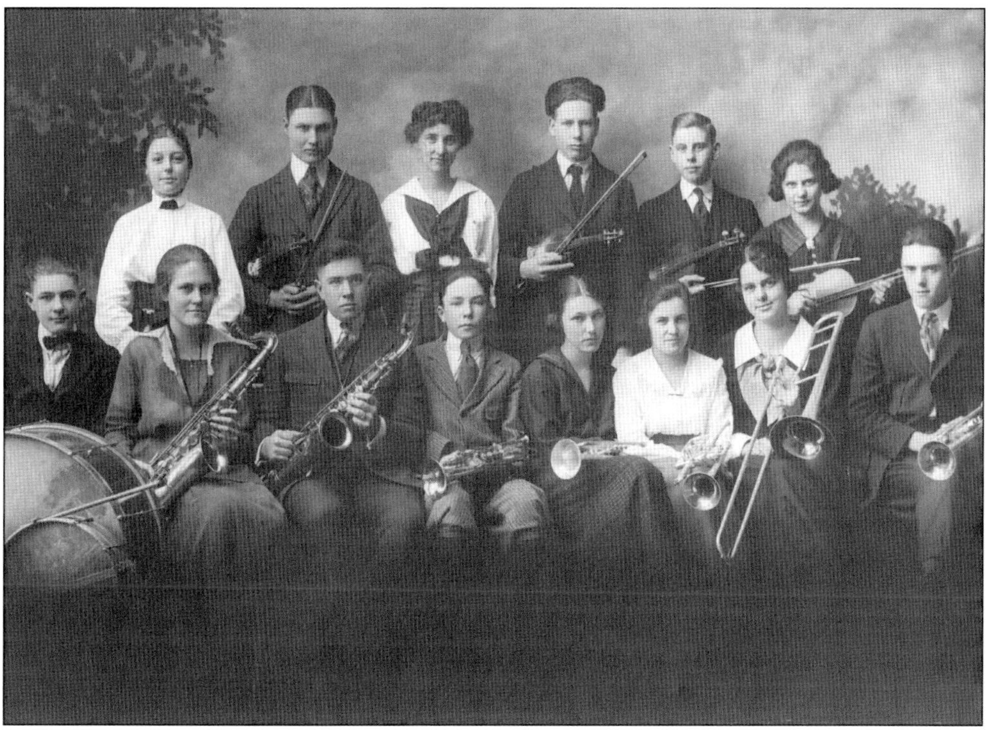

ADRIAN HIGH SCHOOL ORCHESTRA. From the Middle Ages, the study of music was one of the liberal arts and believed to be vital to the development of a well-rounded person. A traditional orchestra contains four families of instruments: brass, strings, woodwinds, and percussion. This group photograph of the 1921 Adrian High School Orchestra would be considered such by a purist, as all families are included.

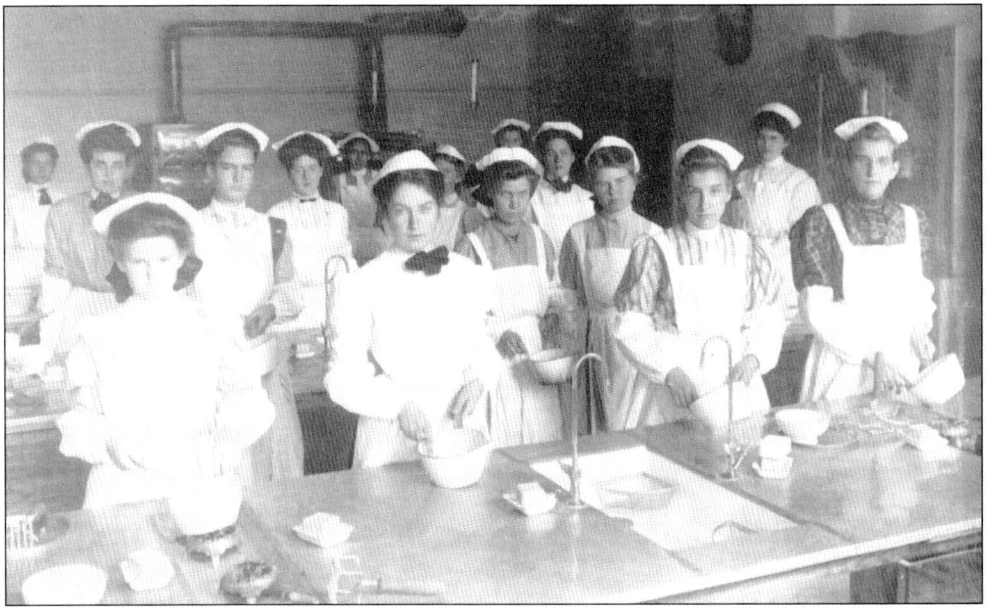

Domestic Science Class. Although the roots of the curriculum date to the mid-19th century with reformers like Catherine Beecher, home economics was not widely adopted in the school systems until the early 20th century, primarily for young women. Subjects such as nutrition, childcare, housekeeping, clothing production, interior design, and consumer studies all hoped to create a scientifically managed home and a more orderly society.

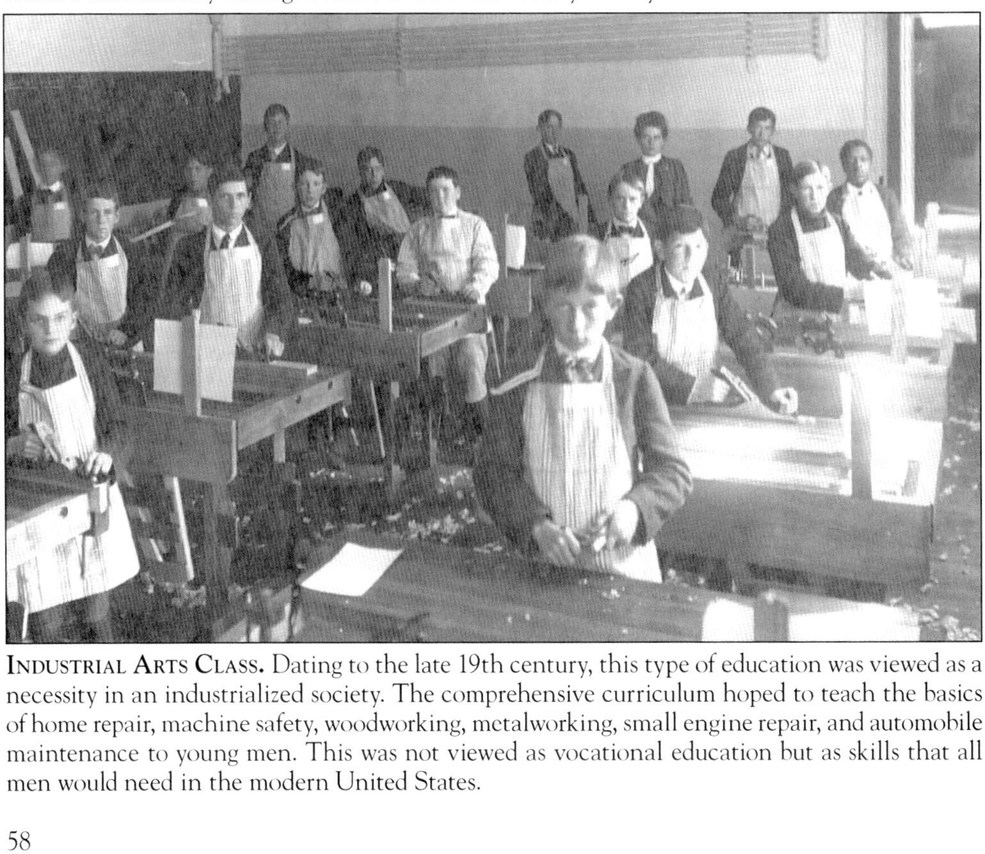

Industrial Arts Class. Dating to the late 19th century, this type of education was viewed as a necessity in an industrialized society. The comprehensive curriculum hoped to teach the basics of home repair, machine safety, woodworking, metalworking, small engine repair, and automobile maintenance to young men. This was not viewed as vocational education but as skills that all men would need in the modern United States.

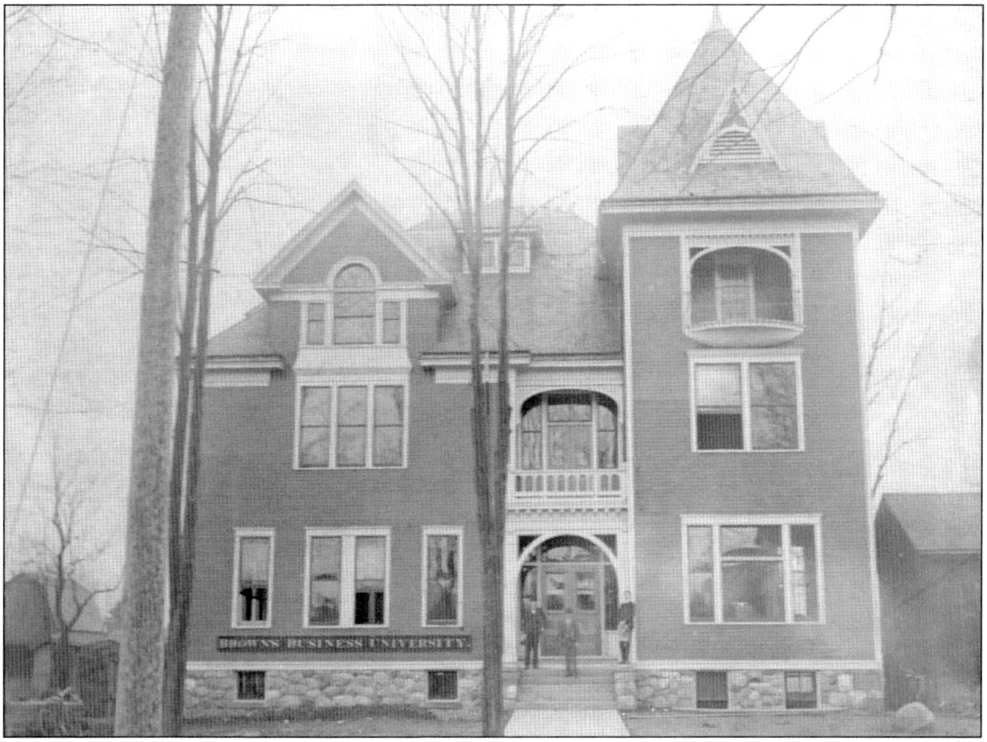

Brown's Business University. Lynn Brown founded this business school in 1884. Initially classes were offered at various locations downtown, until the opening of its own building in 1902, shown here in two images. The university offered a course of study in stenography, primarily for women, and in business, primarily for men. Classes included banking, commercial law, bookkeeping, shorthand, typewriting, and rapid dictation. Both Lynn and his wife, Clara, taught at the school until it closed when they retired in 1923.

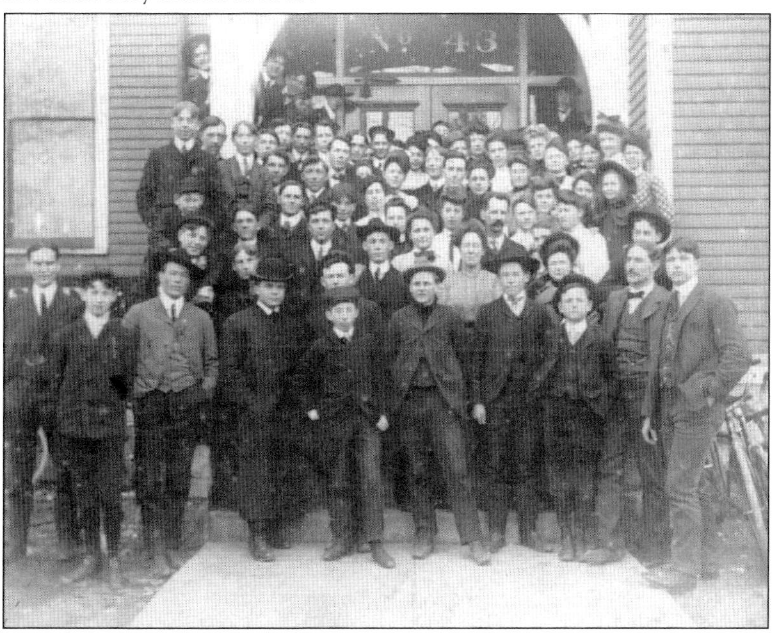

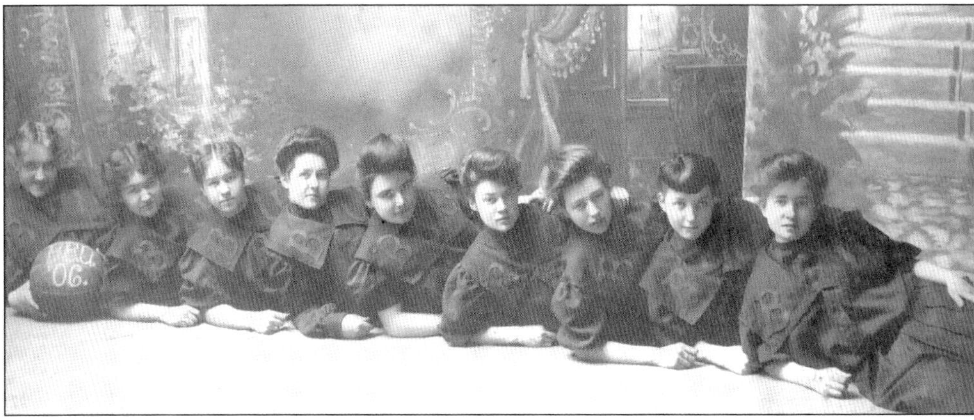

Brown's Business University. By the early 20th century, Brown's Business University had a student body of 175 young men and women when the new building opened. With the growth in the student population, there was also an increase in opportunities for extracurricular activities, such as a school newspaper and athletics. Above is a team photograph of the 1906 girls' basketball team, and below is a graduating class.

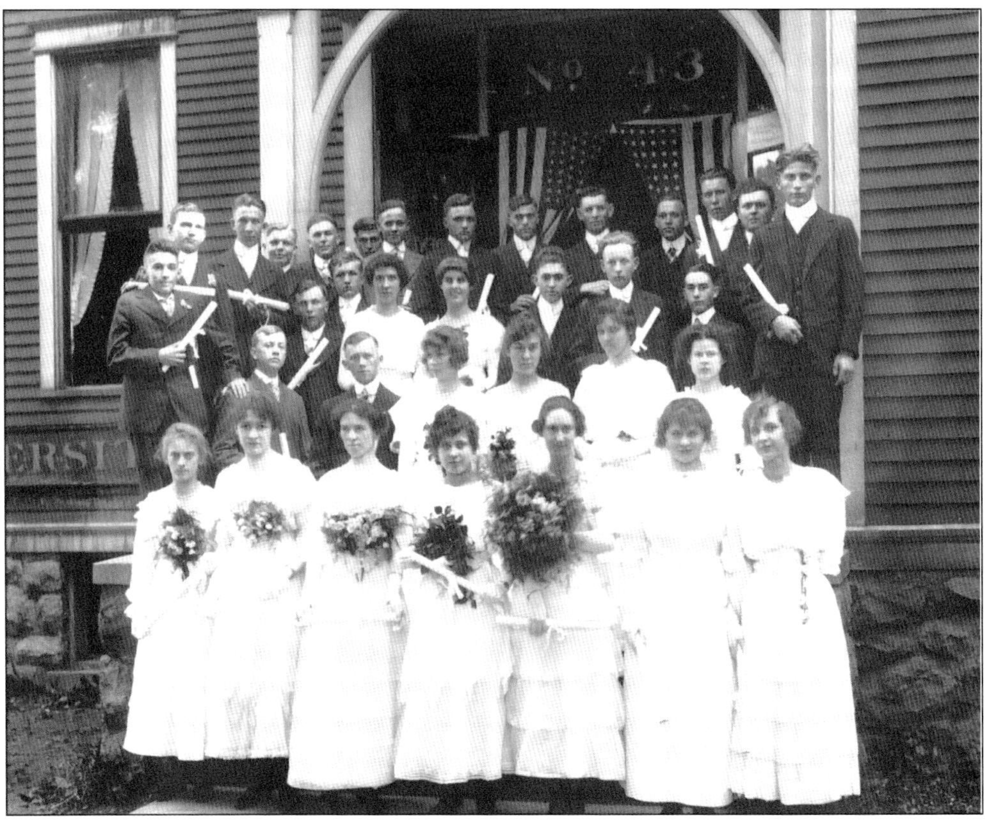

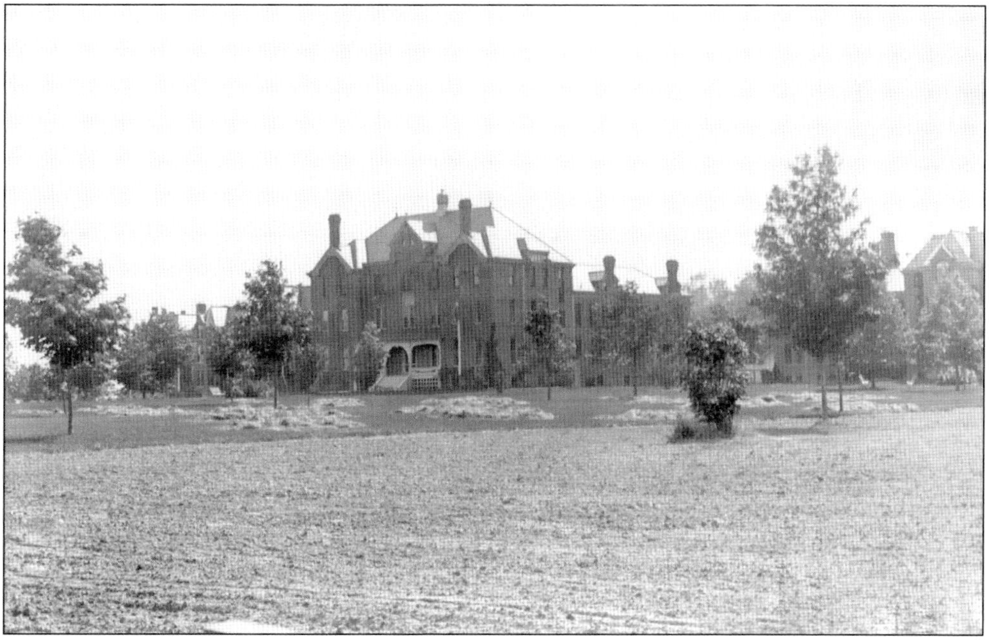

Adrian College. This college, originally Michigan Union College, was sponsored by the Wesleyan Methodists and moved from Leoni to Adrian in 1859. Rumor was that the temperance stance of the college was not welcome at Leoni. Initially it had in addition to the college a musical conservatory, theological seminary, and preparatory school. Adrian College's first president was Dr. Asa Mahan, a well-known educator, abolitionist, and former president of Oberlin College. Above is a photograph of the campus, and below is a photograph of the football team.

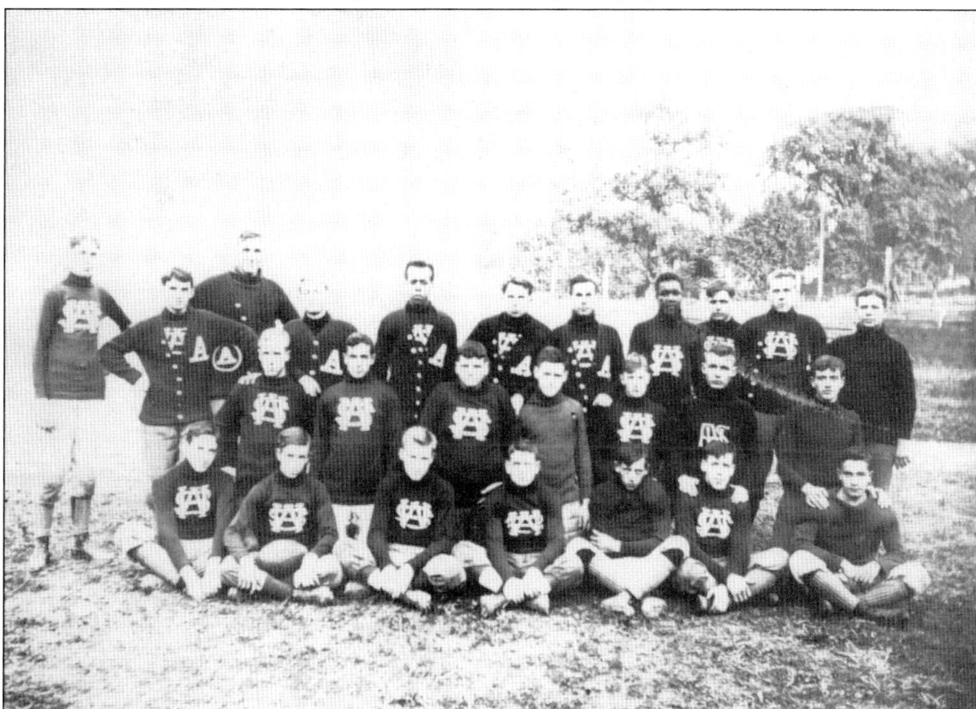

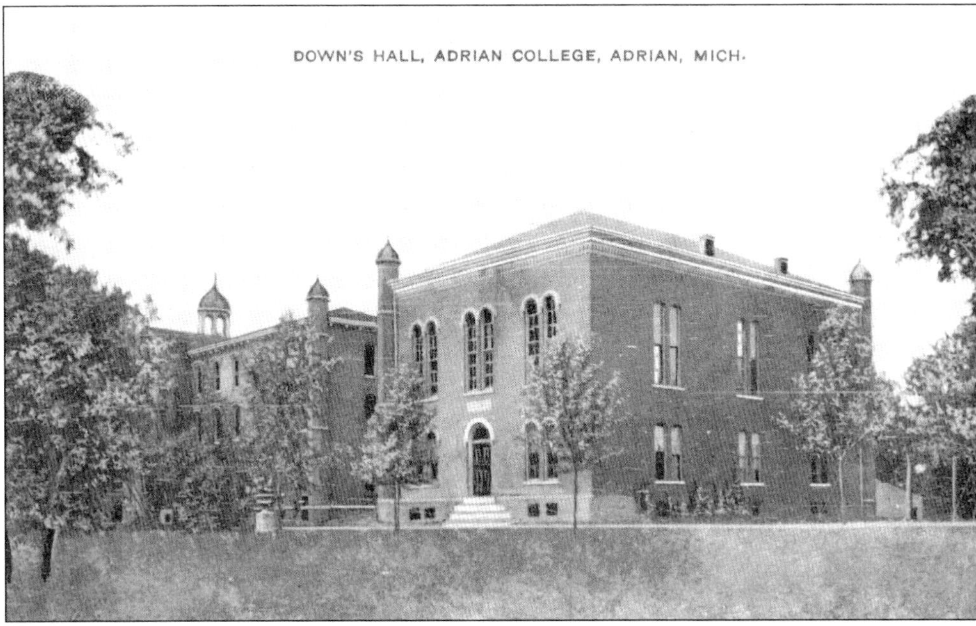

ADRIAN COLLEGE. The image above is of Downs Hall, which still stands on the campus and dates from 1860. Classrooms were located on the first floor, and the auditorium was located on the second floor. Each school day started out with chapel services held in the auditorium. The photograph below shows North Hall and the Science Building. North Hall contained the men's dormitory, president's office, administrative offices, library, YMCA office, and gymnasium. The science building housed lecture rooms and laboratories.

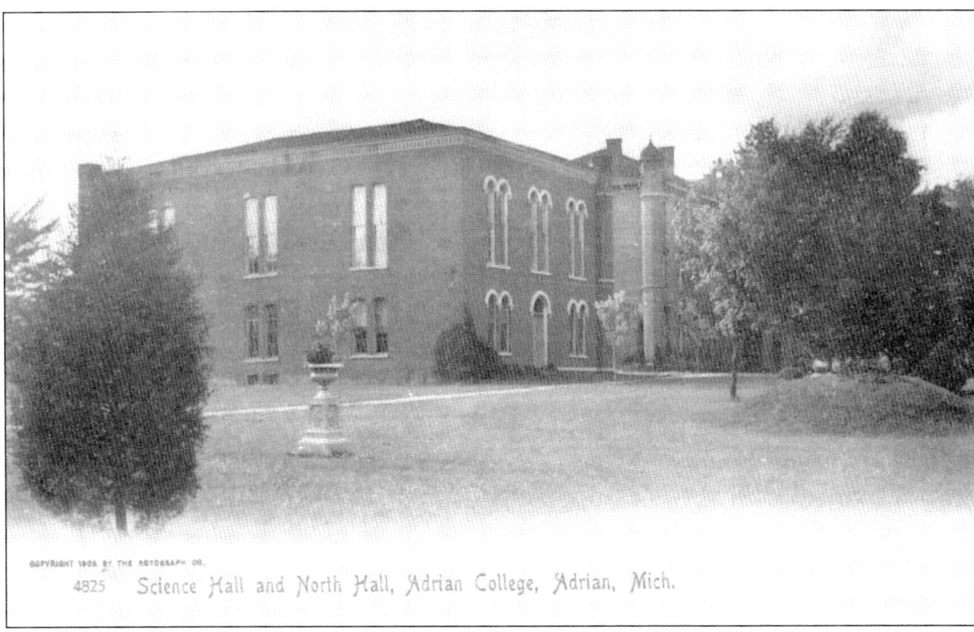

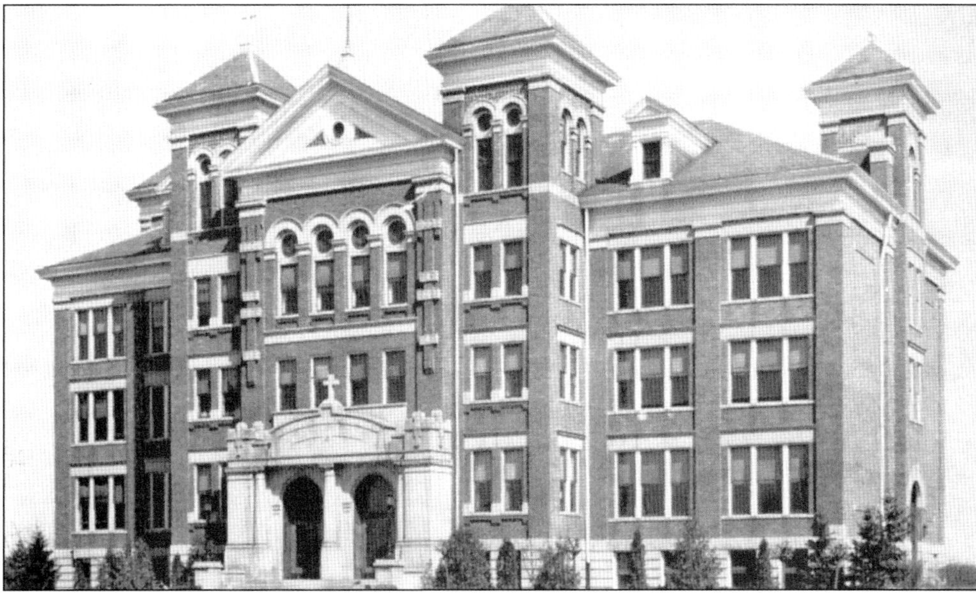

St. Joseph College. The Adrian Dominican Sisters founded this women's college in 1919. Initially it shared a space with St. Joseph Academy. The first dedicated building for the college opened in 1922 with Sacred Heart Hall, seen above. In the early years, the academic focus was upon the liberal arts and sciences and teacher education. Dominican Sisters served as the faculty, such as Sr. Marcine Klemm, seen below. In 1939, to avoid confusion with the academy, the school was christened Siena Heights College, after St. Catherine of Siena, and became coeducational in 1969.

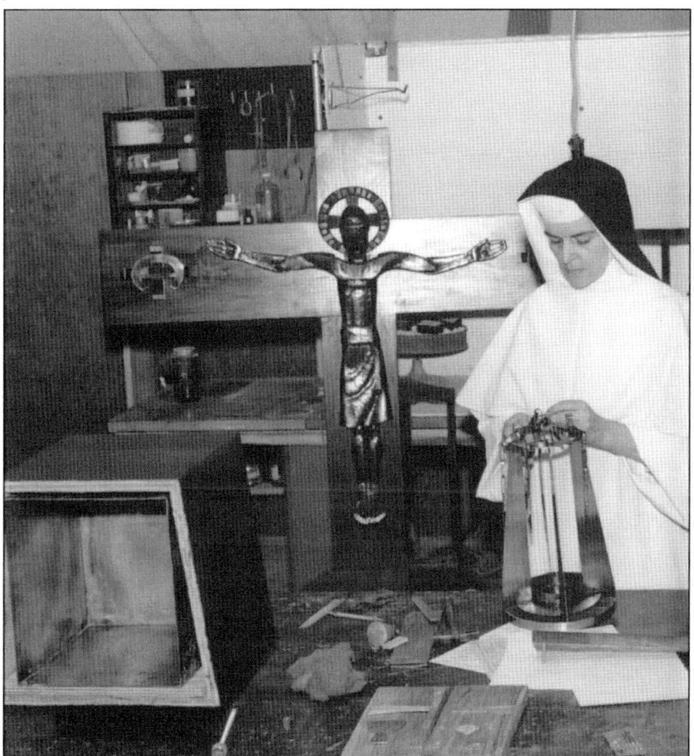

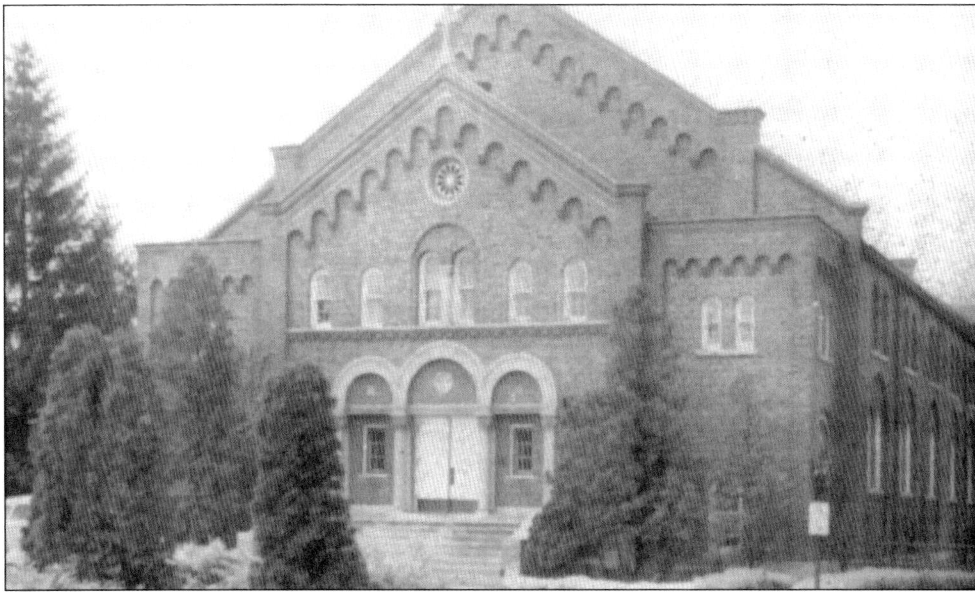

St. Joseph College. Walsh Hall opened in 1925 as the second building to serve the college. It included an auditorium for musical and theatrical events. It also had a gymnasium for sporting events at the college. Early athletic teams included both basketball and volleyball. This building has been called Sage Union since 1972 and now serves as a student center. With the expansion into more areas of study and graduate programs, this institution was renamed Siena Heights University in 1998.

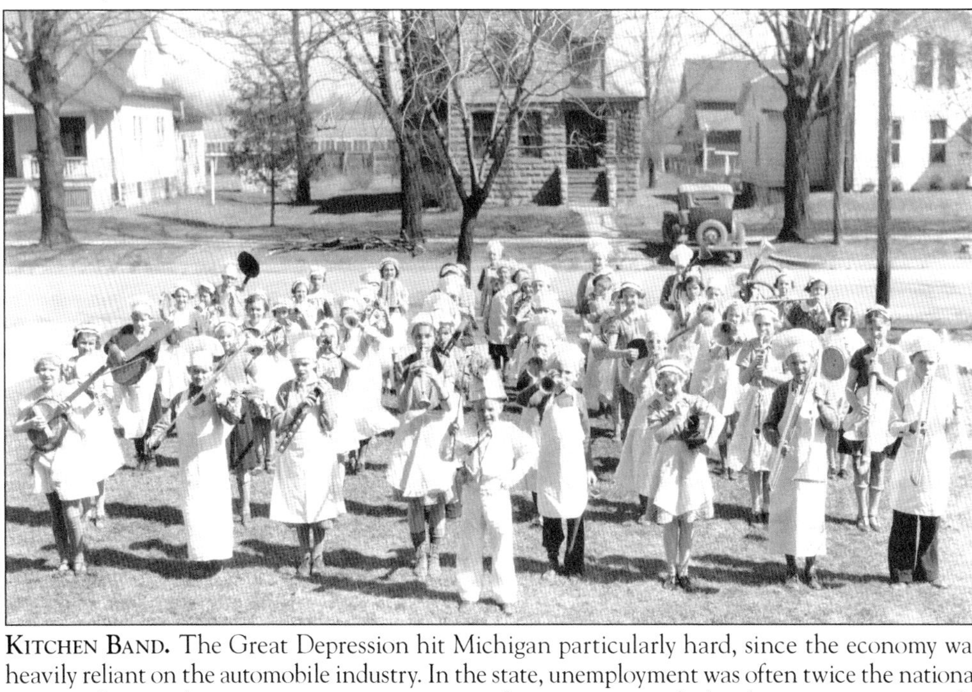

Kitchen Band. The Great Depression hit Michigan particularly hard, since the economy was heavily reliant on the automobile industry. In the state, unemployment was often twice the national average. Poverty, however, was not going to result in a poverty of school spirit or ingenuity for these fourth graders in 1936. Instead of traditional instruments, they have borrowed funnels, pots, and pans to create a kitchen band.

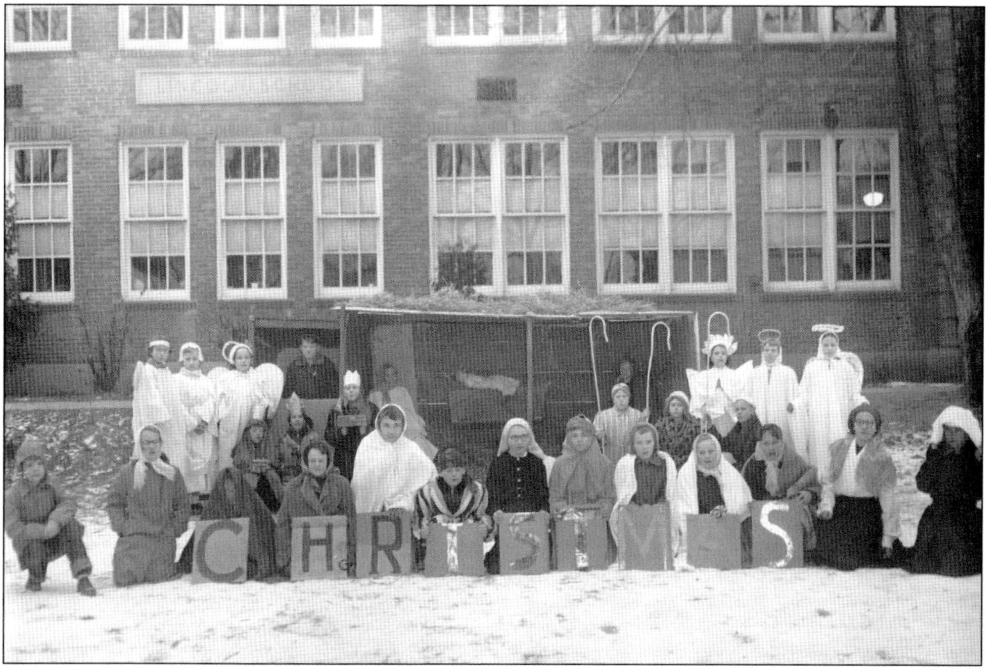

Nativity Pageant. Classroom celebrations were believed to be a wonderful way to create a sense of belonging for the students. Recognition of the major seasonal holidays was especially popular in many school systems. Above is a photograph of a Christmas Nativity Pageant from Lincoln Middle School and below is a fifth-grade Halloween masquerade party also from Lincoln.

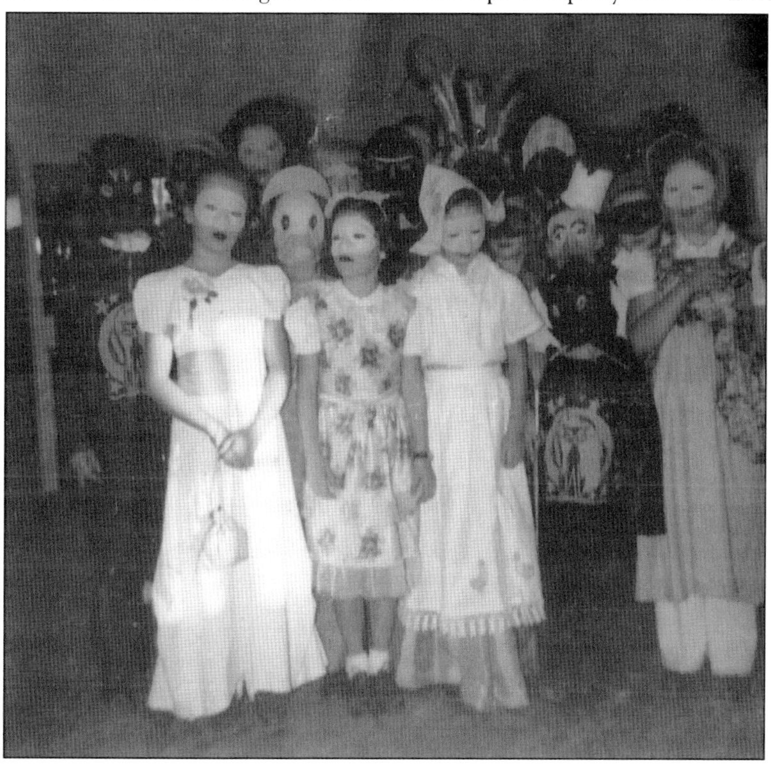

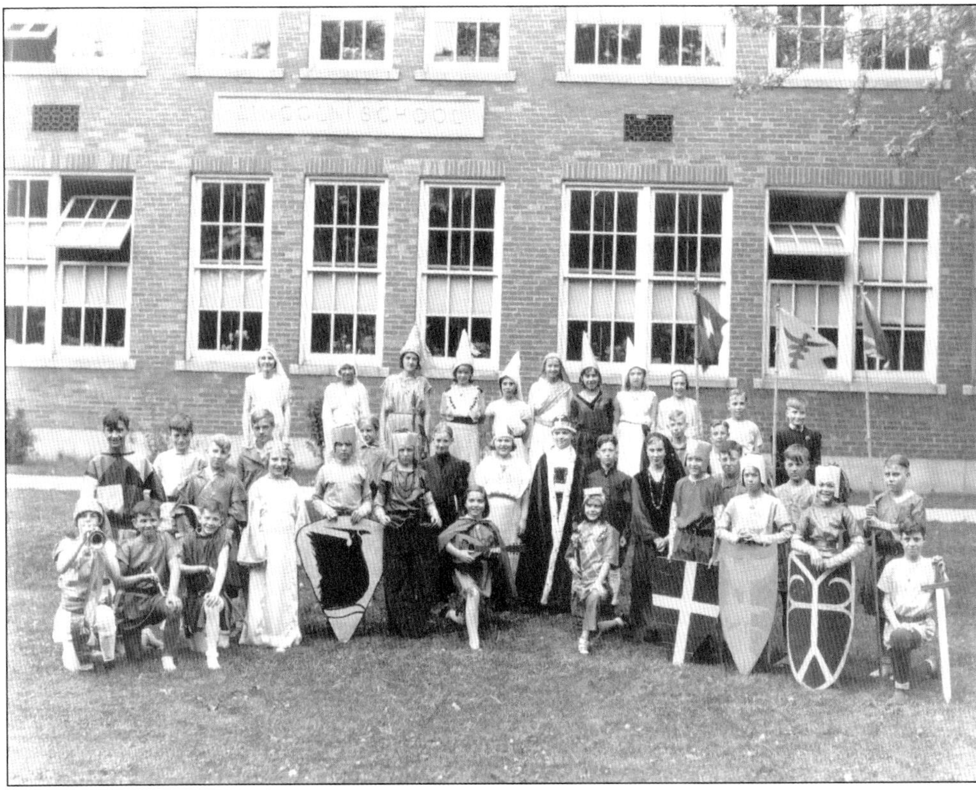

School Assemblies. Any type of assembly that could bring the various grades together was also considered important for developing school spirit. Lectures, performances, and field days were all utilized for this purpose. Often students themselves provided the entertainment. The above image is from 1933, with sixth graders re-creating the Middle Ages, and the image below is from 1921, with fifth graders acting as fairies.

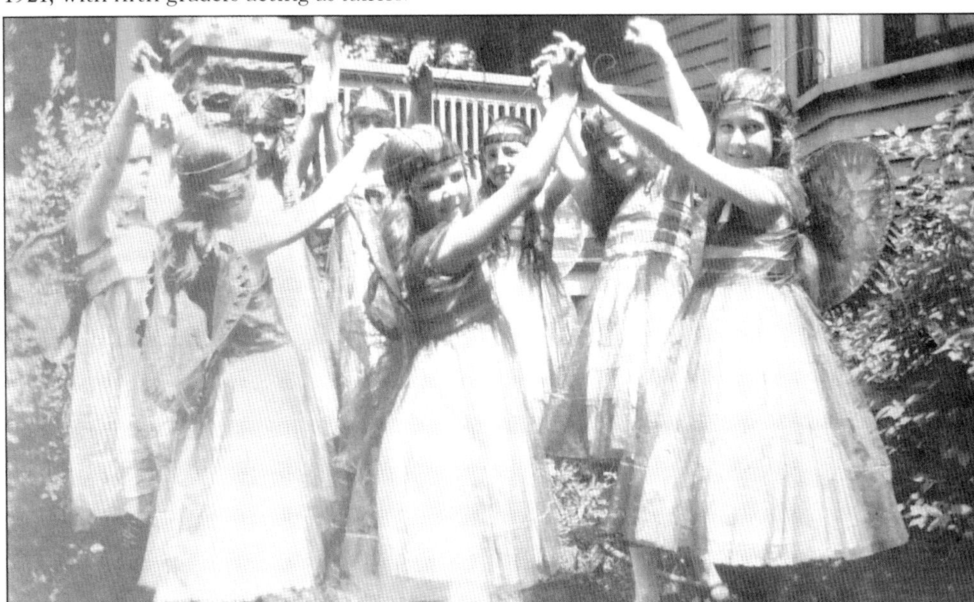

Four

Religious and Social Organizations

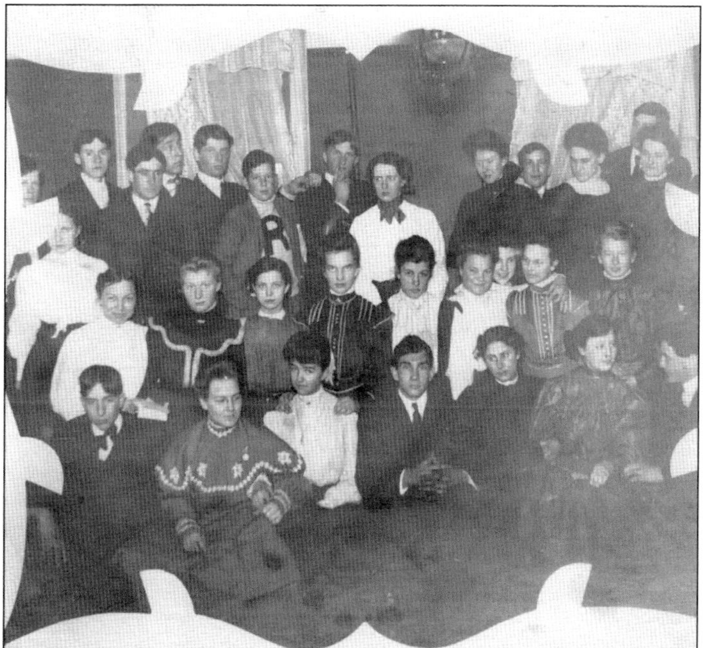

Bible Study Social, Raisin Valley Institute. The Raisin Valley Institute hoped to educate young people of all denominational backgrounds and also provide opportunities for them to socialize together. This photograph highlights a party thrown at the school that was also a Bible study. This would have been a common practice at organizations where everyone was of the same religious faith, however, it could have been quite interesting considering the diversity of this student body.

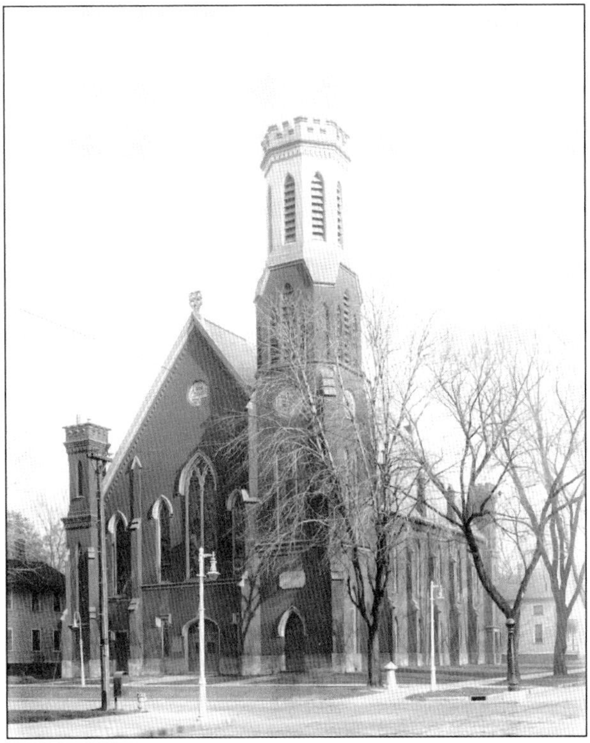

METHODIST EPISCOPAL CHURCH. A group of the faithful began to meet in their private homes in 1827, eventually being added to the Monroe circuit and then to the Tecumseh circuit as the population grew. A schism over governance issues caused a group to leave and form a Methodist Protestant church in 1830. Adrian had its own Methodist station in 1837, with the Methodist Episcopal church completed in 1840.

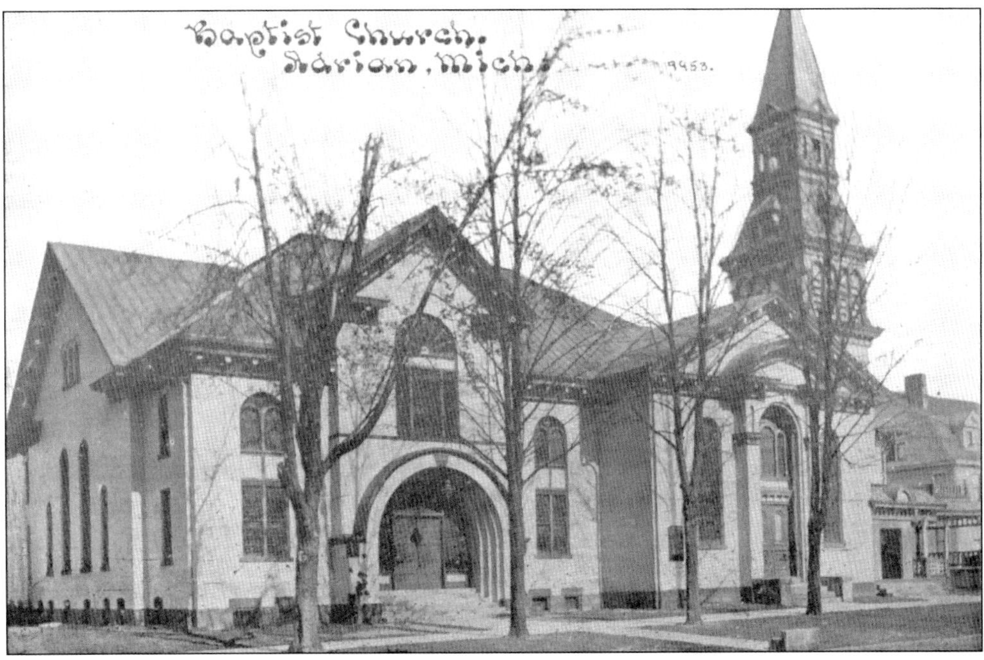

FIRST BAPTIST CHURCH. A group of 24 people began meeting regularly in the home of John Hutchins in 1831. By 1838, this group was able to purchase the land to build this church upon in the Greek Revival style. By the turn of the 20th century, First Baptist was the largest Protestant church in Adrian, with around 700 members. Unfortunately, with declining membership, the church closed in 2010 and the building was gifted to the Crossroads Community Church.

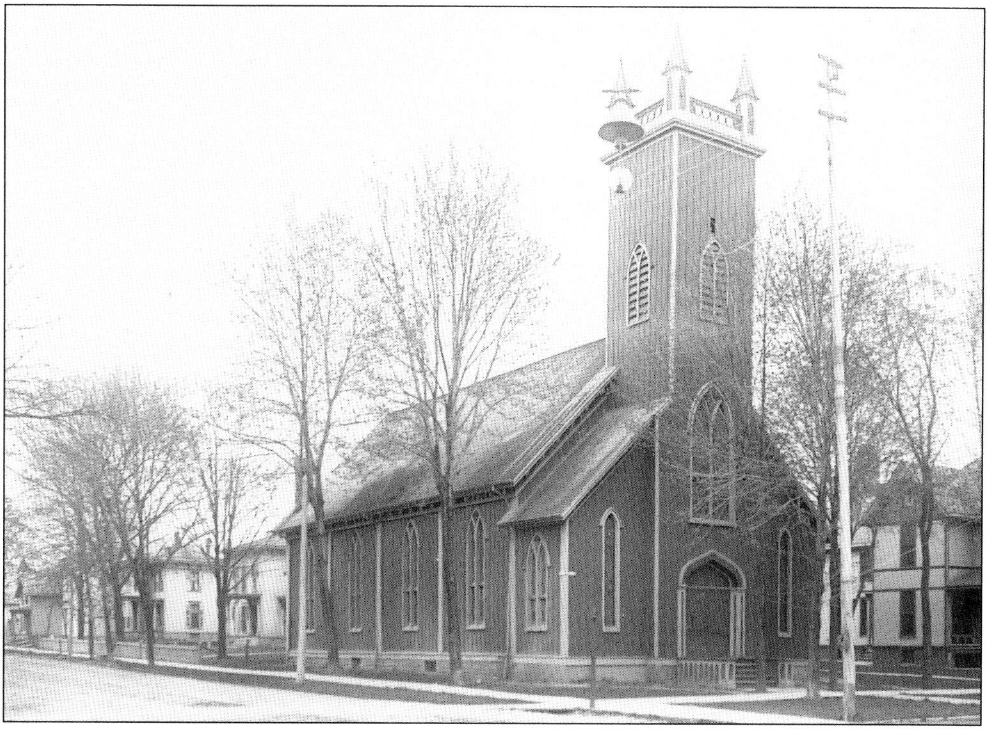

Christ Episcopal Church. In 1836, meetings were held in the log home of Ebenezer Selleck, who was a mason and farmer, to start an Episcopal society. By 1838, they were officially organized and had their first church building in 1851. The stone church was built on the same location in 1898 as the first church. It had to have massive repairs after a fire in 1958. Above is an image of the first church, and below is an image of the second church.

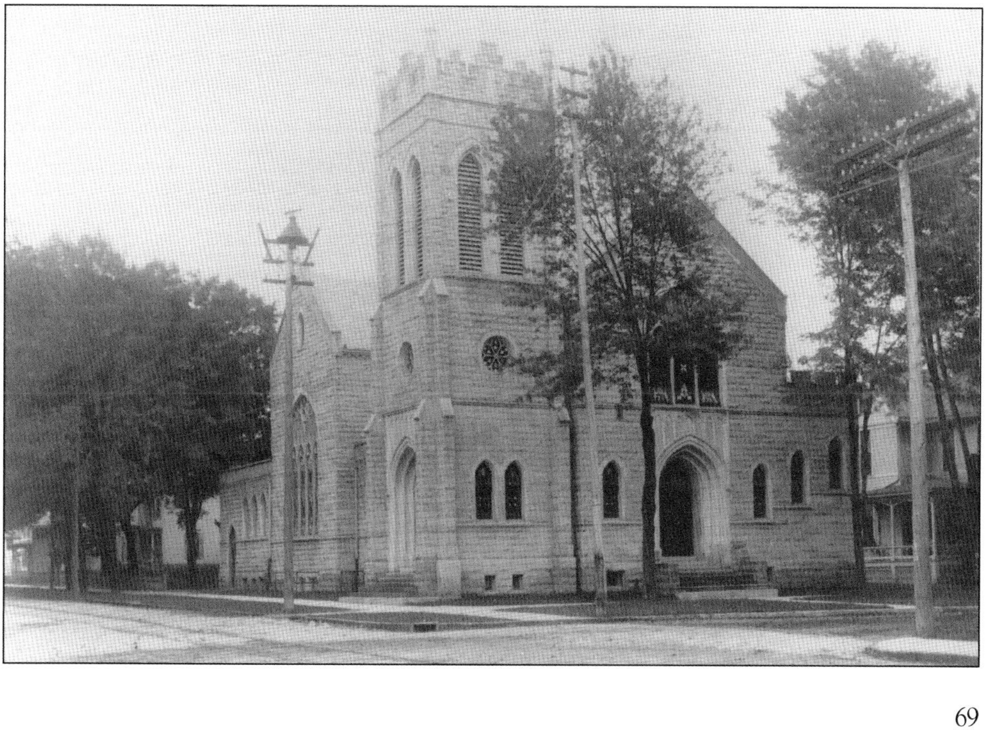

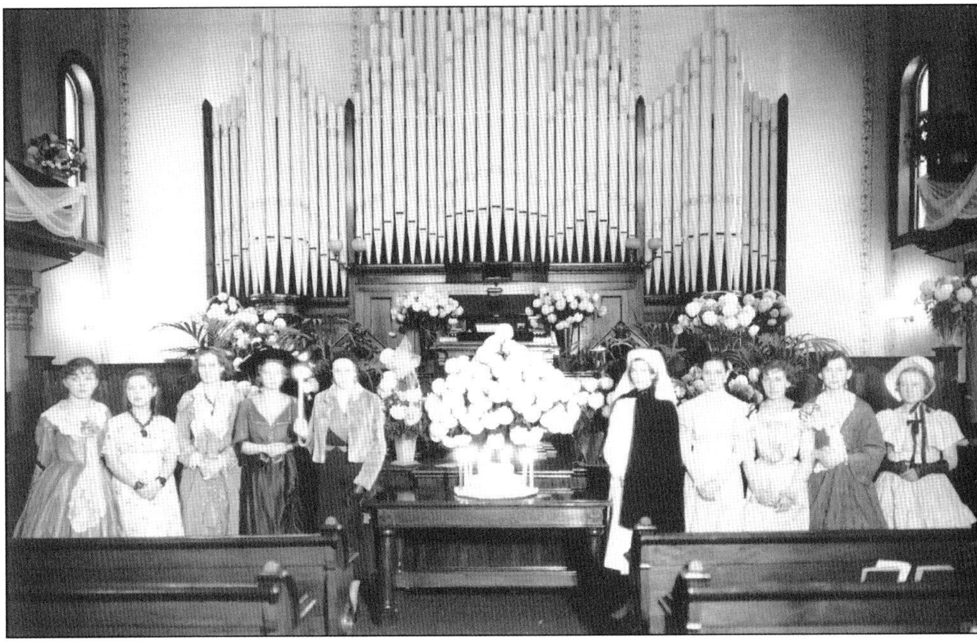

First Presbyterian Church. Although these young women are all smiles on the 100-year anniversary of First Presbyterian Church, its history is perhaps one of the most contentious in the county, which even involved the state legislature at one point. A group of Congregationalists and Presbyterians began meeting in homes by 1832. The congregation shifted between the two denominations until the final schism, with the Congregationalists leaving to form Plymouth Church in 1854.

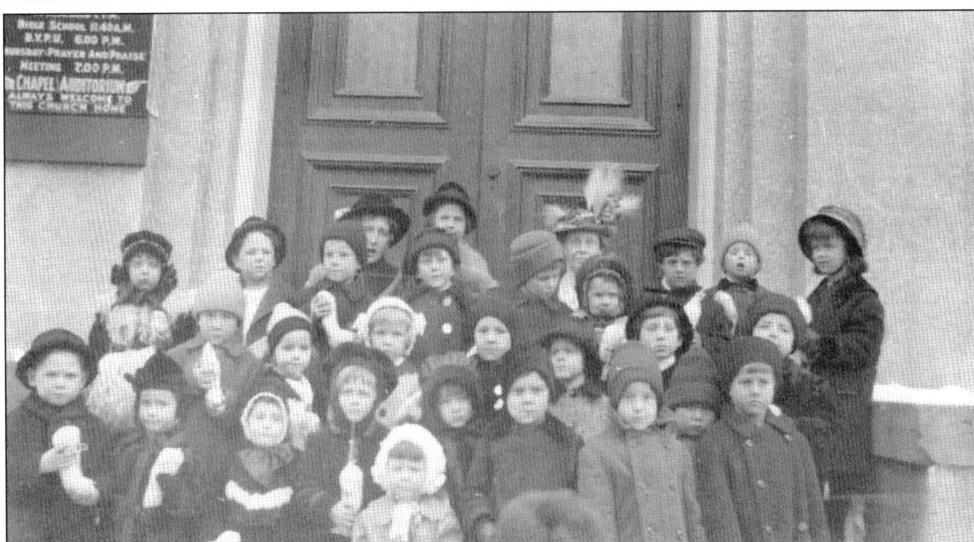

Sunday School, First Baptist Church. The Sunday school movement started in England as a religious mission to teach children of the poor basic literacy and ethical behavior. This model spread to the United States by the late 18th century. However, with the development of the common school, Sunday schools became primarily concerned with religious instruction for the children of church members by the late 19th century. This photograph depicts a Sunday school class from the First Baptist Church of Adrian.

METHODIST PROTESTANT CHURCH. After the split with the Methodist Episcopal Church, this body was served by itinerants for a period of time until Dr. Asa Mahan became their pastor. This congregation purchased Adrian College in 1868, so it was often referred to as College Church. In 1880, this group was able to purchase the former Plymouth Congregational Church as its new home, which is shown here.

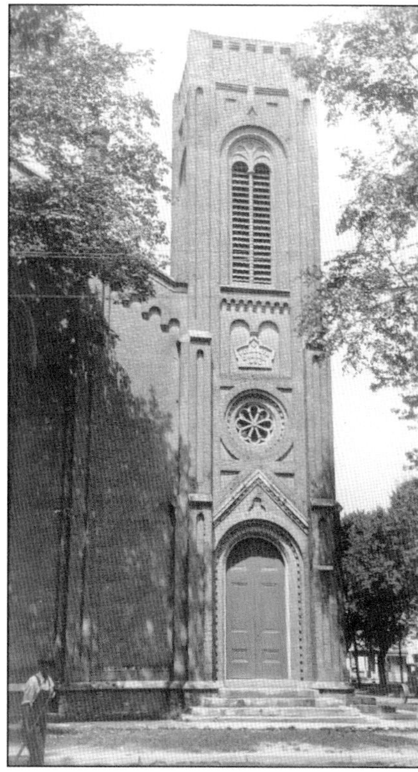

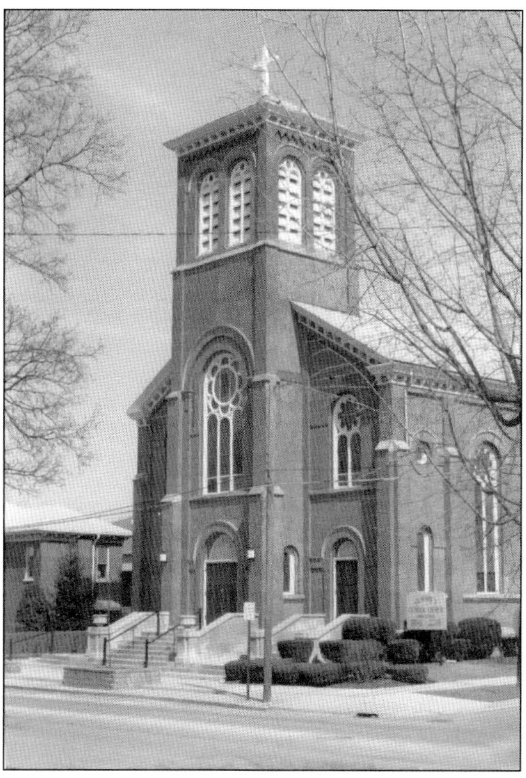

ST. MARY'S CATHOLIC CHURCH. A Catholic mission was begun in 1840 by Father Smoulder, who visited monthly from Monroe. With a growing Irish and German Catholic population, the first church was created in 1845, with the second structure (shown here) built in 1869. St. Mary's started the first parochial Catholic day school in the county for the children of its parishioners. Even with the schism, St. Mary's boasted a large church body of nearly 1,000 in 1900.

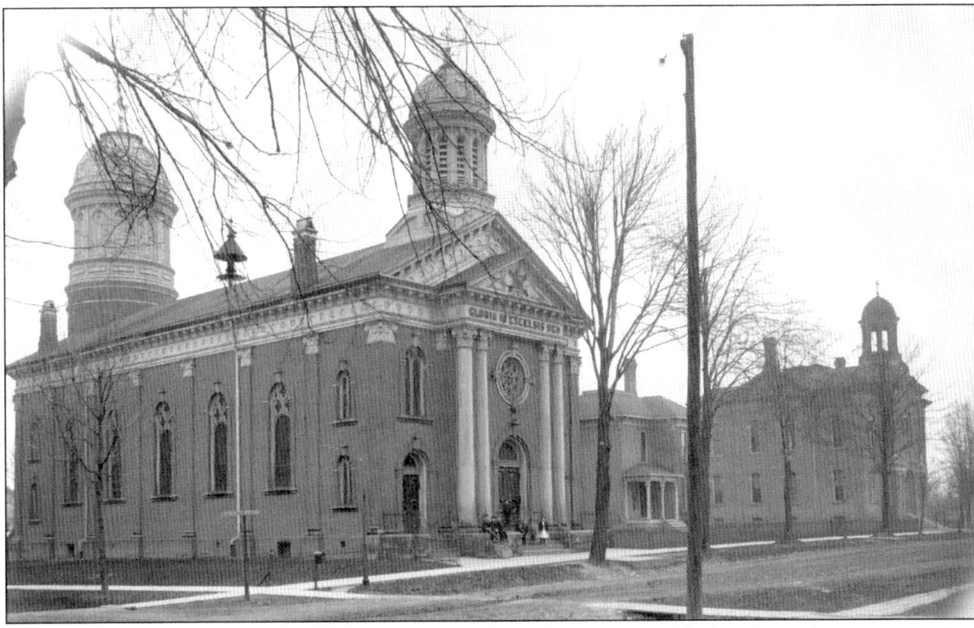

St. Joseph Catholic Church. Members of a group of German Catholics desired services in their own language, so they broke away from St. Mary's Church in 1862. For approximately three years, this new congregation was ministered to by Redemptorist monks from Detroit until receiving their own priest in 1865. With a growing population, they began building this church in 1873, which also had a rectory and a day school.

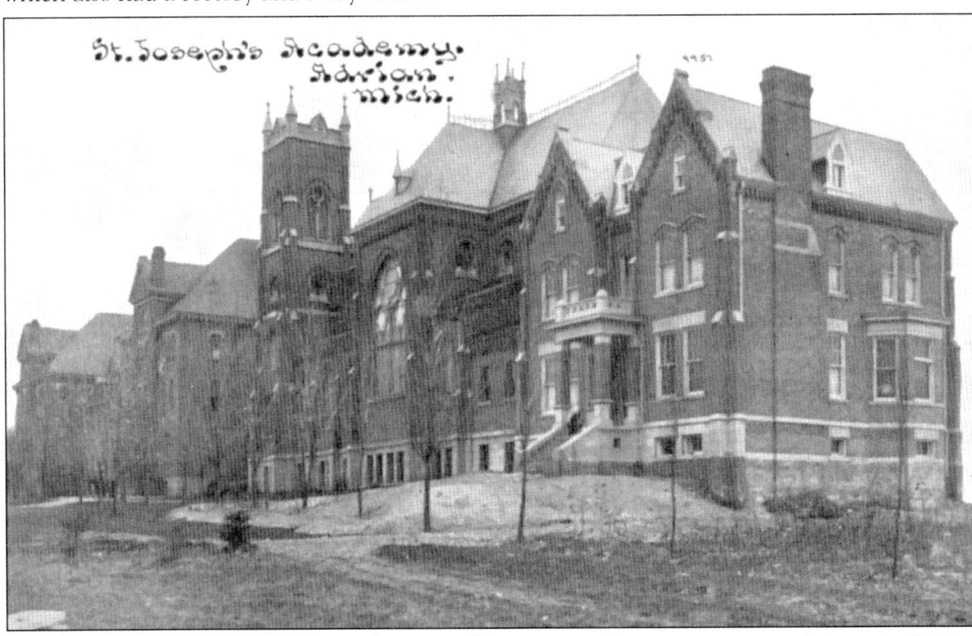

Dominican Motherhouse. A small group of Dominican Sisters was sent to Adrian in 1879 to serve a growing Catholic population, acting as teachers for St. Mary's Parish. More Sisters also were sent to the area in 1884 to establish a hospital for the aged. Under the direction of Mother Camilla Madden, the Sisters soon opened institutions to serve the educational needs of Catholic females, and in 1886 a new building was erected to house the Sisters, students, and patients.

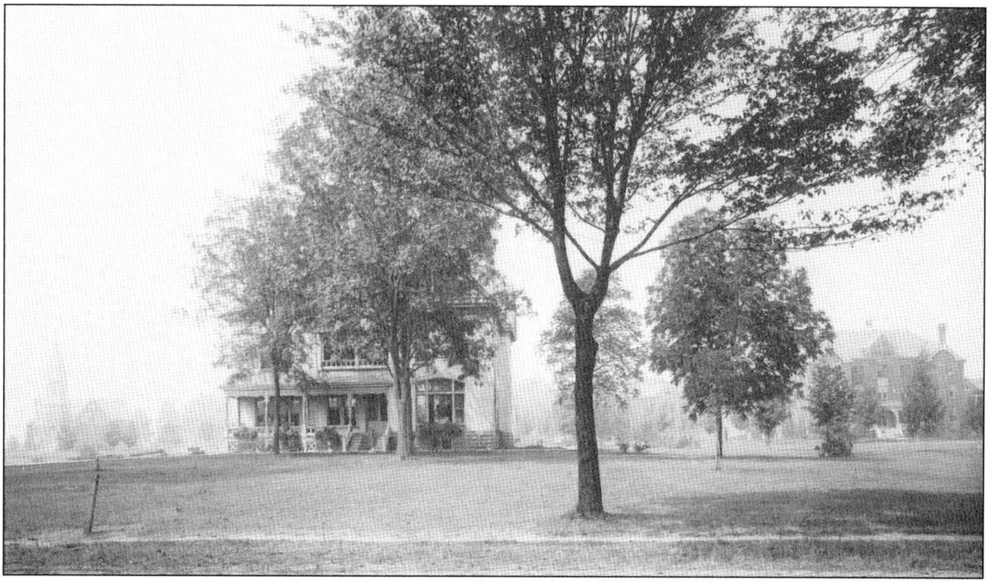

Michigan Industrial Home for Girls, Chapel. Religious services were an integral component to help delinquent children in the reform school movement. As was common, the chapel was the central focus on the campus. The Michigan Industrial Home for Girls was unusual in that both Protestant and Catholic worship services were offered to the girls at this school. Nationally, usually only Protestant faiths were promoted in the reform systems.

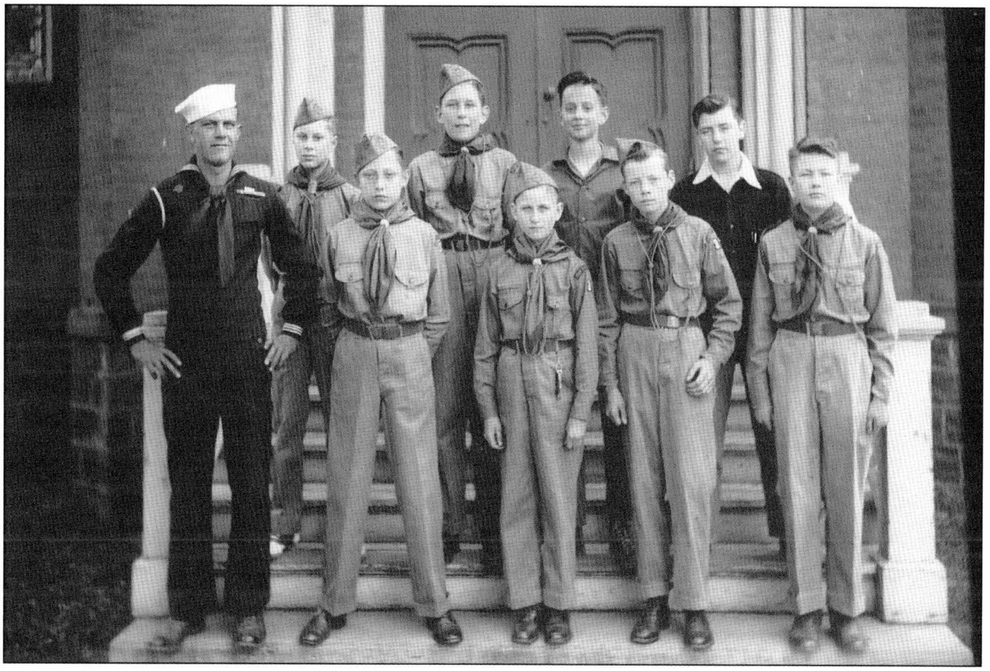

Boy Scouts. The Boys Scouts of America was incorporated in 1910 with a mission to teach, especially through outdoor educational programs, patriotism and self-reliance to young men. Hands-on learning was believed to be extremely important in building confidence and leadership skills. The traditional division in the group was younger boys being Cub Scouts and the older boys being Boy Scouts. These Adrian Boy Scouts are posing in front of St. John's Lutheran Church.

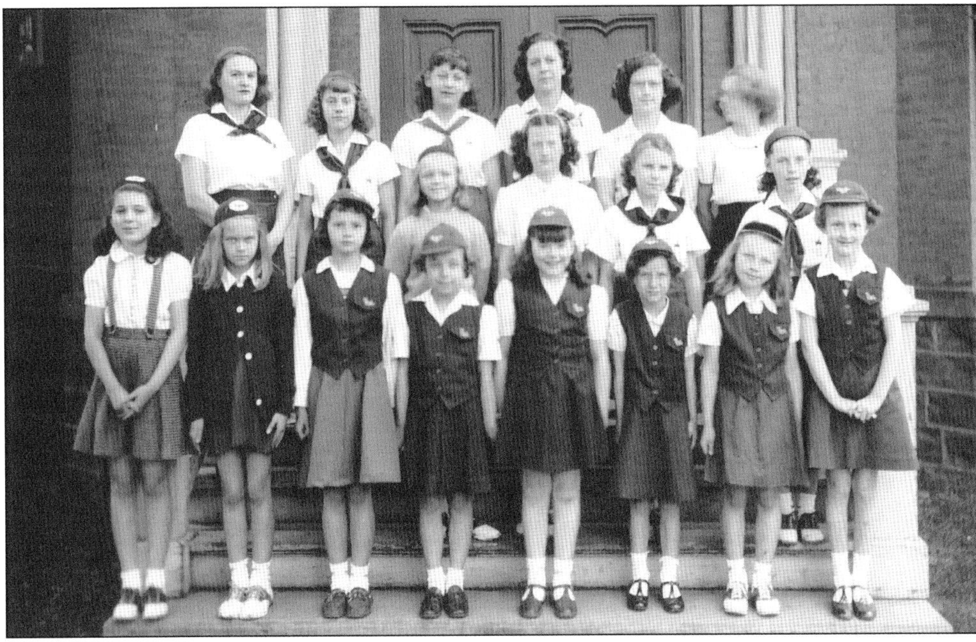

Campfire Girls. The Campfire Girls organization began in Vermont in 1911 as a way to offer educational opportunities for young women in the great outdoors similar to what the Boy Scouts offered for young men. Campfire Girls had summer camps and in 1913 started an outreach to younger girls called the Bluebird program. This image includes both Campfire Girls and Bluebirds from Adrian.

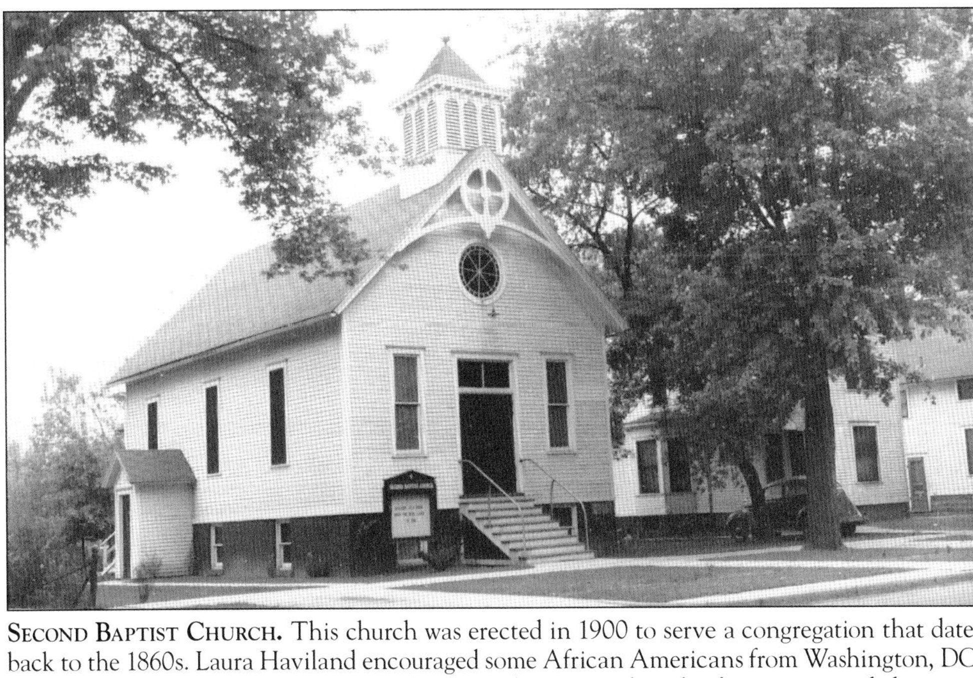

Second Baptist Church. This church was erected in 1900 to serve a congregation that dates back to the 1860s. Laura Haviland encouraged some African Americans from Washington, DC, to immigrate to Adrian. The Reverend A.I.J. Jackson served as the first pastor, and the group initially worshiped in a hall downtown for many years before purchasing the current property on North Broad Street.

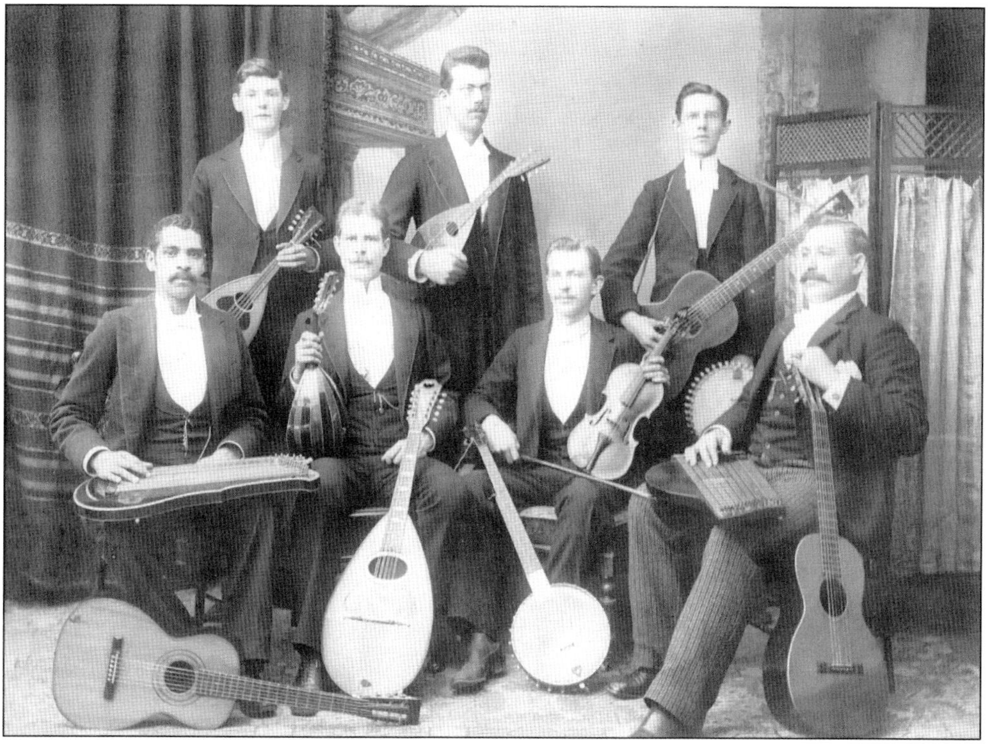

Adrian Mandolin Club. Mandolin groups were popular from the late 19th century until about 1920 in many US cities. Such orchestras highlighted instruments from the mandolin family, and the repertoire of music played could range from popular marches to classical pieces. This 1892 photograph shows several instruments that would have been typical, like the mandola, as well as less common instruments, such as the violin.

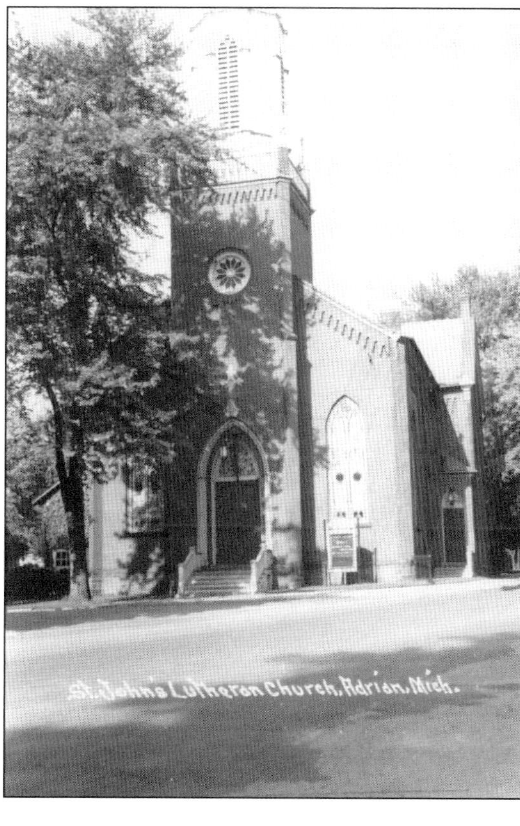

St. John's Lutheran Church. Affiliated with the Missouri Synod, St. John's was the first Lutheran congregation established in Lenawee County. German-Lutherans began to immigrate to the region in the 1840s and were served by a missionary pastor from Monroe until 1847, when they could found their own church and issue a call for a minister. The congregation also opened a parochial school for their children and built a more impressive place of worship in 1861.

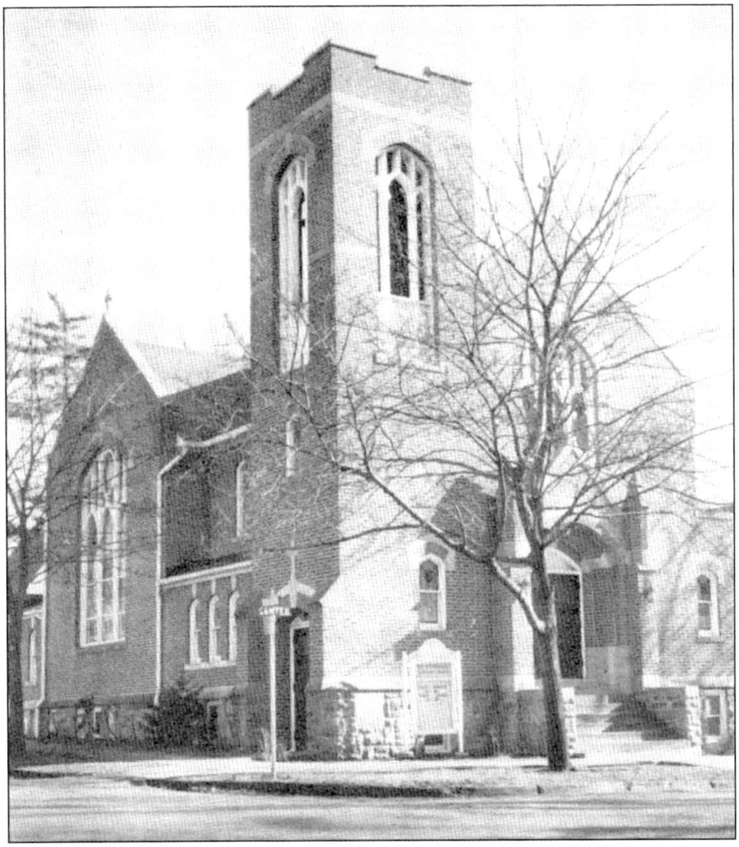

ST. STEPHEN'S LUTHERAN CHURCH. Now affiliated with the Wisconsin Evangelical Lutheran Synod, St. Stephen's Lutheran Church was formed after a schism at St. John's caused 11 members to leave and form a new church of the Michigan Synod in 1860. The first church was originally located at Toledo and Center Streets. They also started a Lutheran parochial school for the children of the congregation. At left is an image of the second church, and below is an image of one of their early choirs.

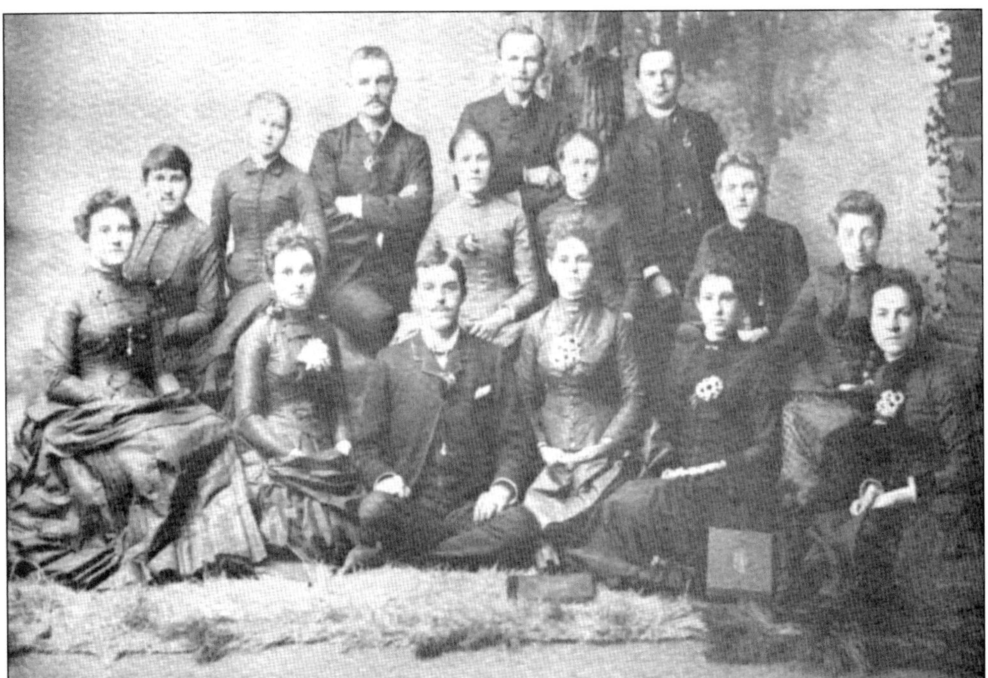

Masonic Temple. Fraternal organizations were extremely popular in the 19th century, and Adrian reflected this trend. Often, leading figures of the community were among the members who pledged mutual support to one another. By the late 19th century, Adrian had chapters of societies such as the International Order of Odd Fellows, Freemasons, and the Grand Order of the Eastern Star, one of few that accepted both men and women as members. Pictured to the right is the temple, and below is a view inside the lodge.

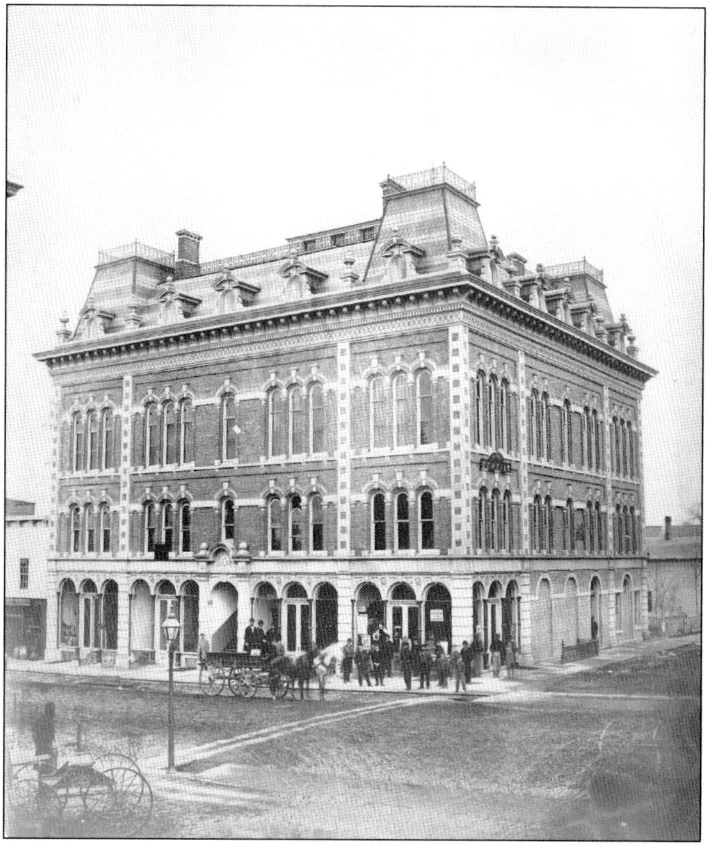

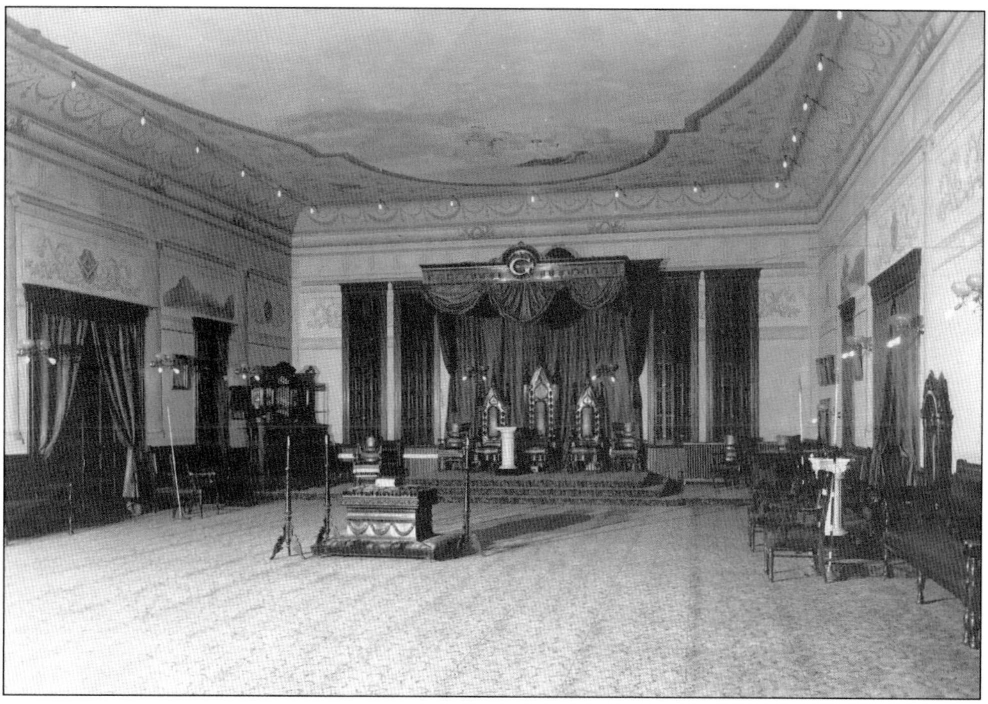

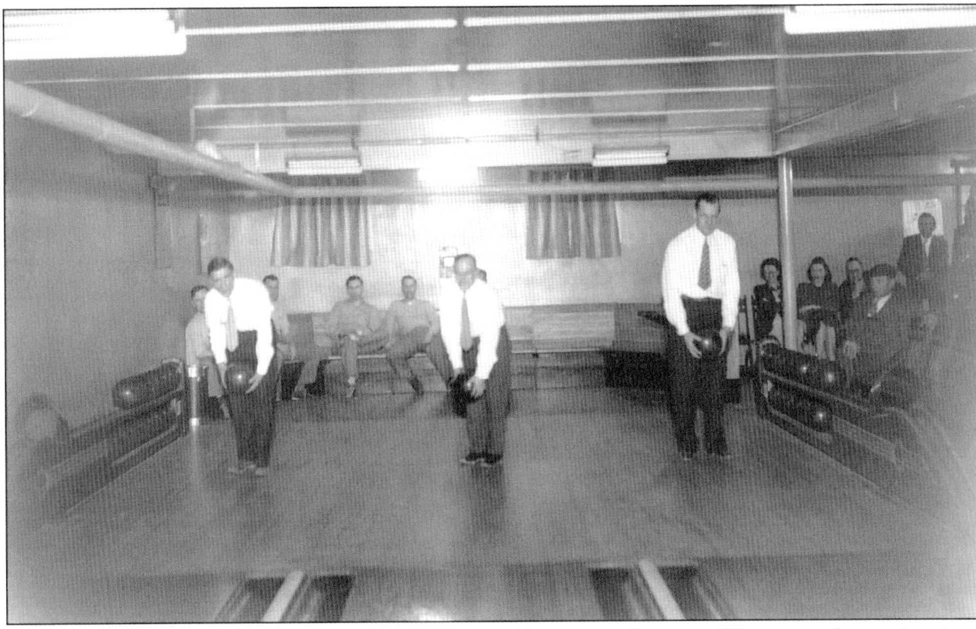

Young Men's Society, St. John's Lutheran Church. Certain Christian denominations were suspicious of fraternal organizations such as the Masons due to secret rites and fears of either an antireligious stance or an endorsement of liberal theology. Many started their own social groups for church members. Here is a photograph of the Young Men's Society enjoying fellowship and bowling.

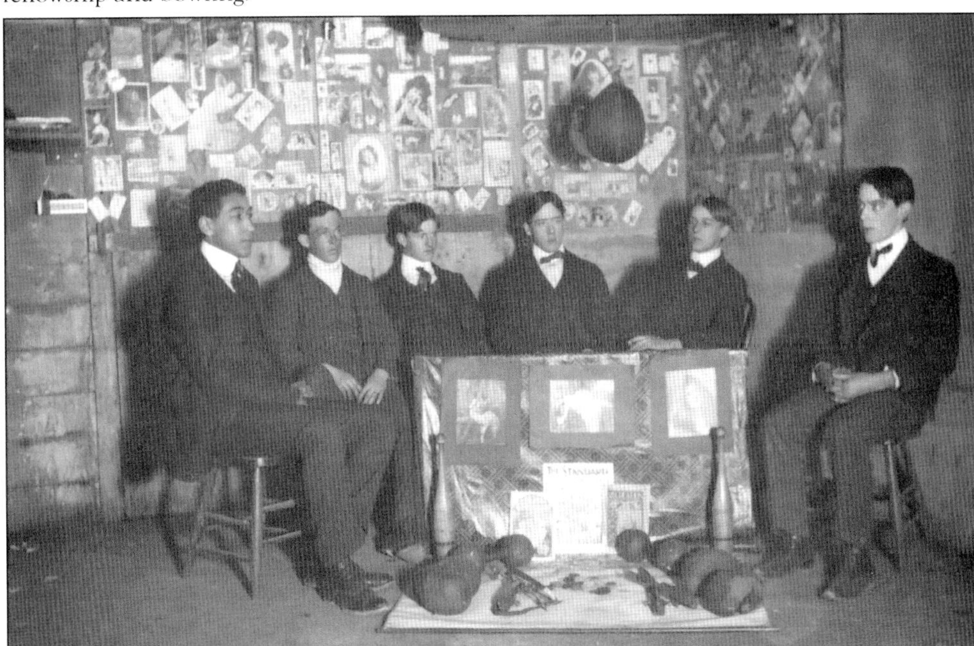

Adrian Camera Club. In 1890, the Adrian Scientific Society organized a section for an amateur camera club. Members would meet twice a month to share techniques and new technologies, as well as display their recent photographs. The society had a darkroom set up specifically for members. Once a year, the club would also hold excursions to area attractions of photographic interest.

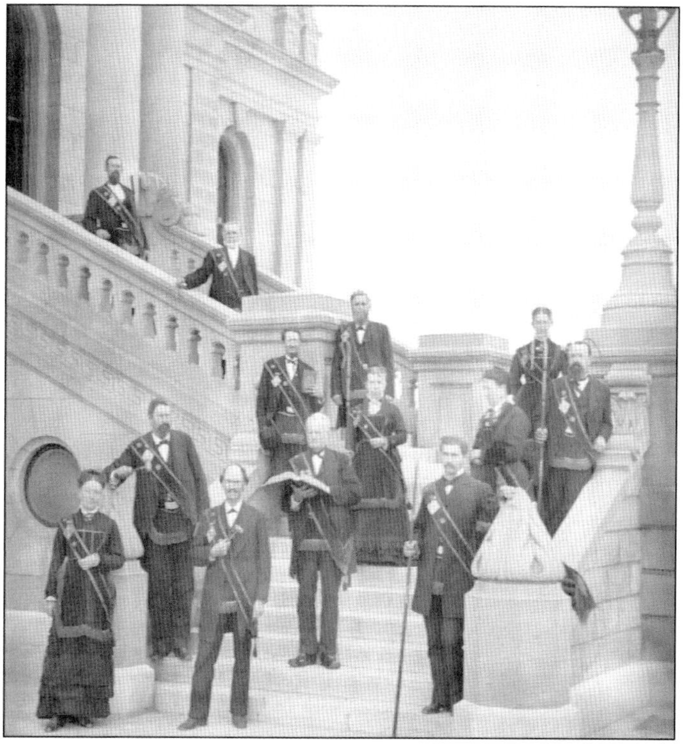

THE NATIONAL GRANGE OF THE ORDER OF PATRONS OF HUSBANDRY, ADRIAN OFFICERS. The Grange began in 1867 as a fraternal organization for farmers to help serve their interests. Headquartered in Washington, DC, this organization lobbied for rural free delivery, regulation of railroad and grain elevator fees, temperance, and suffrage. Men and women were equal members in this group, and local chapters also often held social events. For example, the chapter in Adrian once had a tree-planting party.

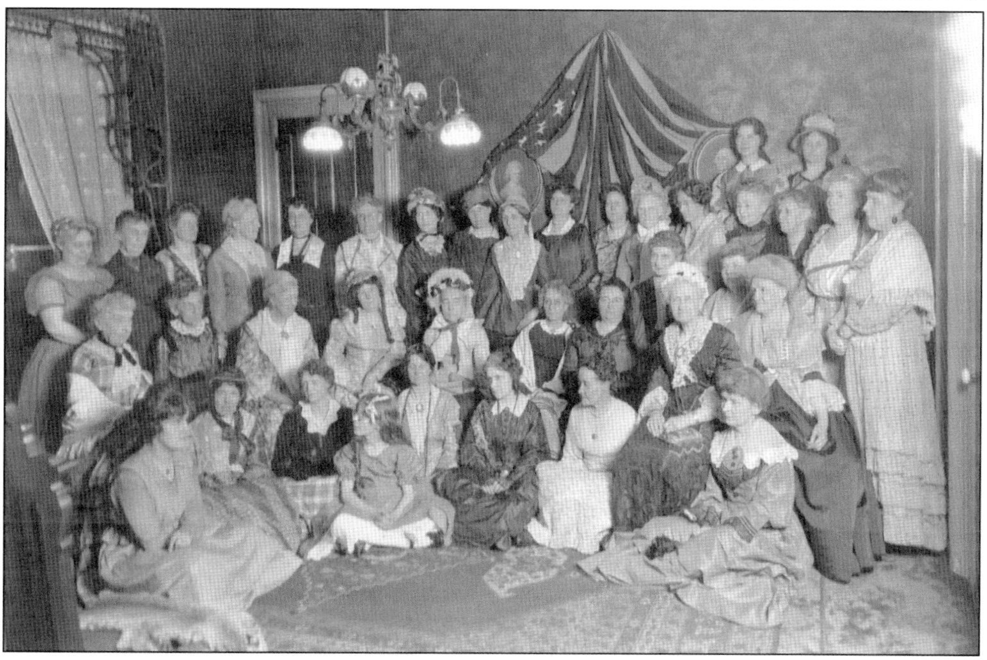

DAUGHTERS OF THE AMERICAN REVOLUTION, LUCY WOLCOTT BARNUM CHAPTER. The DAR was created in 1890 as a woman's service club, with a primary focus on encouraging patriotism, historic preservation, and education. One requirement for membership was to be a blood descendant of a person who was directly involved in the struggle for US independence. Here the Adrian chapter has gathered to celebrate George Washington's birthday with a party in 1919.

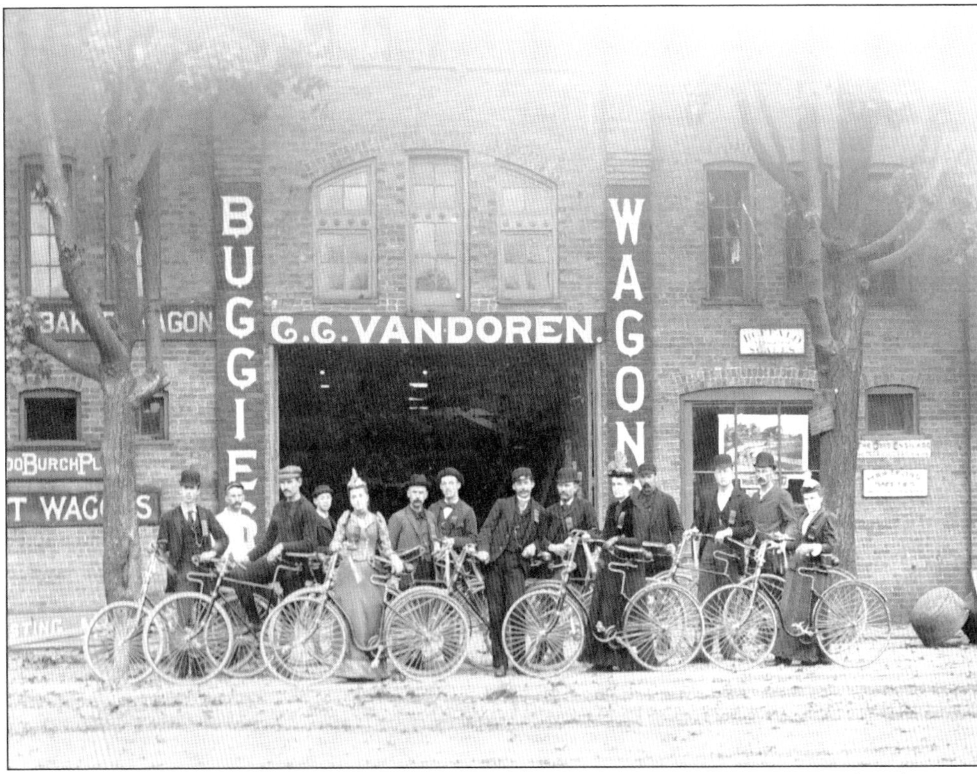

ADRIAN BICYCLE CLUB. Two decades before cycling became all the rage nationwide, when improvements such as inflatable rubber tires and cushioned seats made riding more comfortable, bicycling was a popular pastime in Adrian. The Adrian Bicycle Club was organized in 1870, and with the founding of the Maple City Cyclists in 1884, Adrian could boast of two clubs. These organized groups not only cycled together but also held dances, parades, and formal teas.

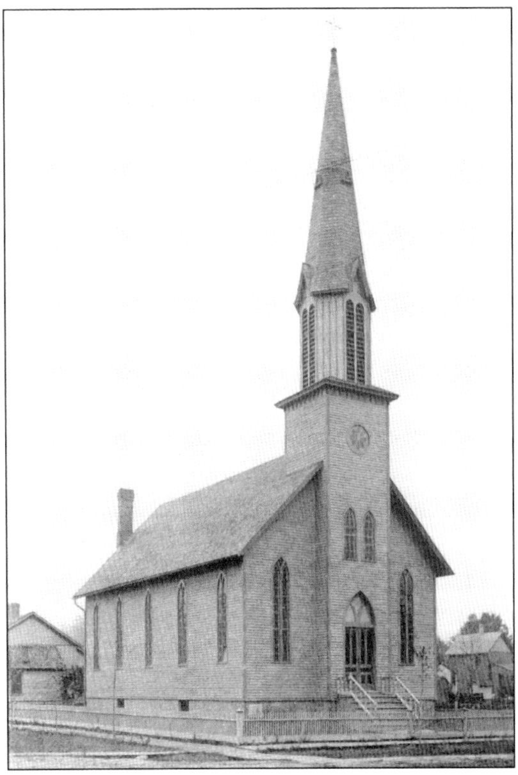

IMMANUEL EVANGELICAL CHURCH. This congregation was formed by a former teacher, Rev. J.B. Meister, from St. Stephen's Lutheran School in 1892. Many of the congregants of St. Stephen's followed him and became affiliated with the German Evangelical Synod of North America, which had roots in both the Lutheran and Reformed traditions. Their structure was influenced by the Gothic style, as evidenced by its pointed arches and tall, vertical lines.

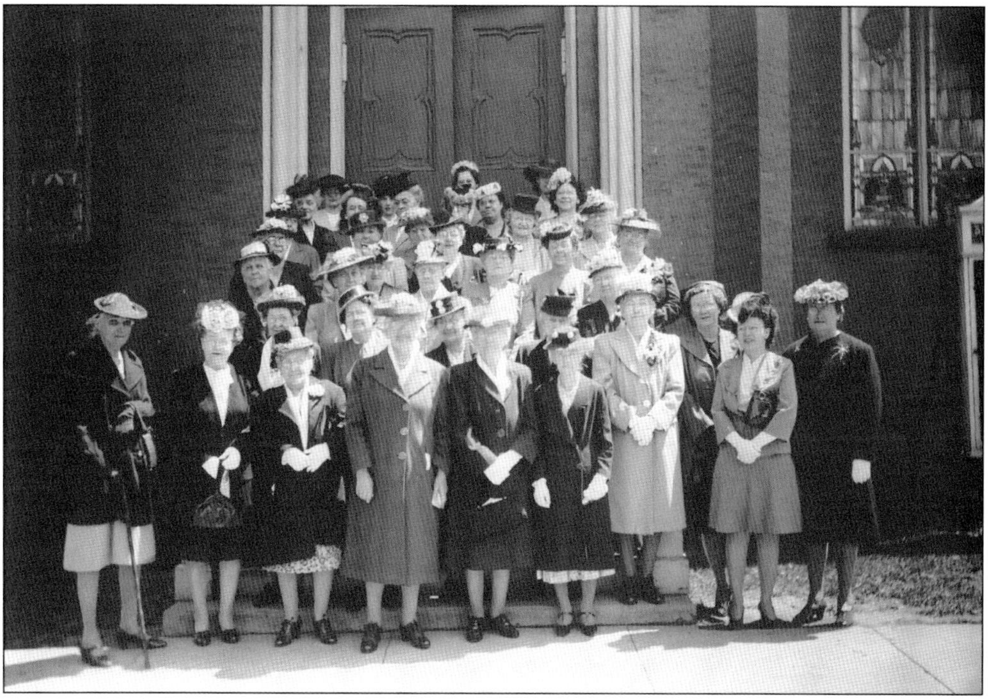

Ladies' Aid Society and Tabea Society. Many Lutheran congregations of the Missouri-Synod had women's missionary societies by the early 20th century. The purpose of these women's groups was to raise funds for both foreign and domestic missions. The Tabea Society sewed products to sell, and the Ladies' Aid Society often collected spare change with mite boxes. The above image is of the Ladies' Aid Society, and the image below is of the Tabea Society.

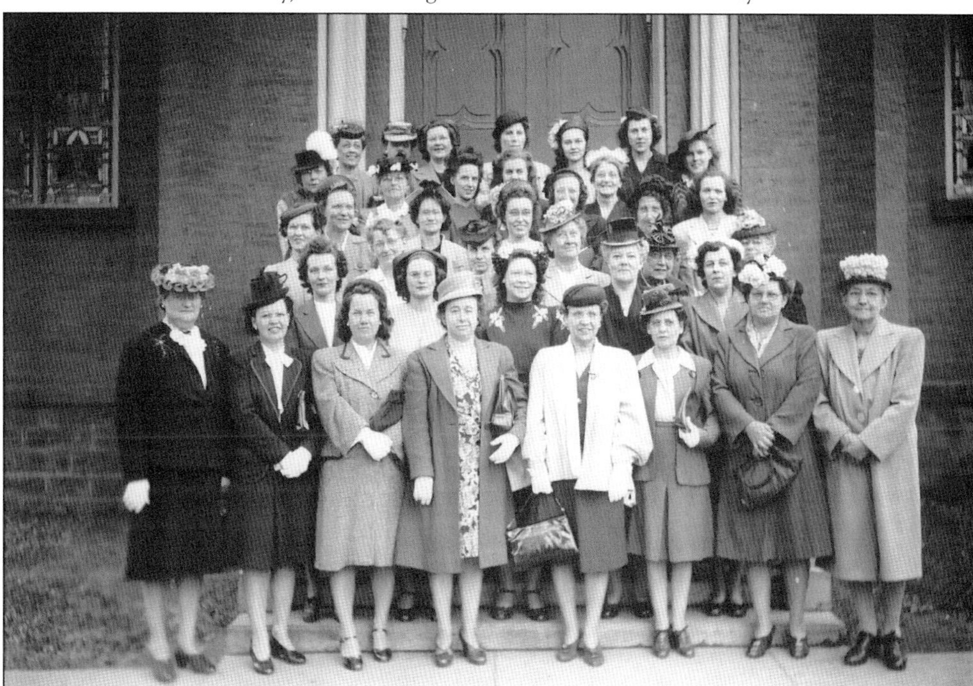

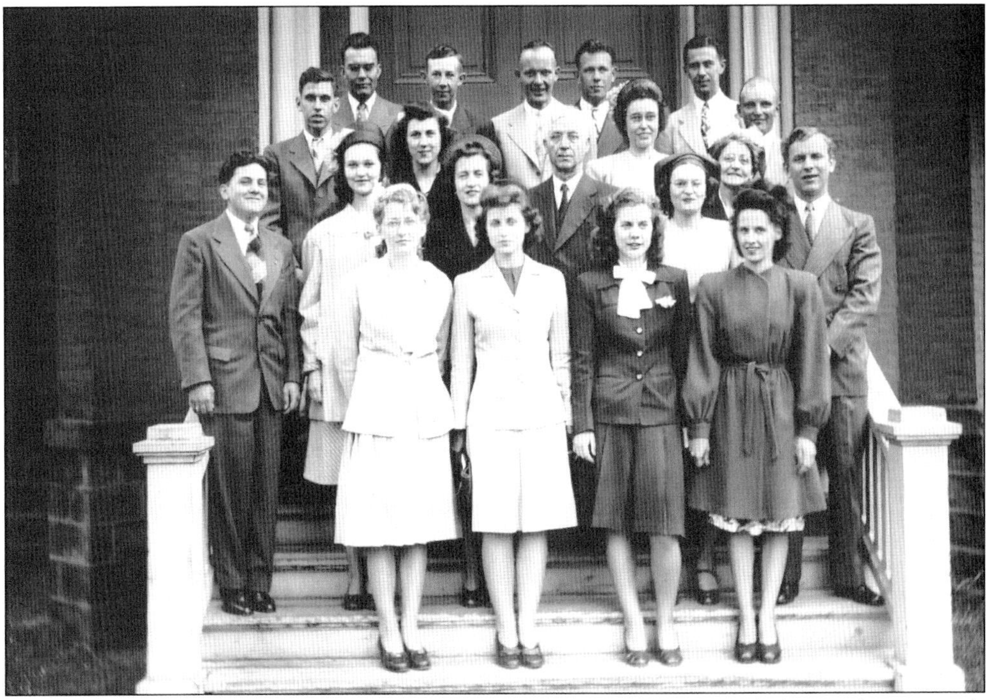

Walther League. Named for the first president of the Missouri-Synod, this Lutheran youth organization could trace its roots to 1848. These congregational groups provided social gatherings and educational opportunities for young people of the church. St. John's had two such groups directed at different ages, as seen by these images: the Walther League above and the Junior Walther League below.

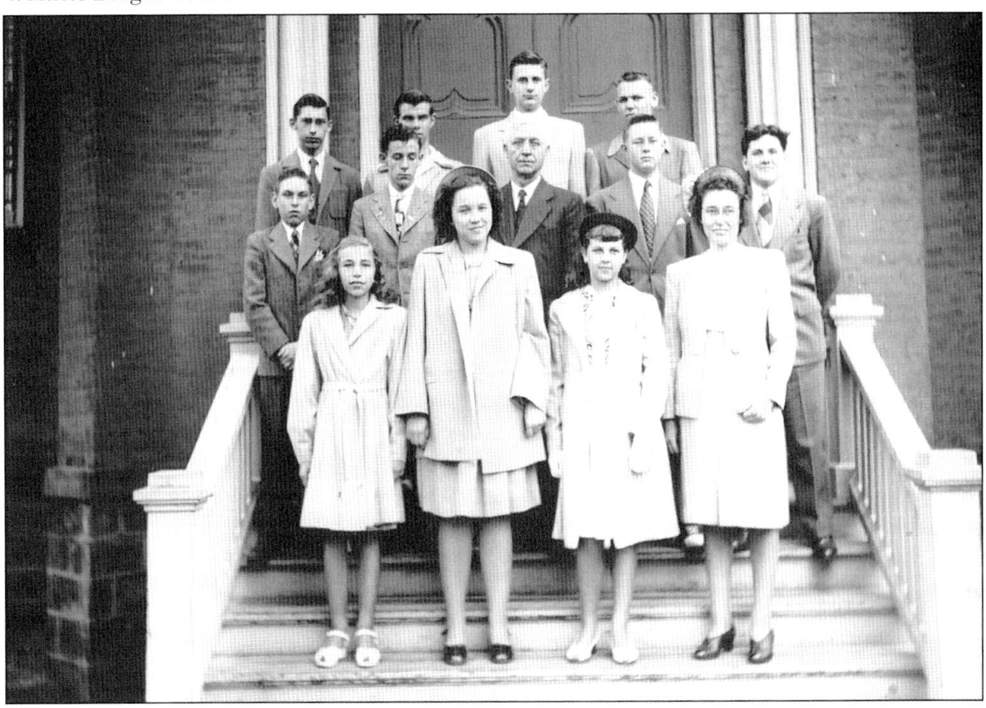

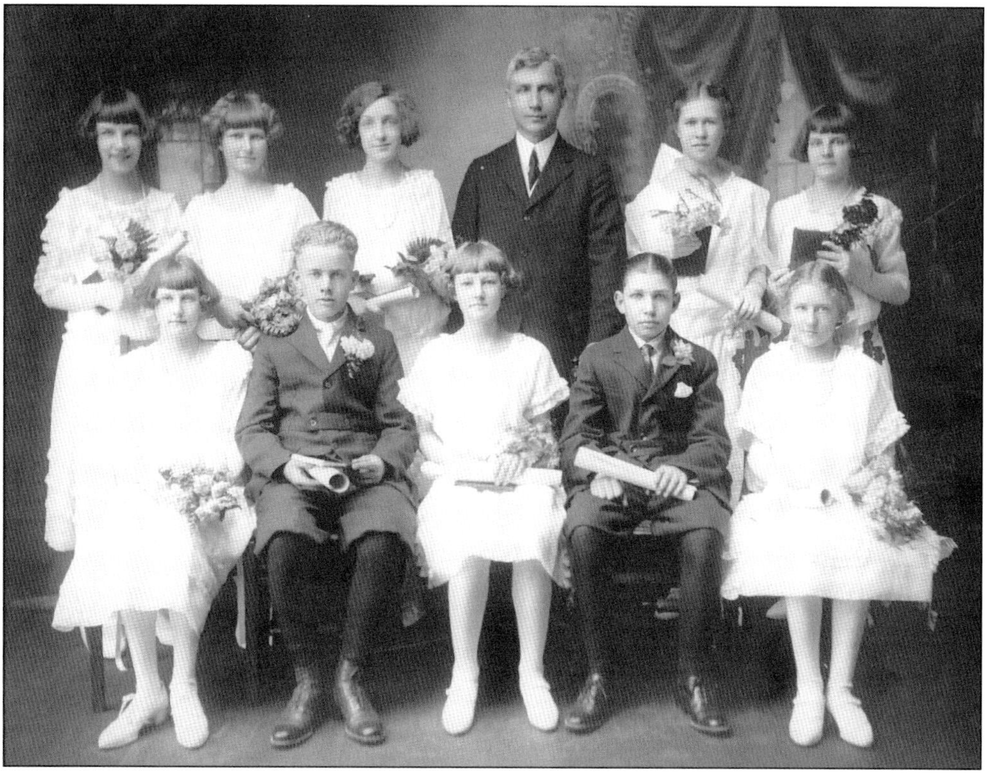

Lutheran Confirmation. Young Lutherans, often around the age of 12, would begin a long period of formal religious instruction in order to become confirmed members of the faith. At a minimum, the prospective confirmand would need to be able to recite the Lord's Prayer, the Apostle's Creed, the Ten Commandments, profess their desire to become a member of the church, and pass inspection by the pastor. The confirmation ceremony was a public recognition of this rite of passage.

Catholic Confirmation. Considered a sacrament, young Catholics, often around the age of seven, would begin their period of religious instruction in order to be in full communion with the faith and then able to receive the Eucharist. Often at confirmation, the confirmand would choose a confirmation name connected to a saint that meant something to them to serve as their patron saint henceforth.

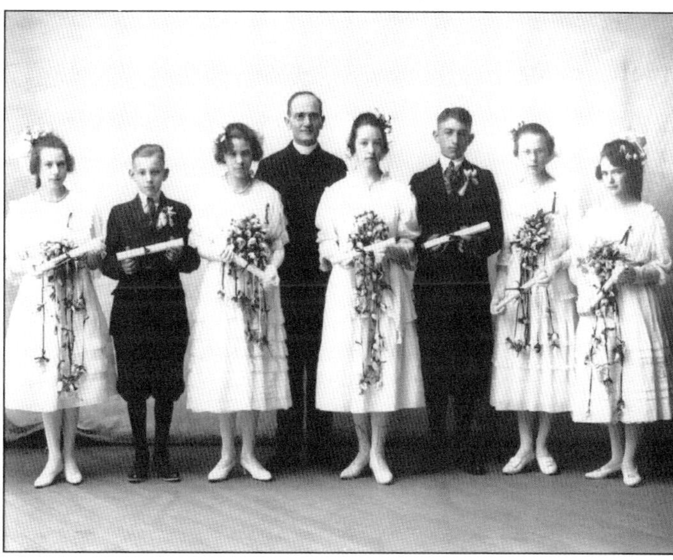

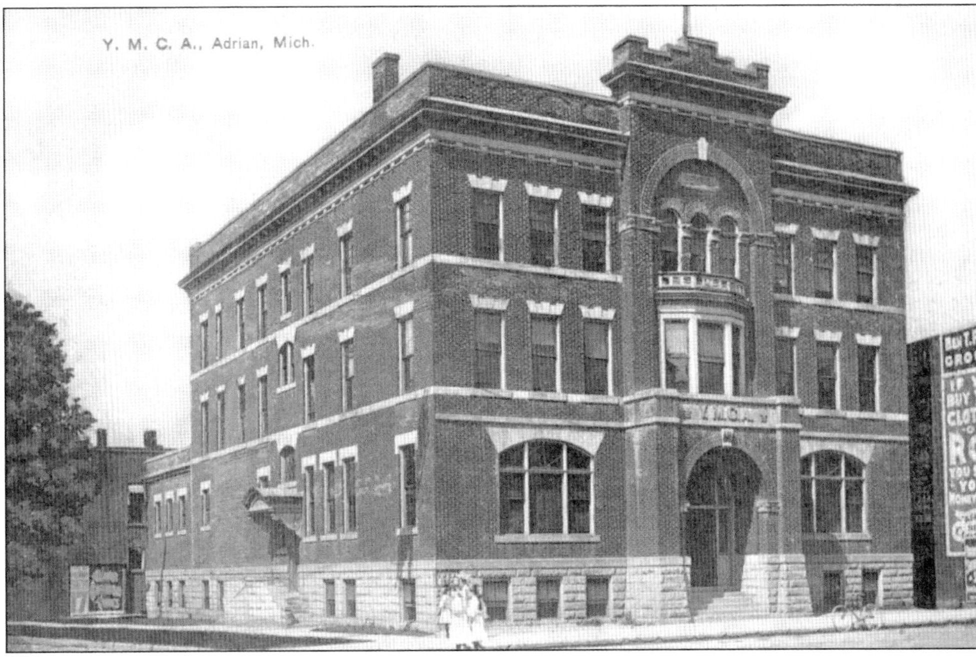

YMCA. This movement to provide wholesome living quarters and activities for young men in urban areas began in Europe. The first chapter opened in the United States in 1851, and Adrian initially had an association at Adrian College and then a full-fledged city chapter by 1892. Adrian's chapter had a reading library, facilities for physical education, and a lecture room. This image is of the modern building constructed in 1911.

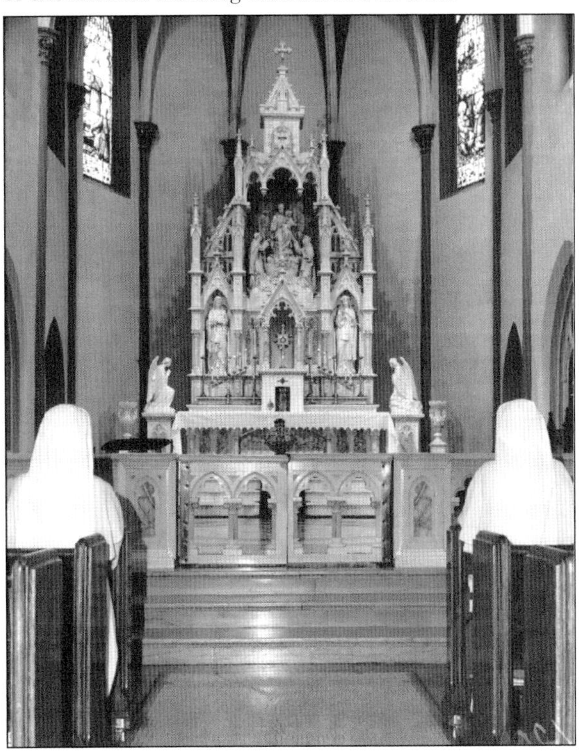

HOLY ROSARY CHAPEL. Completed by 1907, this chapel served the Adrian Dominican Sisters and the students of St. Joseph Academy and Siena Heights College. Worship, celebrations, and graduation ceremonies were all held here. Designed by Detroit architect Peter Dedrich, the chapel is in the Neogothic style and includes stained-glass windows designed by Sr. Helene O'Connor, who taught art at Siena Heights College.

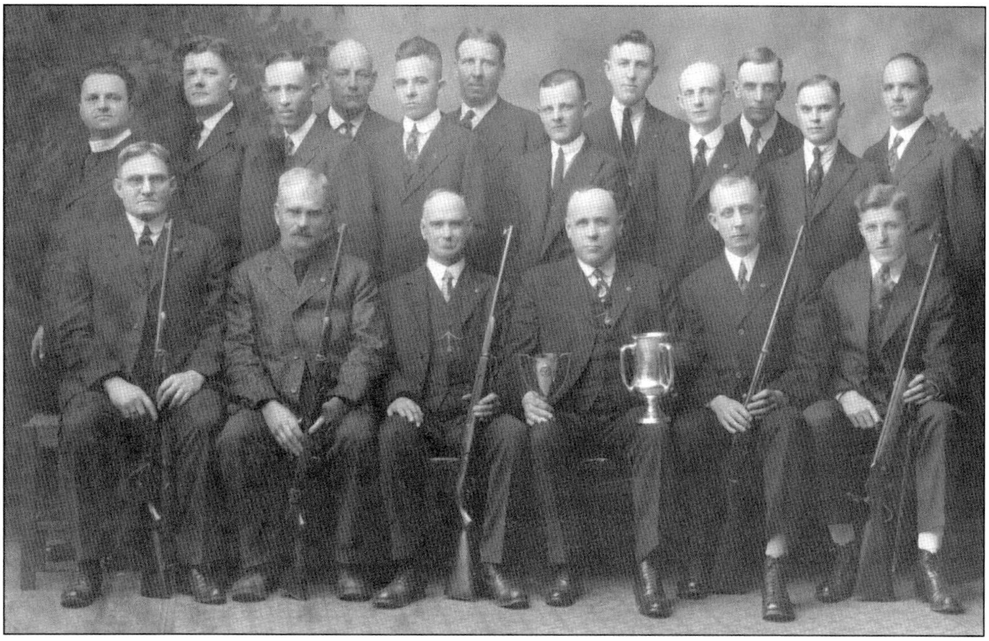

Adrian Rifle Club. This small group was formed around 1910 to promote the shooting sports. Although tiny in numbers, this rifle club was impressive with its results in competition against larger military organizations. For example, in 1911, the club beat the Michigan National Guard in two competitions. The club mainly focused on tests of proficiency with .22-caliber rifles and was in existence until World War II.

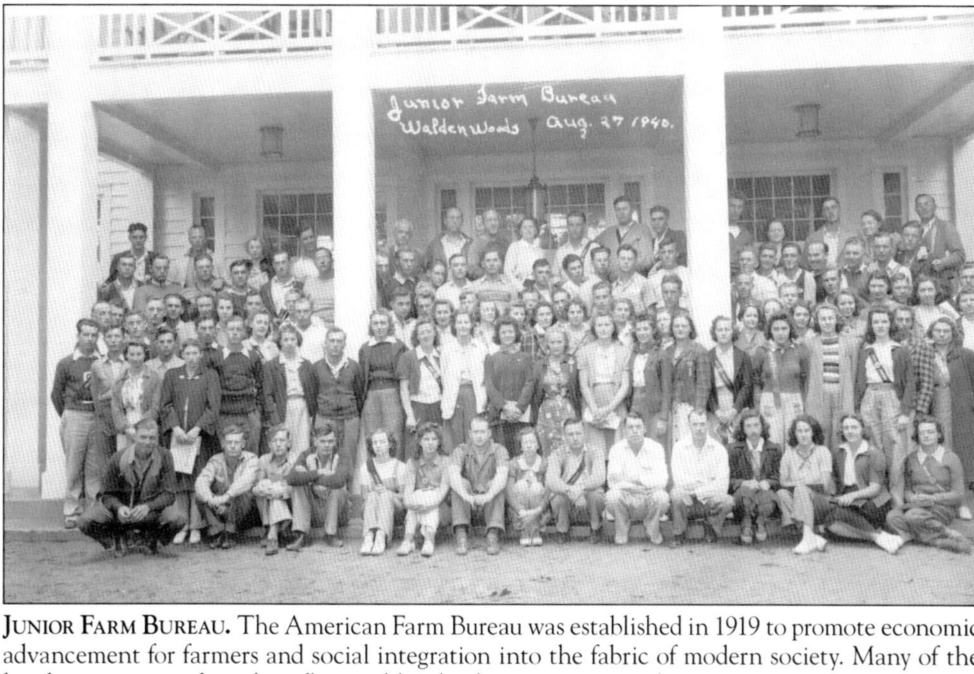

Junior Farm Bureau. The American Farm Bureau was established in 1919 to promote economic advancement for farmers and social integration into the fabric of modern society. Many of the local groups were directly influenced by the farm extension education movement out of land grant colleges, such as Michigan State University. This photograph displays the chapter for young people of this group at the Waldenwoods Resort, located in Hartland, Michigan.

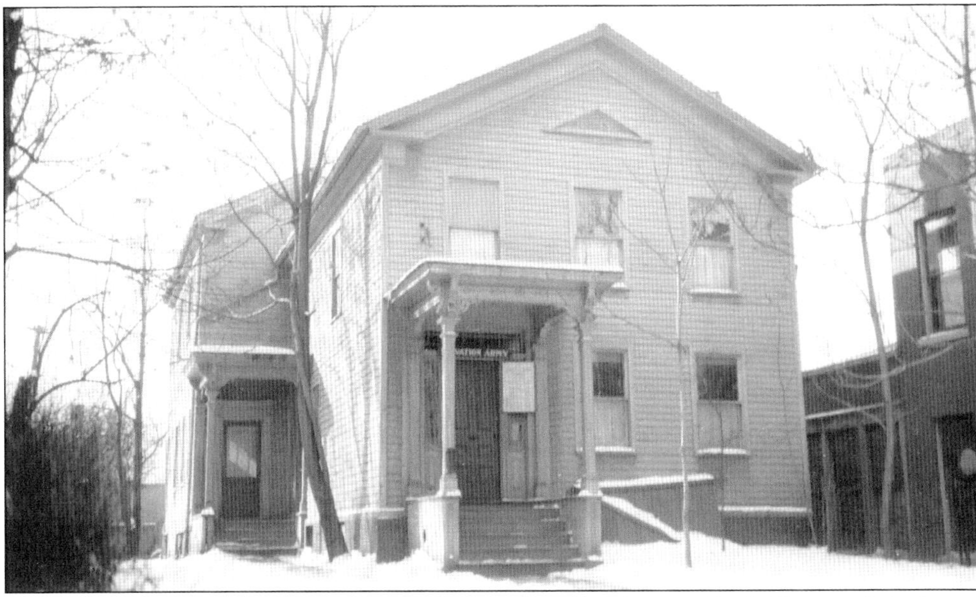

SALVATION ARMY. This church had its beginning in England, started by William and Catherine Booth in 1865. Its particular mission was to help the downtrodden, poor, and hungry by focusing both on spiritual and physical needs. By the 1880s, the Salvation Army had spread to the United States, with the Booths' daughter Evangeline serving as first field commissioner from 1904 until 1934. Her tenure proved that women could be effective in ministry.

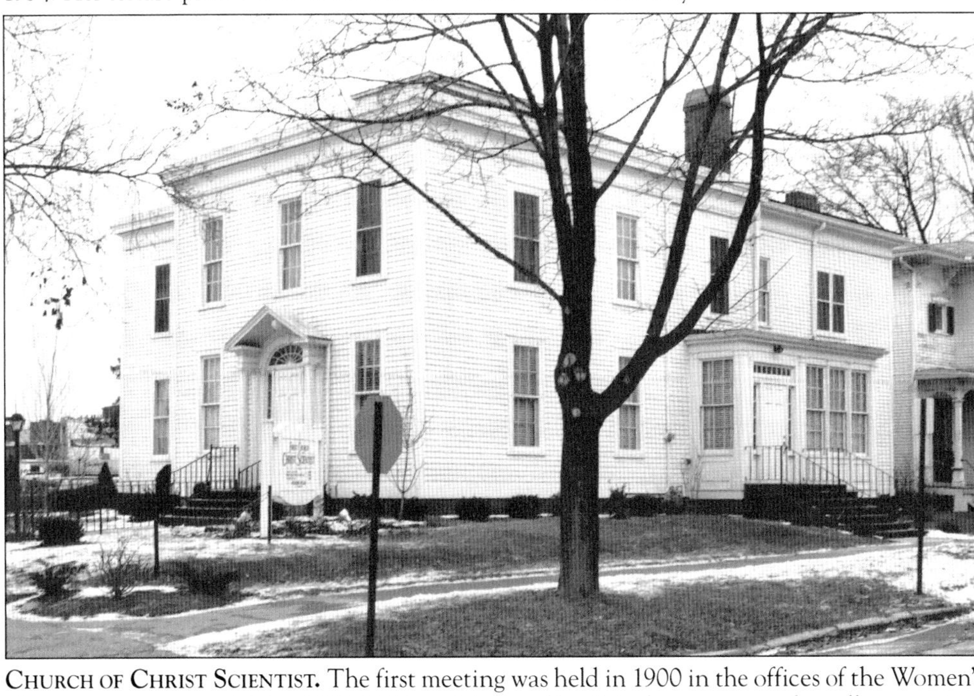

CHURCH OF CHRIST SCIENTIST. The first meeting was held in 1900 in the offices of the Women's Christian Temperance Union (WCTU) in Adrian, and by 1901 the society was formally recognized by the national organization. In 1905, this group disbanded temporarily in order to secure church status by the state. Meetings were held at various locations until 1907 with the move to this building located on West Maumee Street. The congregation numbered about 25 people at that time.

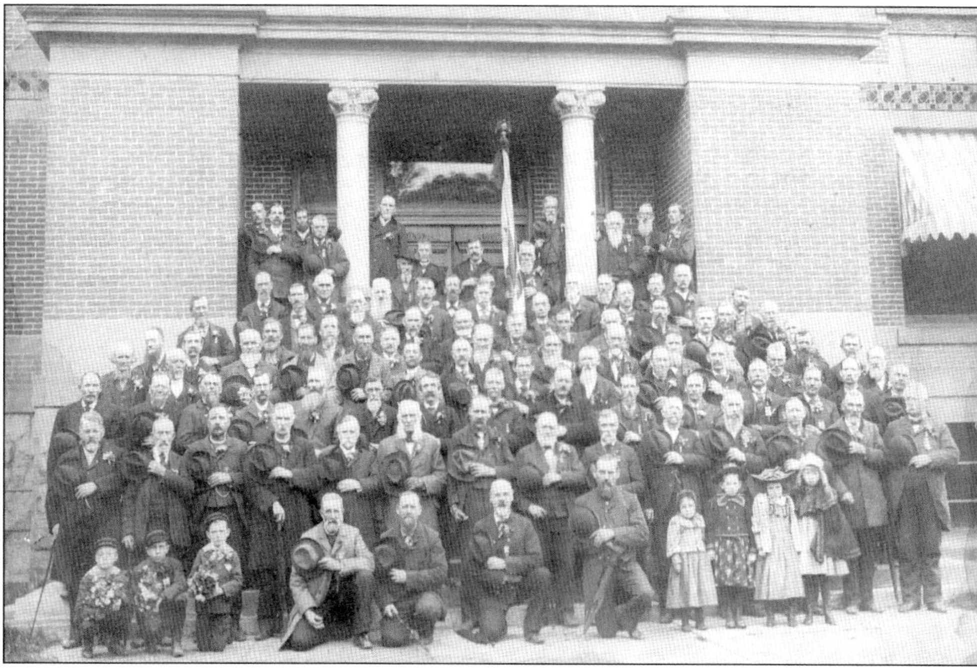

Grand Army of the Republic. Begun in Illinois by Benjamin Stephenson in 1866, the GAR was a fraternal organization for Union veterans of the Civil War. Initially focused on social events, it also became involved in political activism, especially in supporting Reconstruction. Although the GAR declined in many states, it grew in Michigan and was incorporated in 1883. The GAR officially disbanded with the death of its last member in 1953.

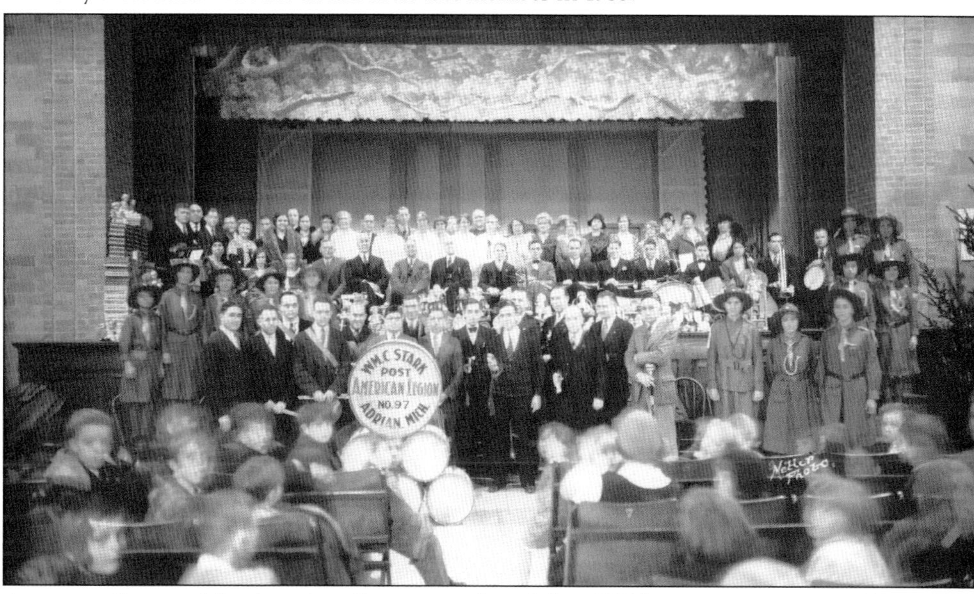

American Legion. The American Legion was founded in 1919 by veterans returning from World War I as a mutual aid society. Granted a charter by Congress, the American Legion developed job programs, social programs, and over time expanded to include veterans from other conflicts. The American Legion has been instrumental in the creation of the Department of Veterans Affairs and lobbying for the interests of service people.

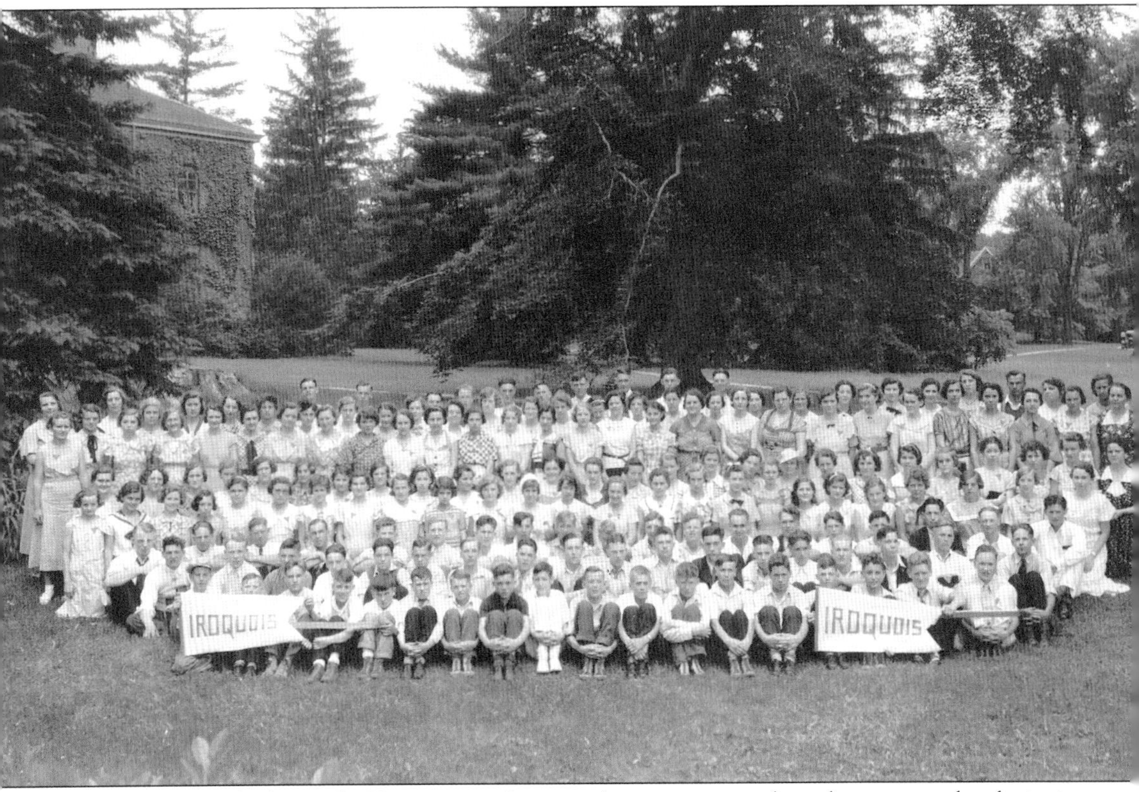

4-H CLUB. The focus of 4-H was as an educational program to rural youth on new technologies in agriculture and home economics. Nationally organized in 1914, an experiential learning approach was encouraged to benefit these young people. Summer camps and county fair programs became closely affiliated with these clubs, which eventually became affiliated with the Cooperative Extension Service of the USDA.

Five

RECREATION

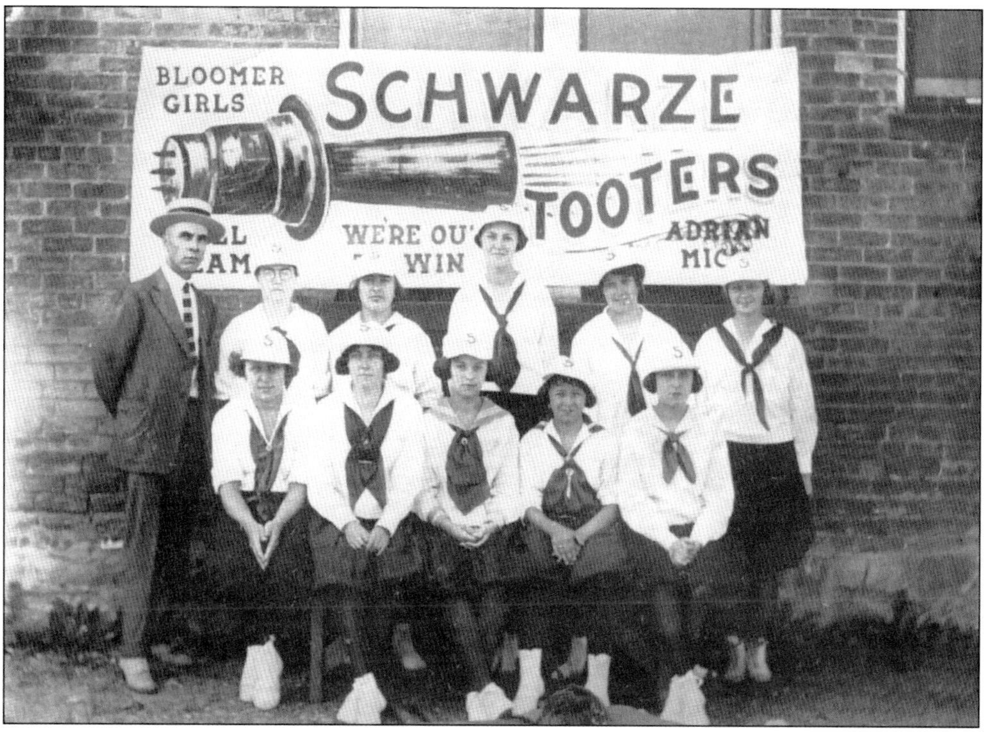

SCHWARZE TOOTERS BALL CLUB. Schwarze Electric Company sponsored a women's baseball club to promote its business. Considered a "bloomer team," such groups commonly traveled the United States barnstorming from community to community from the 1890s through the 1930s. They would play other bloomer teams and semiprofessional and professional ball clubs. At times, some bloomer teams would include men dressed as women.

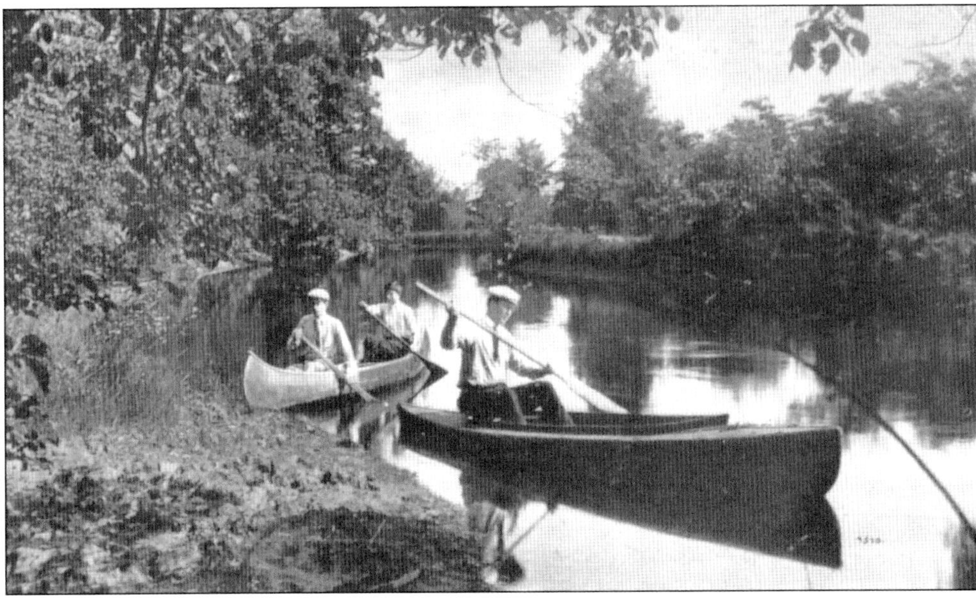

River Raisin. Named such by the French for the wild grapes growing along its banks, this river flows through southeast Michigan to Lake Erie. Many towns such as Adrian sprung up along its banks due to its benefit for both agriculture and industry. It never became widely used for transportation, as it is claimed to be the most crooked river in the world. Below is a person enjoying its scenery, while above canoeists are testing their skills on the river for entertainment.

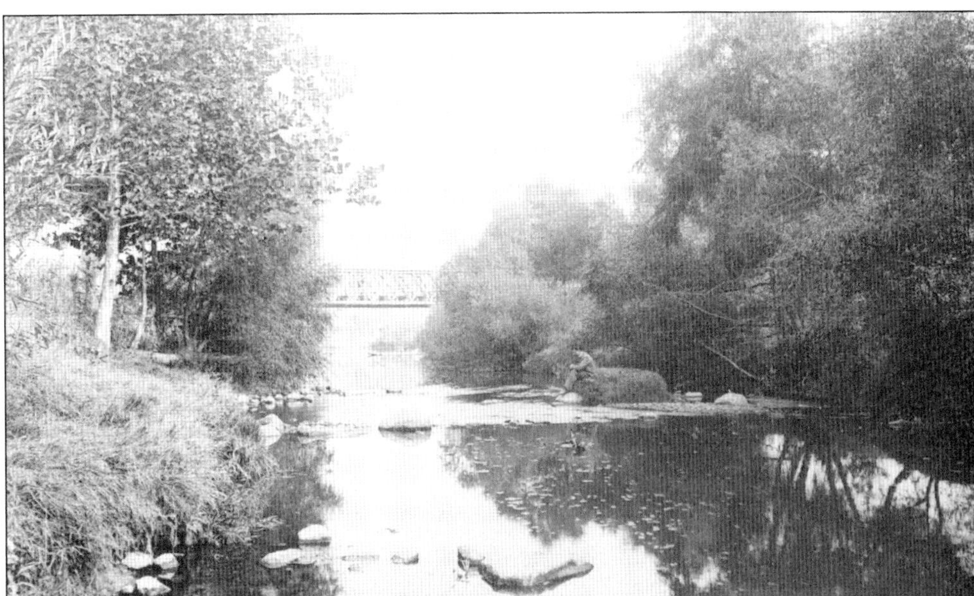

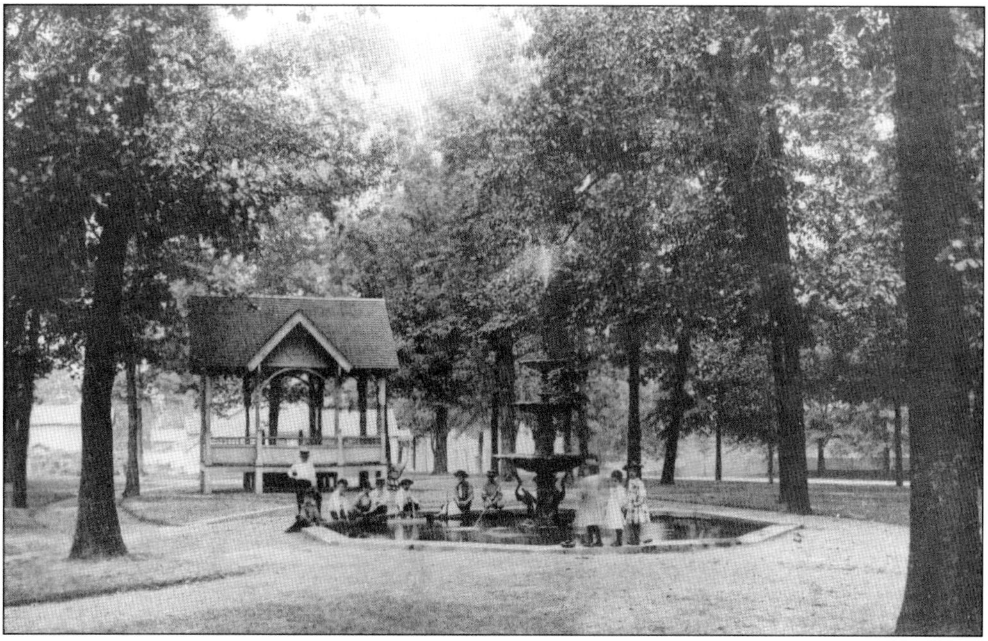

Parks. Adrian still has many areas where nature can be enjoyed by its citizens. Multiple public parks are located within the city, such as Riverside Park, Island Park, and Heritage Park. Oakwood Cemetery was influenced by the garden cemetery movement, so it was developed as a memorial garden. Hidden Lake Gardens, located northwest of the city, was developed by Adrian businessman Henry Fee. Above, people are enjoying a day at South Park, and below these young people are picking wildflowers near Adrian College.

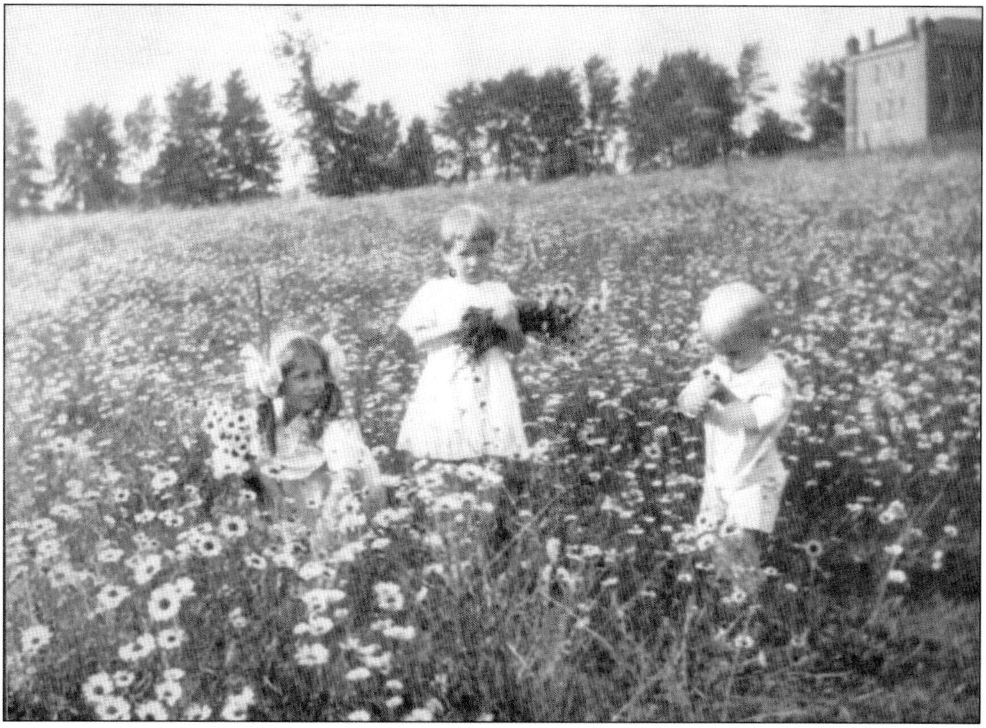

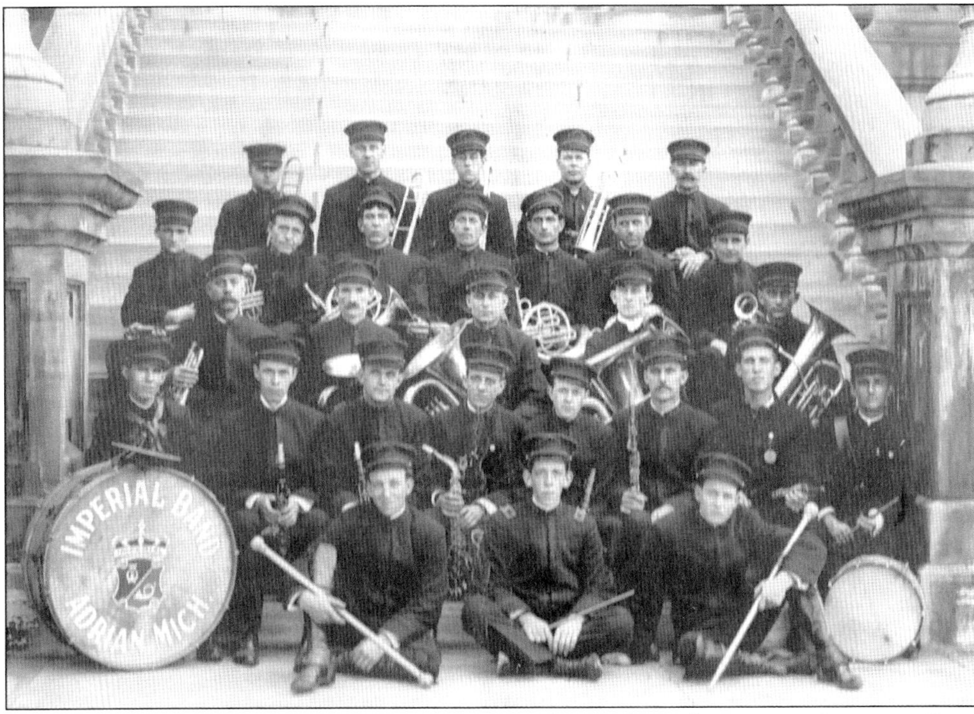

Imperial Band. Adrian had many musical groups that performed at various functions. Some were connected with businesses, some with church groups, some with fraternal organizations, and some were independent entities. The Imperial Band, seen above, was quite popular, even winning third place in a state competition in 1908. Below is a photograph of St. Joseph's Catholic Church Band.

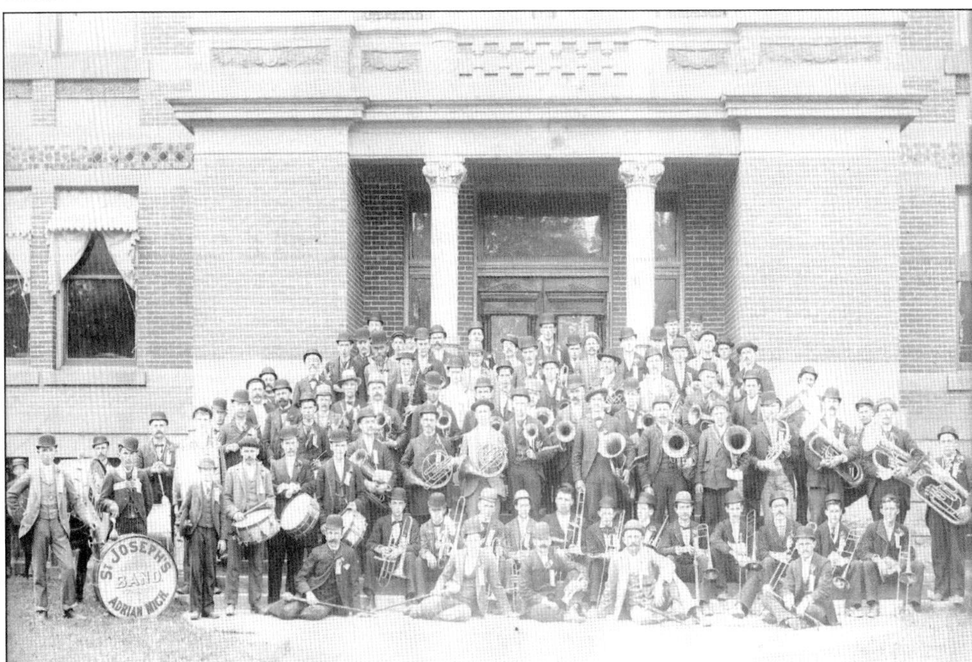

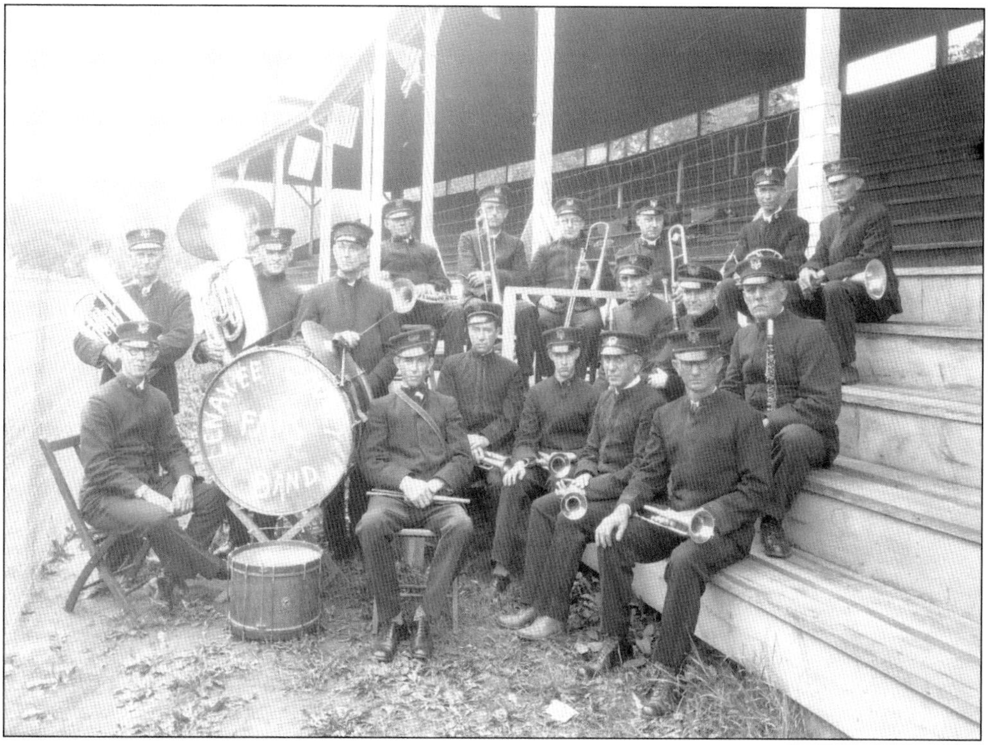

LENAWEE COUNTY FAIR. Since 1839, the Lenawee County Fair has been held in Adrian, and it is one of the oldest fairs in the state. It has been located at the current fairgrounds since 1879. A variety of entertainments could be experienced by the fairgoers. Musical arts, horse racing, carnival rides, and contests were common from the beginning. Above is a photograph of the fair orchestra, and below is a scene of attendees from 1889.

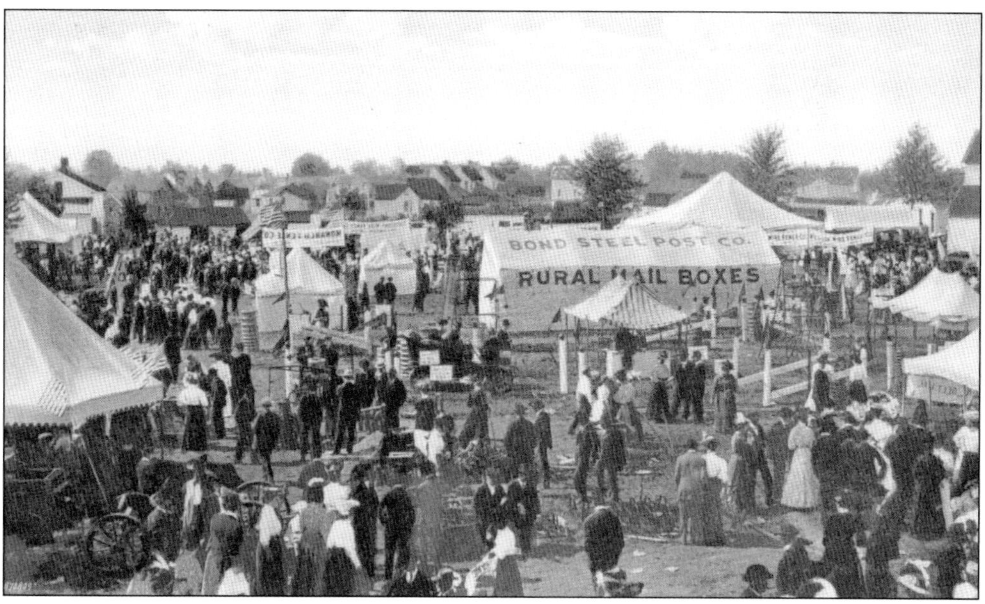

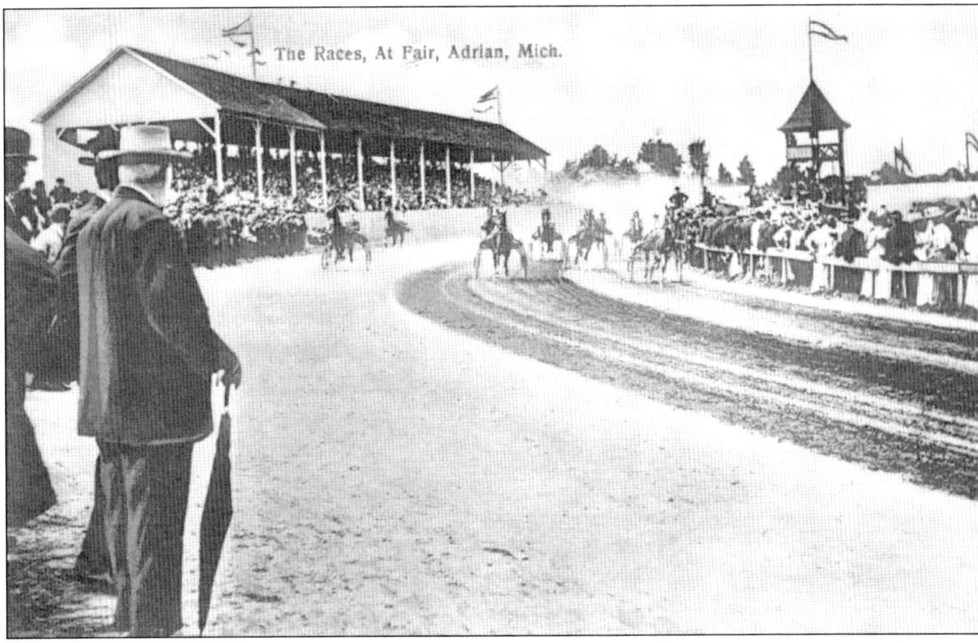

LENAWEE COUNTY FAIR. Contests focused on agricultural excellence are a mainstay of county fairs. Adrian, with its agricultural heritage, also follows this pattern. Contests include judging livestock, flowers, canning, and baked goods. As the fairgrounds include a track, horse racing was extremely popular, as evidenced by the image above. The young man below received multiple 4-H awards for his winning sheep. (Below, author's collection.)

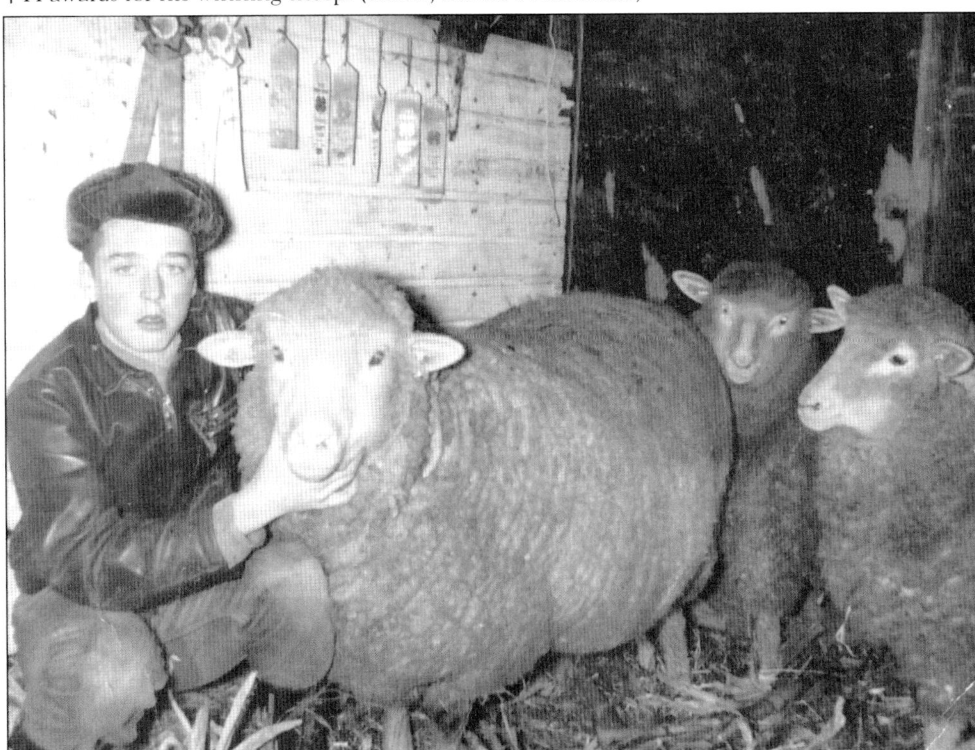

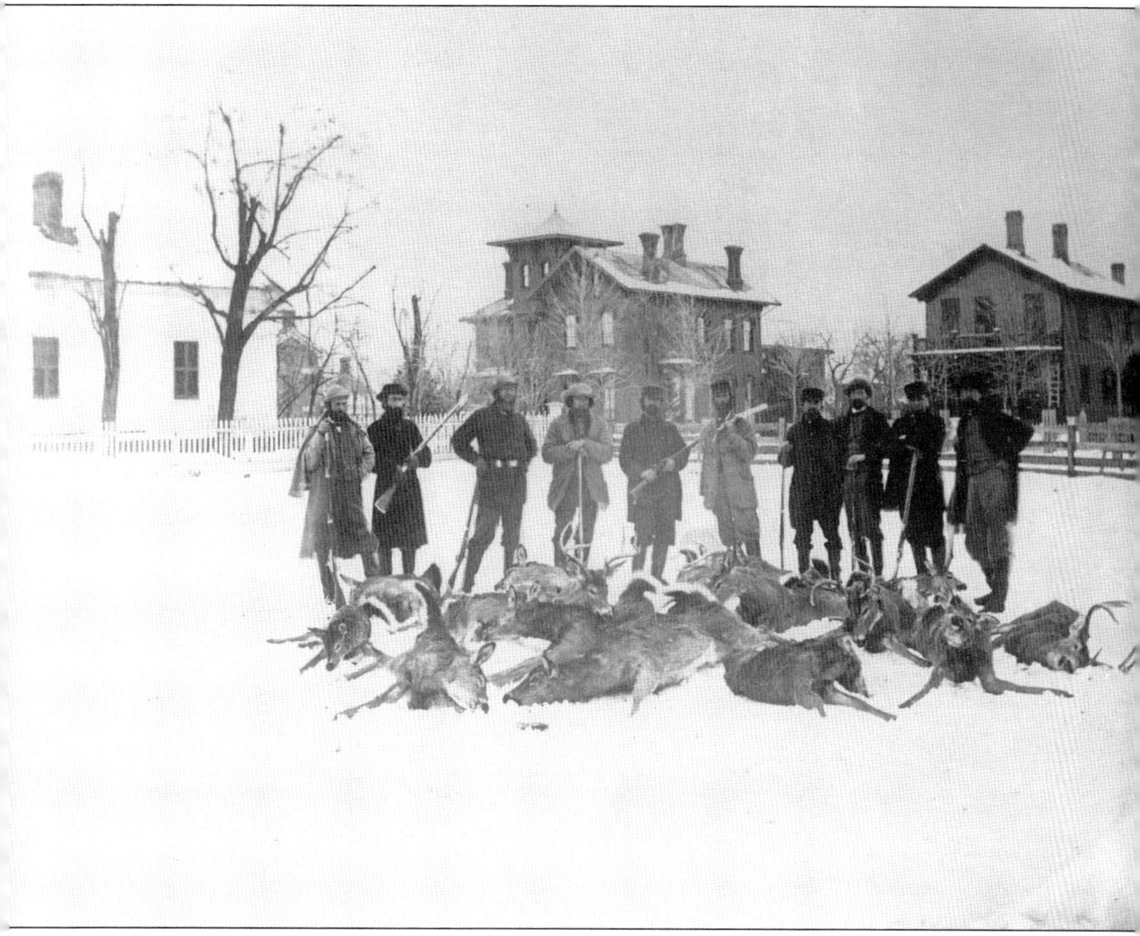

Declining Deer Populations. In the 19th century, many who hunted did so as a profession, selling the meat to both local and national markets. Concerned with the decimation of deer populations, in 1859 the state legislature created a four-month hunting season for the species, with violators fined $5. Continued over-harvesting caused the Anti-Market Hunting Act to be passed in 1880 forbidding commercial hunting of deer.

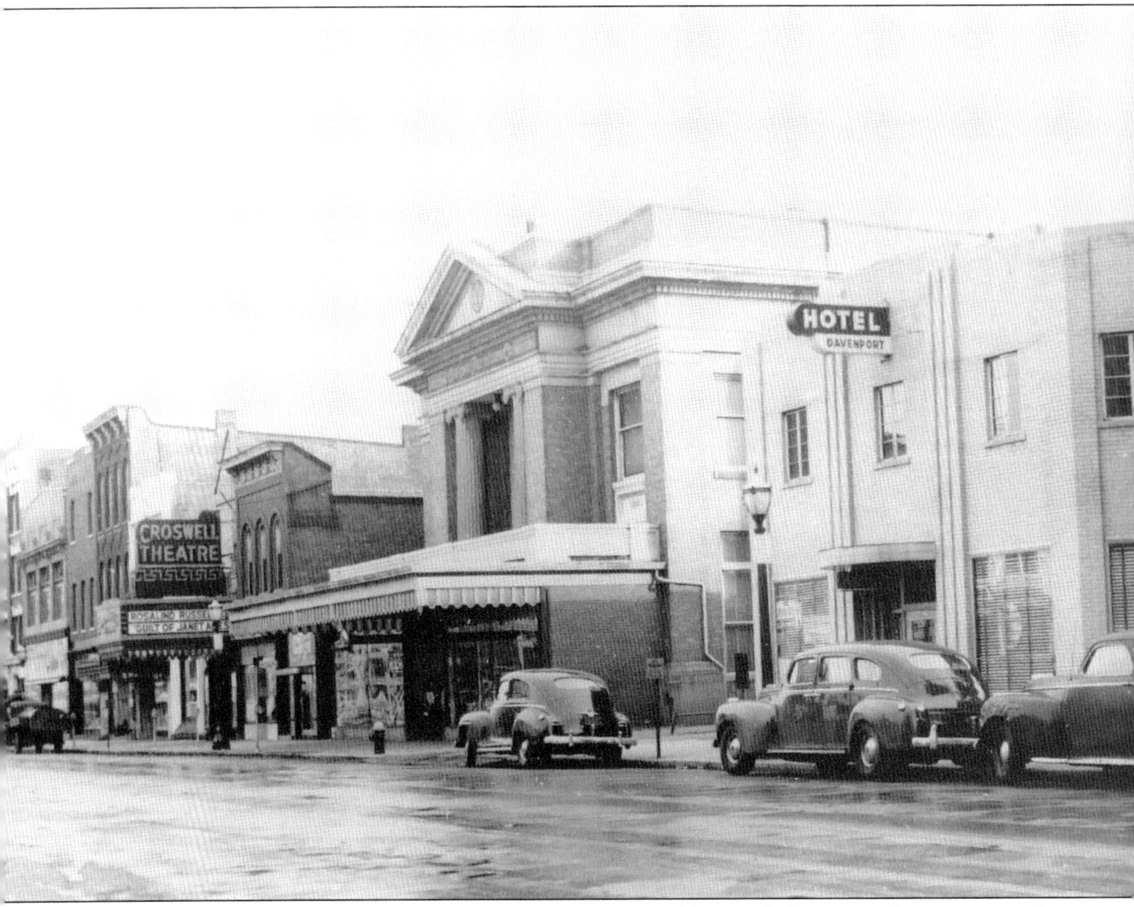

Croswell Opera House. Opened in 1866, the Croswell provided a venue for concerts, plays, and lectures. Noted speakers on this stage included Frederick Douglass and Susan B. Anthony. In 1967, this building was saved from the wrecking ball and became an official Michigan historic site in 1976. The theater underwent a renovation and continues to serve as an entertainment venue, making it the oldest continuously operating theater in the state.

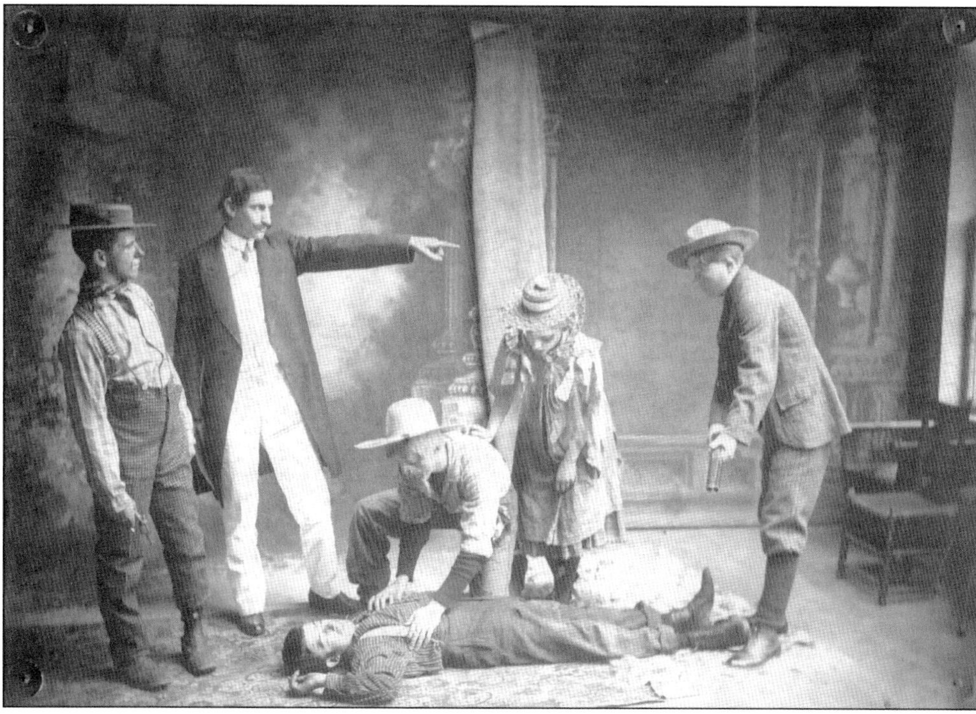

CROSWELL OPERA HOUSE, PRODUCTION PHOTOGRAPHS. Professional theater companies, community productions, and high school plays were all showcased at the Croswell. The above image includes local Henry Kaiser, who was in numerous productions, along with his relatives. The image below is from an amateur community revue created in 1917 entitled *A Whirl of Pleasure*. In the 1920s, the Croswell began to show films as well.

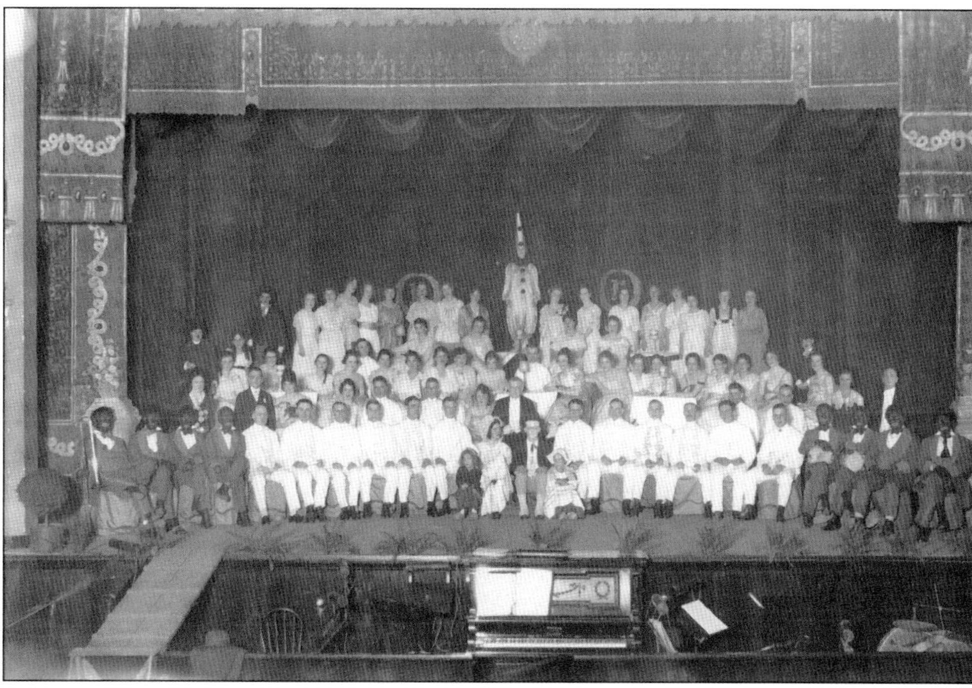

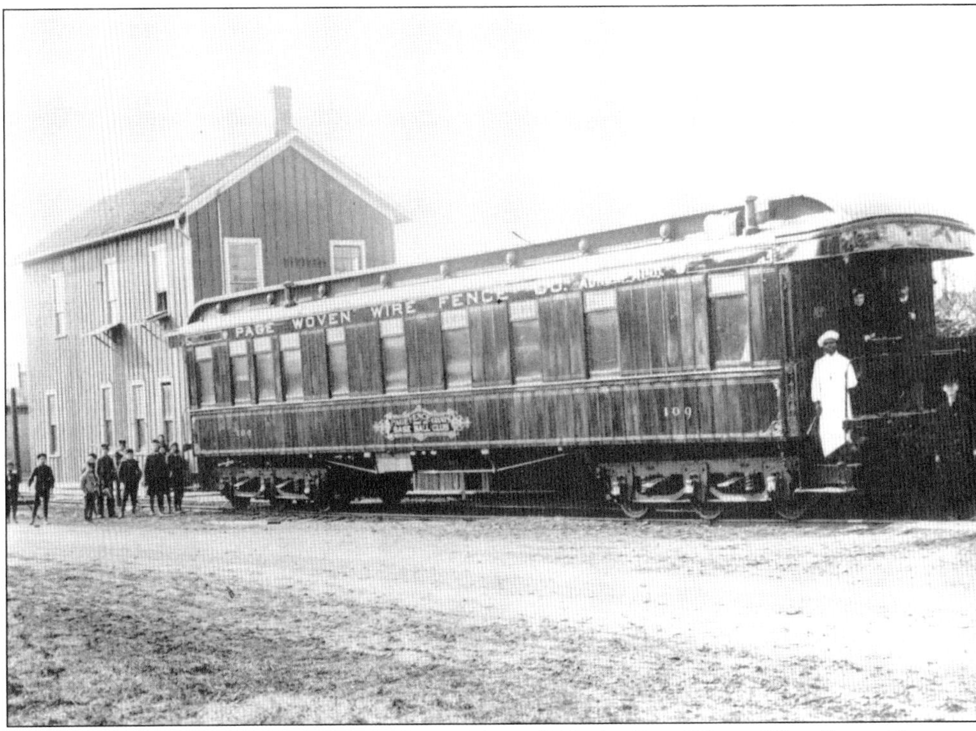

PAGE FENCE GIANTS BASEBALL TEAM. From 1894 to 1898, the Page Woven Wire Fence Company of Adrian sponsored an all–African American baseball team. The Giants, with an impressive record, traveled across the country playing both African American and white baseball clubs. To overcome the problem of segregated restaurants and hotels, the team traveled on its own private railway car with its own cook. The above image is of the car, and the image below is a publicity shot of the team.

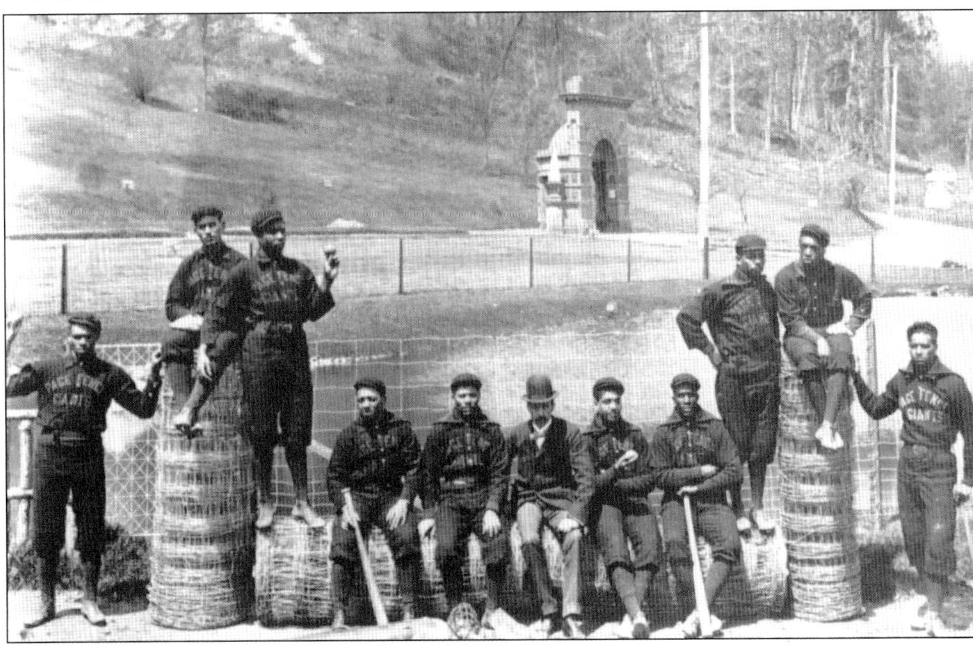

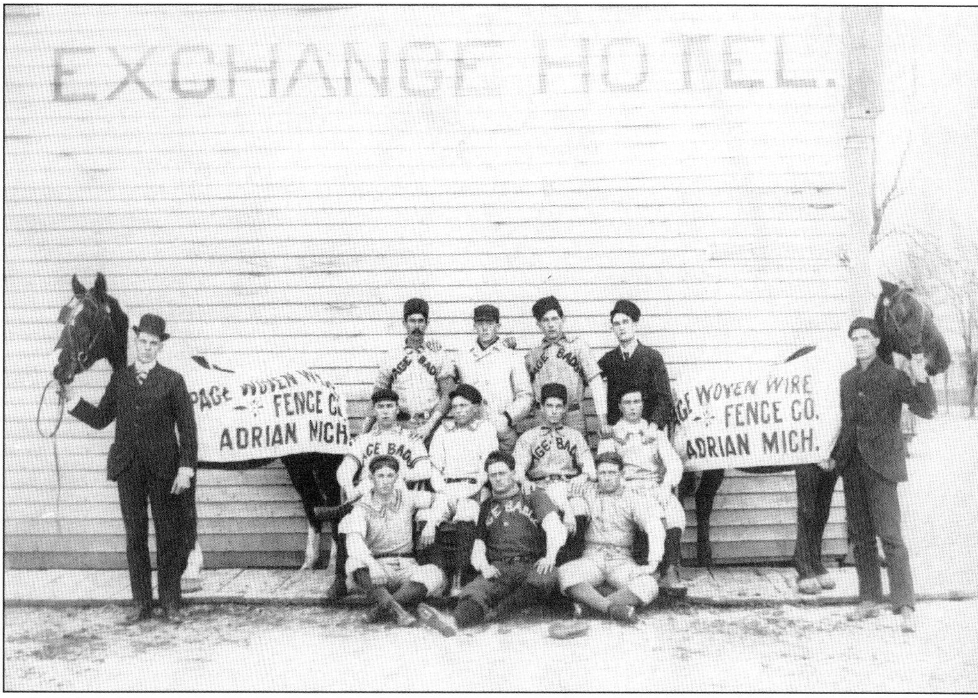

PAGE FENCE PROMOTIONS. Though not as famous as the Giants, the Badgers baseball team was also sponsored by the Page Woven Wire Fence Company and served as a promotional tool for the business. Page Fence was extremely creative in the variety of promotional activities it sponsored, such as a deer park in Adrian and also exhibits of unusual animals at county fairs penned in with their fencing, such as the camel below.

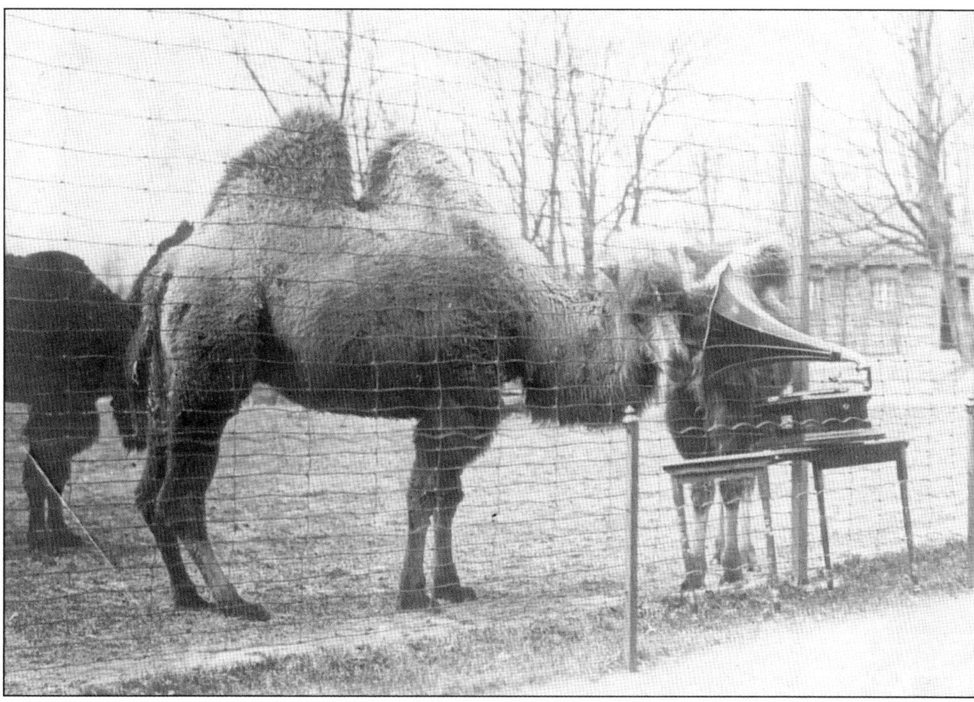

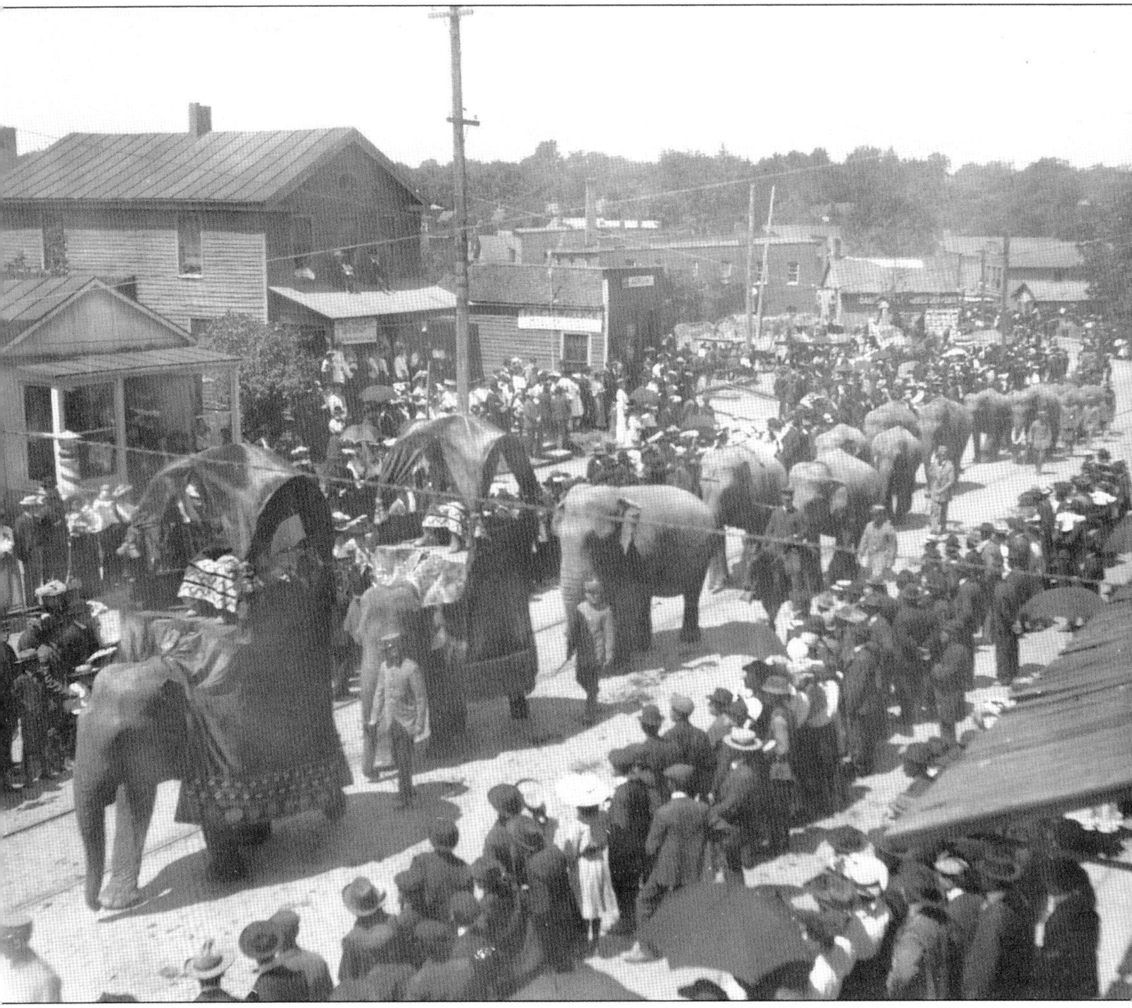

BARNUM CIRCUS PARADE. P.T. Barnum and James Anthony Bailey merged their circuses into one circus company in 1881, and Adrian was a regular stop on the circus route. In 1907, the outfit was purchased by the Ringling Bros., who once again ran them as separate circuses until 1919. Then it became known as the Ringling Bros. and Barnum & Bailey Circus. Typically the circus would open with a parade to drum up business. This photograph is of the Barnum parade of 1916.

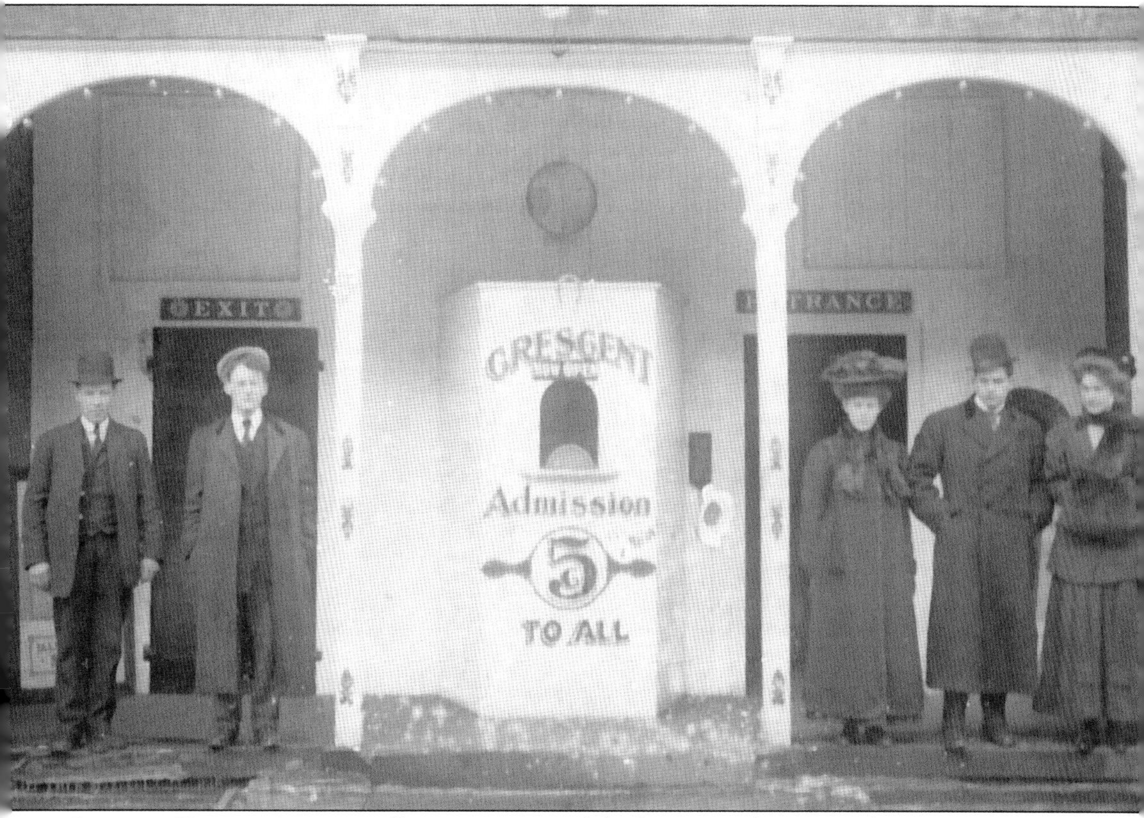

Crescent Theater. In 1907, William Kenan opened the first movie theater in Adrian. Technically the Crescent was a nickelodeon. Nickelodeons were small storefronts that showed short films for a nickel admission price. At times, these silent films would be accompanied by a piano or organ player. The Crescent advertised "a clean, classy program seven days a week." By the 1920s, these movie houses shifted to showing feature-length films by the major studios.

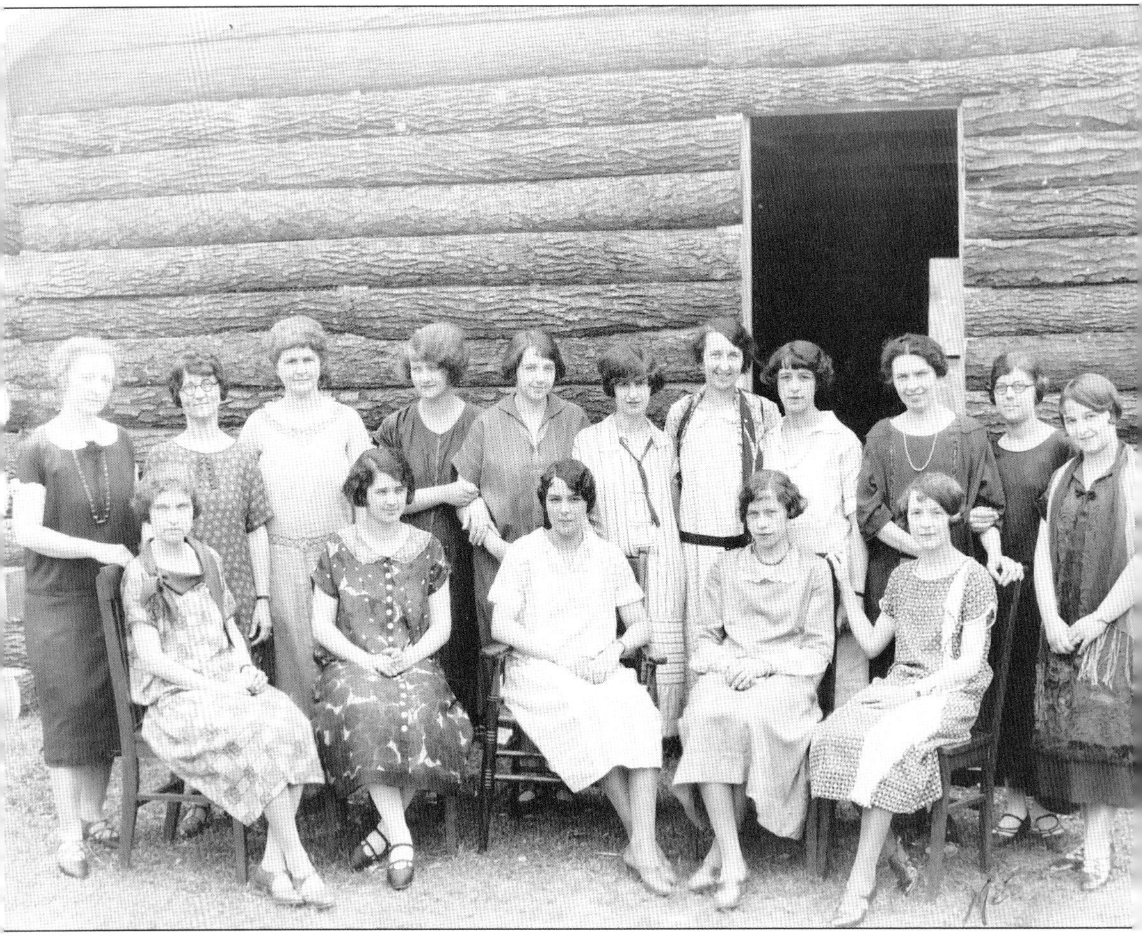

Miss Adrian and Court. The modern US beauty pageant was created by P.T. Barnum in the 1850s, although it was met with public outrage. By the 20th century, beauty contests were commonplace, especially attached to festivals and summer resorts. For example, the Miss America contest of 1921 was initially a ploy to keep tourists around Atlantic City over the Labor Day weekend. In 1925, Adrian held a beauty pageant to crown Miss Adrian as a way to celebrate its 100-year anniversary.

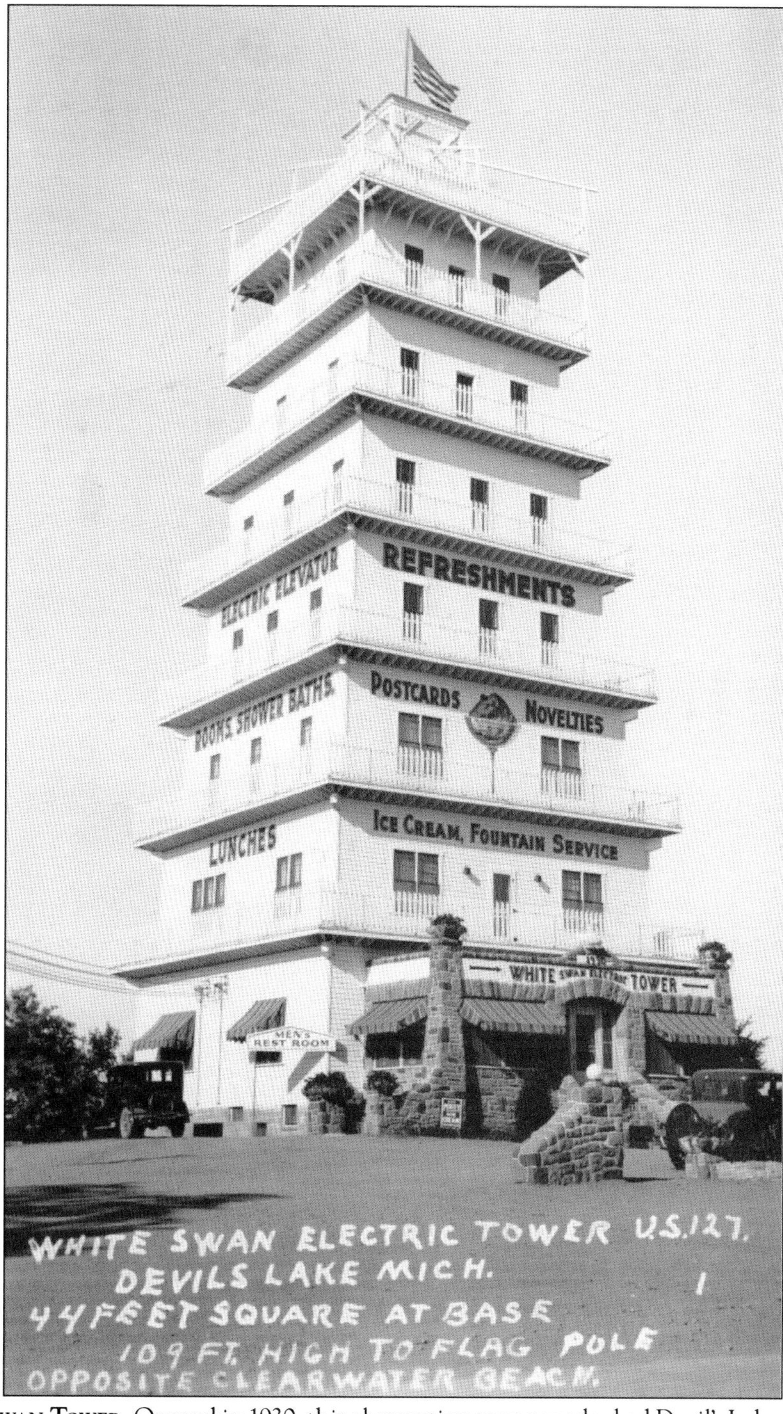

WHITE SWAN TOWER. Opened in 1930, this observation tower overlooked Devil's Lake. It was the last such tower built in the region. Tourists could climb to the top to get a great view of the lake and the surrounding area, buy souvenirs at the store located within, and eat a chicken or steak dinner at the restaurant located on the bottom floor. With the continued economic decline during the Great Depression, the tourist trade died out in this area west of Adrian by the mid-1940s.

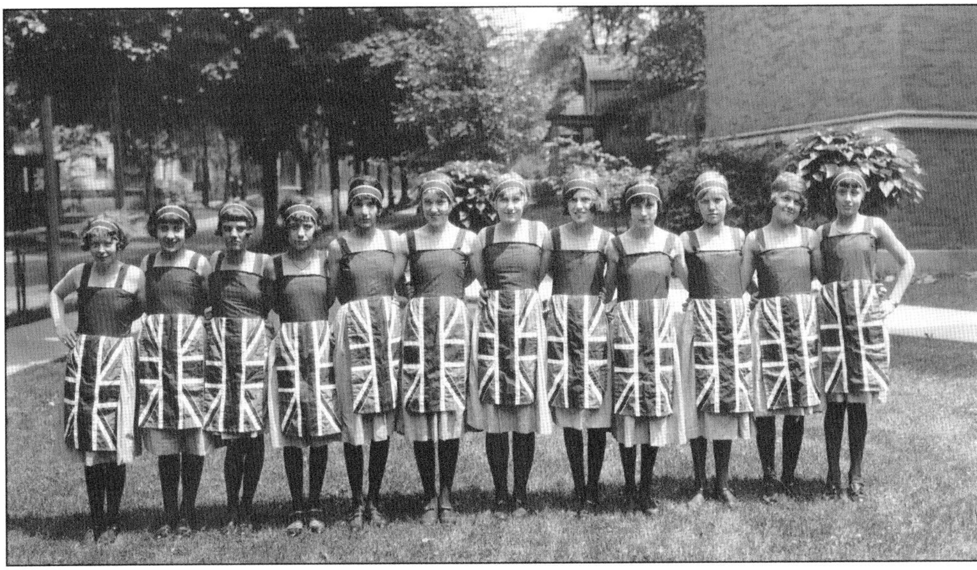

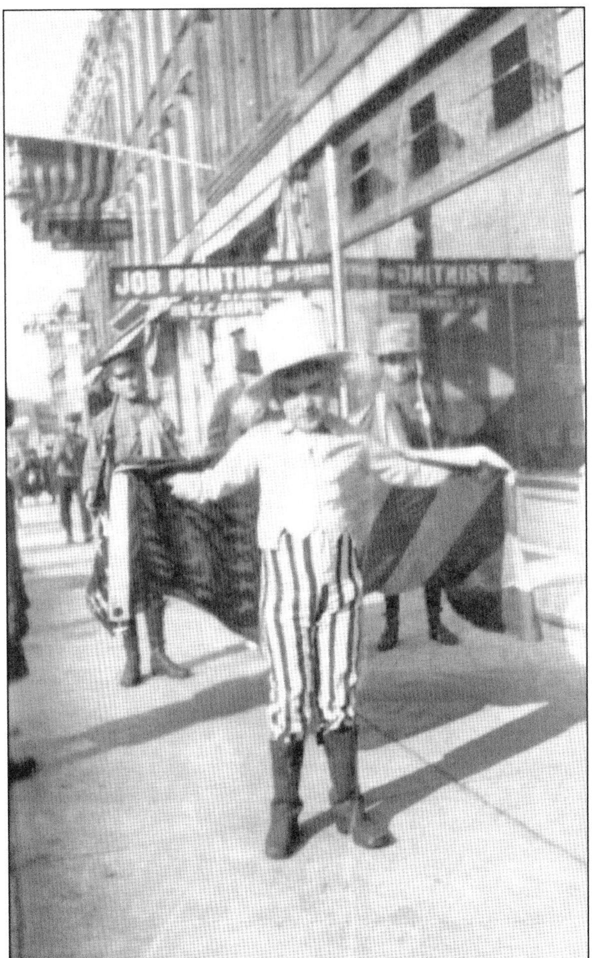

PARADES. As a source of civic pride, Adrian held parades for several occasions, such as national holidays, gala days, and homecoming days. Local businesses, organizations, and city government regularly took part in the fun. The image above is from a parade celebrating the 100th year of the city in 1925, and the young man at left is celebrating the first Armistice Day on November 11, 1918.

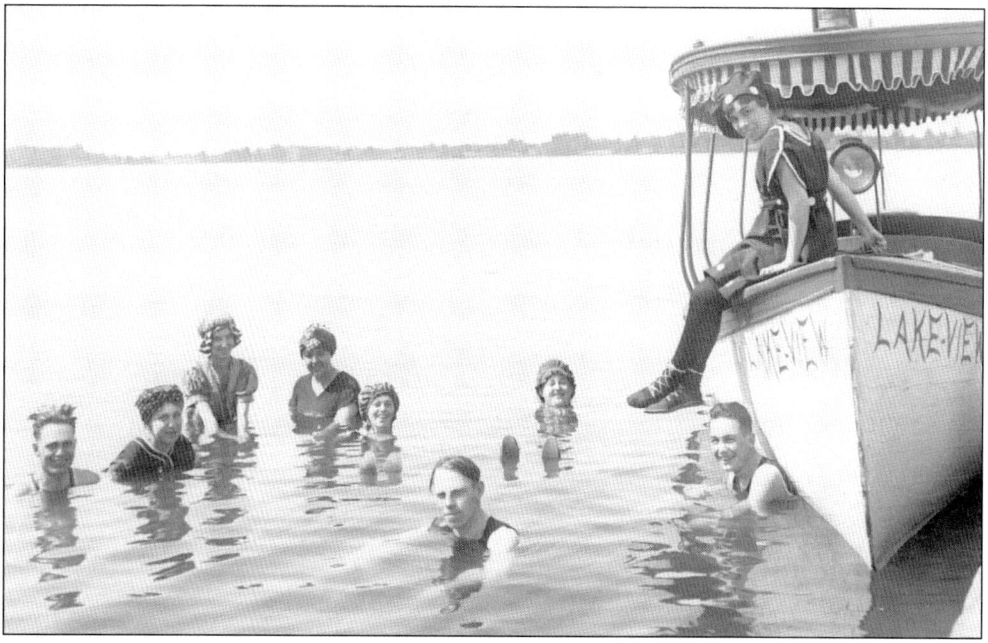

Devil's Lake. This lake is located approximately 15 miles from Adrian. According to legend, Potawatomi leader Meteau believed evil spirits inhabited the lake after his daughter drowned there, hence the name of this body of water. Cursed or not, it did not keep people away, and it was a resort region by the 1830s. Hotels, dance halls, and a water slide all provided a welcome escape during the summer months. Here are two images of people enjoying this area.

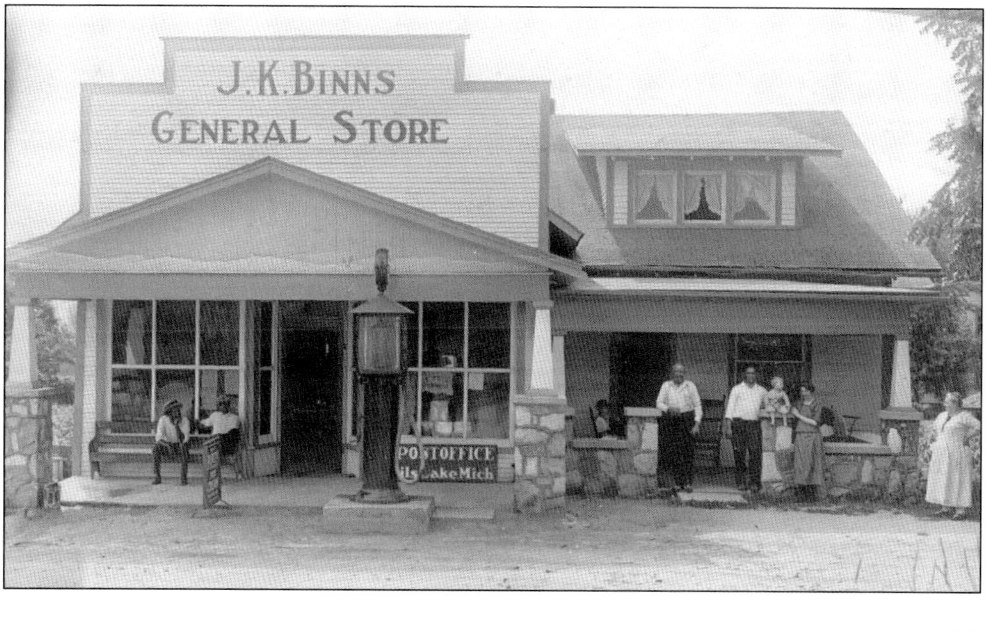

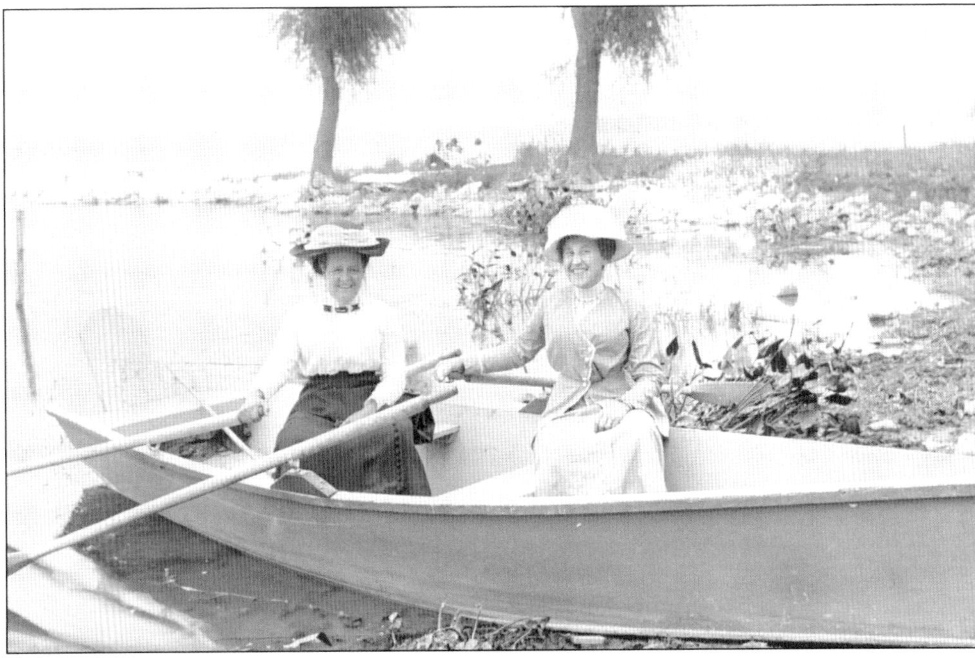

Round Lake. Right next to Devil's Lake was its neighbor, Round Lake. Both are moraine lakes created by glaciers. This area served as a welcome escape from the city via train or automobile. Many people still have summer cabins on these lakes and enjoy swimming, fishing, and relaxing just as people have been doing for generations, as evidenced by these two photographs.

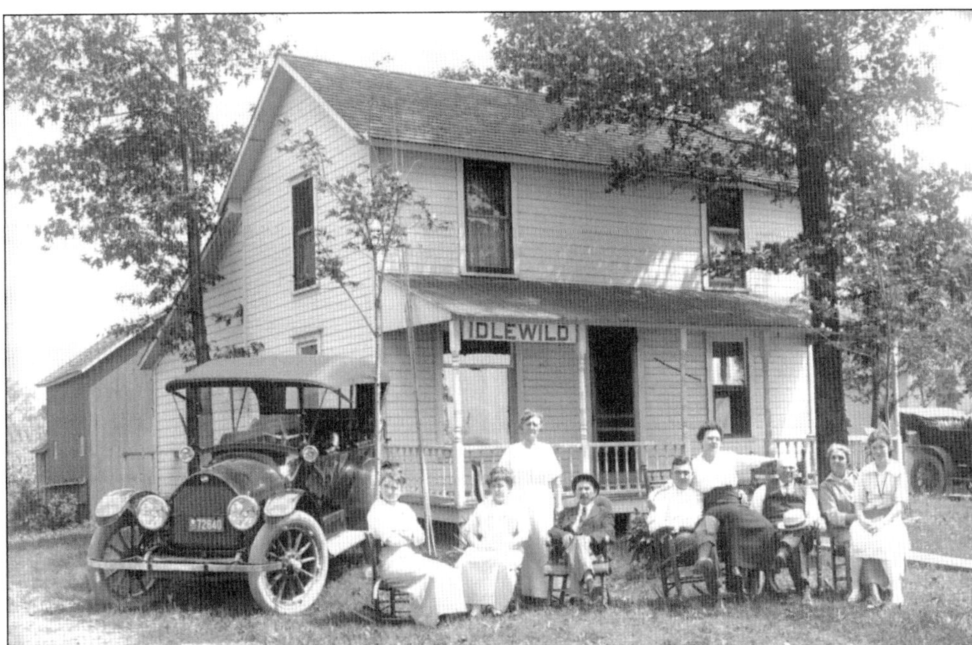

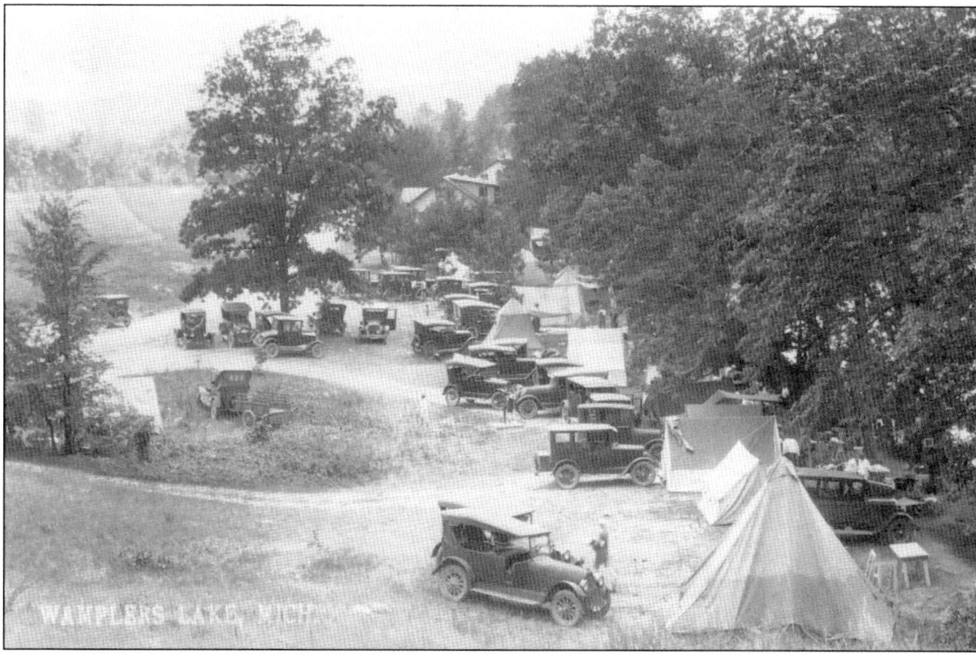

HAYES STATE PARK. During the 1930s, the Civilian Conservation Corps helped to renovate this park and campground located at Wampler's Lake, a 780-acre lake. It originally opened in 1920 as Cedar Hill State Park but was renamed after the family of Sen. W.J. Hayes donated land to this recreation area. Here are two images from the park. Visitors can still enjoy boating, fishing, swimming, and camping at this recreation area.

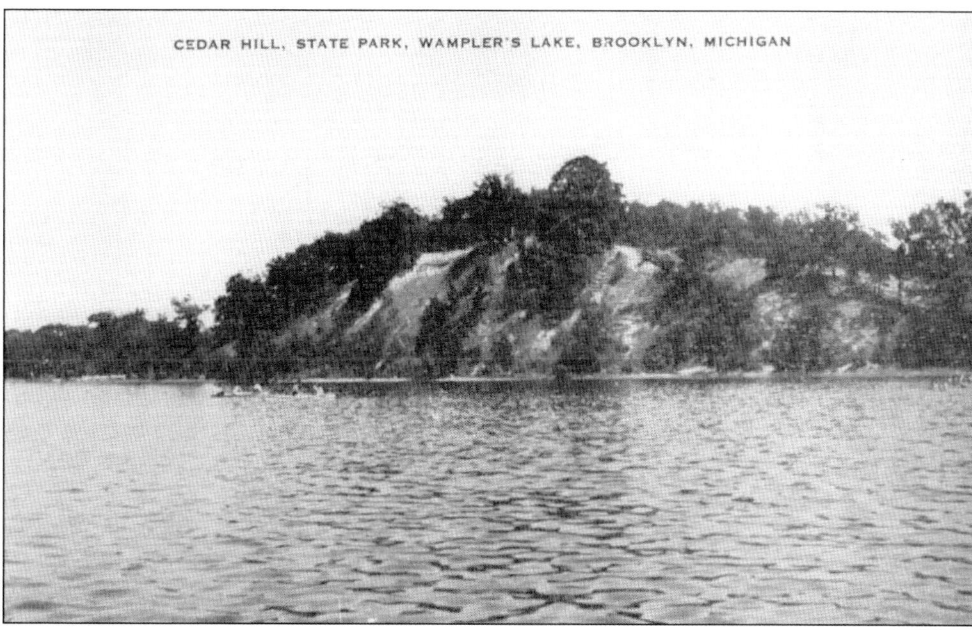

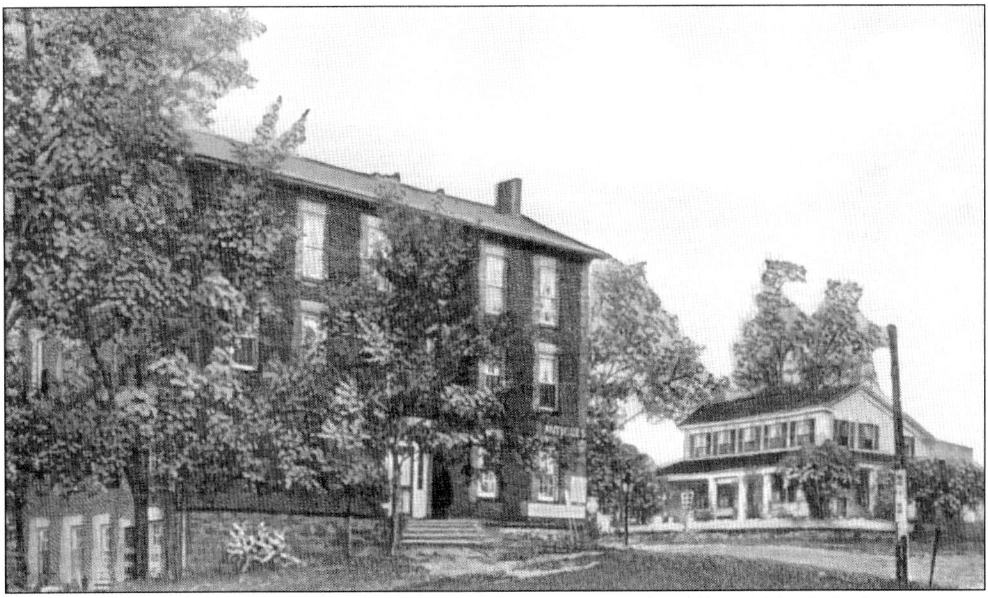

WALKER TAVERNS. Originally a stagecoach stop built in 1832 on the old Sauk Trail, the business was expanded by owner Sylvester Walker, who built a brick tavern here in 1854. In the 1920s, Frederick Hewitt purchased this property to open an antiques shop and tourist attraction; admission was only 15¢. With the advent of automobile tourism, the Irish Hills had become a popular vacation destination, only 18 miles from Adrian. (Author's collection.)

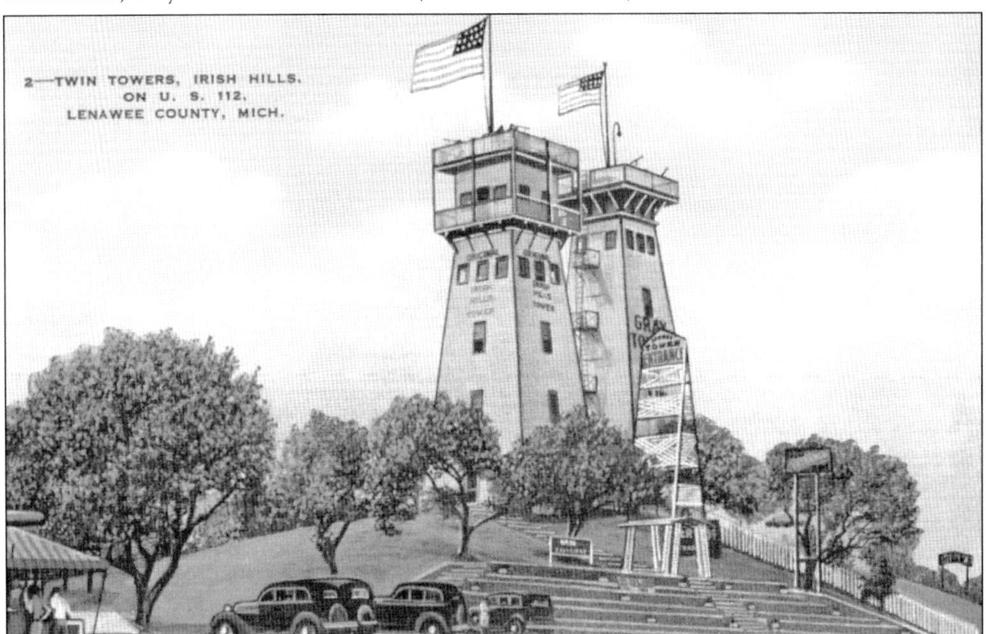

IRISH HILLS TOWERS. Located in the Irish Hills, the first observatory tower was constructed in 1924 by the Michigan Observatory Company so tourists could view the lovely rolling countryside and area lakes. The owner of the neighboring property, Ed Kelly, was not amused and built his own taller tower in retaliation. Not to be outdone, the company added a second viewing platform to its structure, and then Kelly responded in kind. (Author's collection.)

Six

INDUSTRY

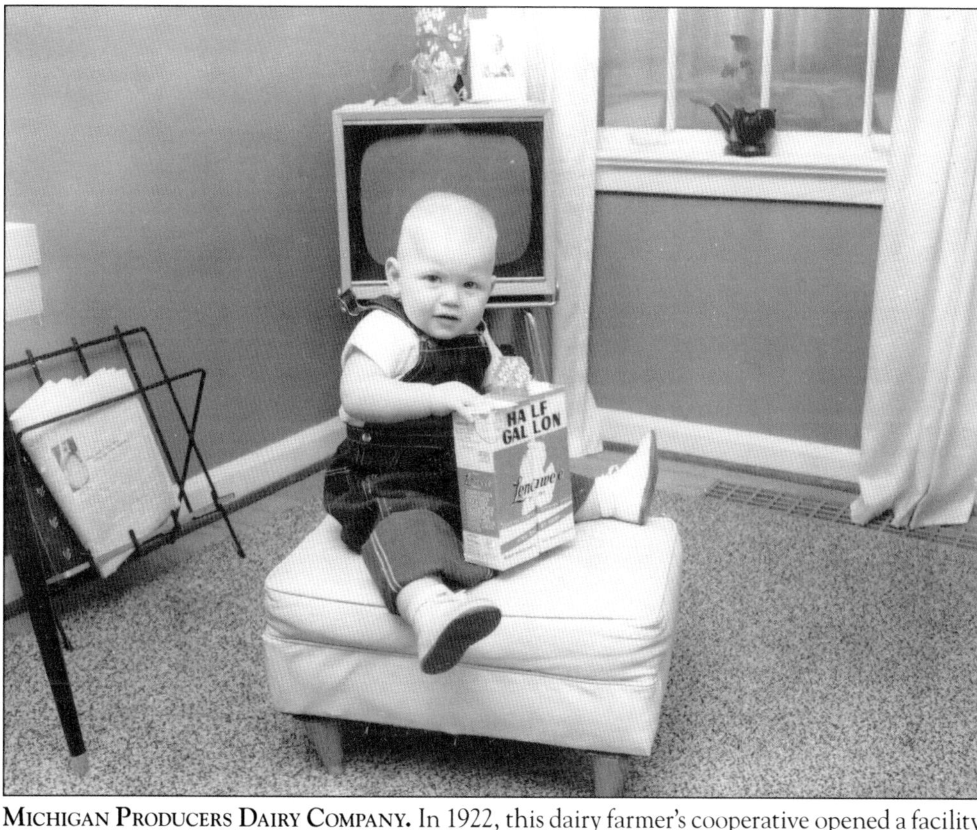

MICHIGAN PRODUCERS DAIRY COMPANY. In 1922, this dairy farmer's cooperative opened a facility in Adrian to primarily produce butter. Over time, milk from the large Holstein herds in the county also was used in the development of Lenawee brand milk, half-and-half, cottage cheese, sour cream, coffee creamer, and powdered milk lines. This publicity shot highlights the wholesome goodness of the brand.

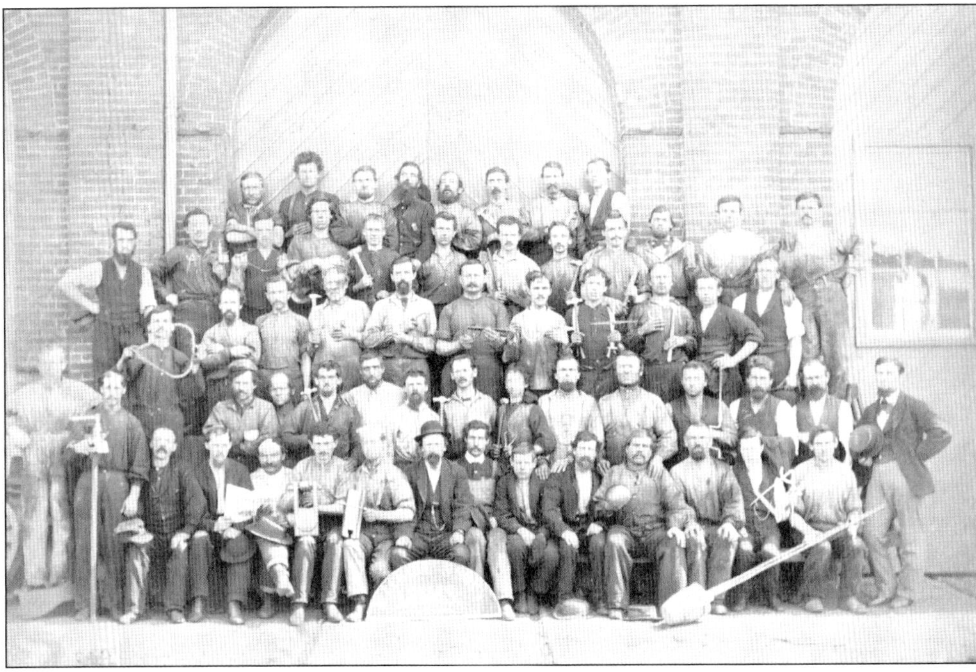

Lake Shore & Michigan Southern. The LS&MS Railway line traveled through Adrian from east to west on the route between Chicago and Buffalo. This business had been incorporated in 1869 after the merger of four earlier railroad companies. Numerous jobs associated with this industry were located in Adrian. Above is a photograph of the machinists typically responsible for on-the-spot repairs to the locomotives, and below is a photograph of line workers.

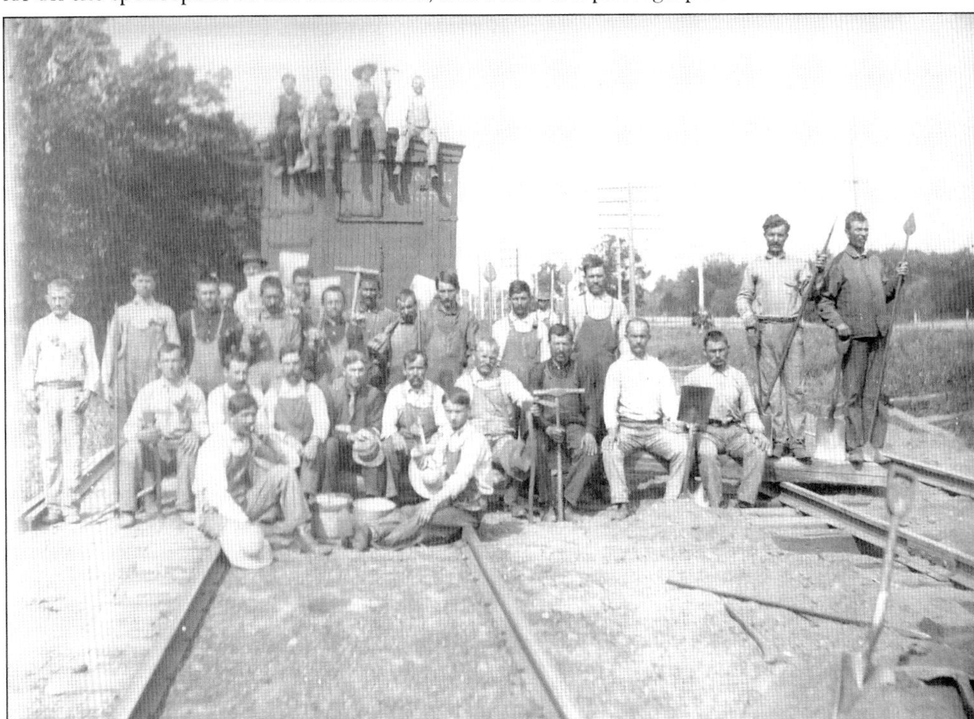

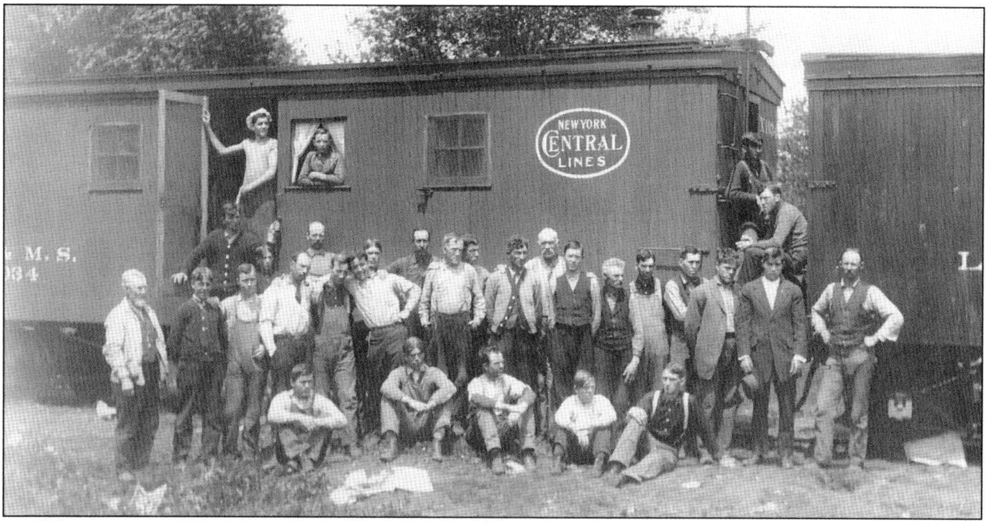

New York Central. The LS&MS Railway allowed for traffic from other companies on its rails, but Cornelius Vanderbilt desired a better deal for his interests in transportation. He secretly bought up stock options in the LS&MS beginning in 1877, after an economic downturn had caused severe distress and layoffs in the industry. The hostile merger was completed by 1914 to create the New York Central Railroad.

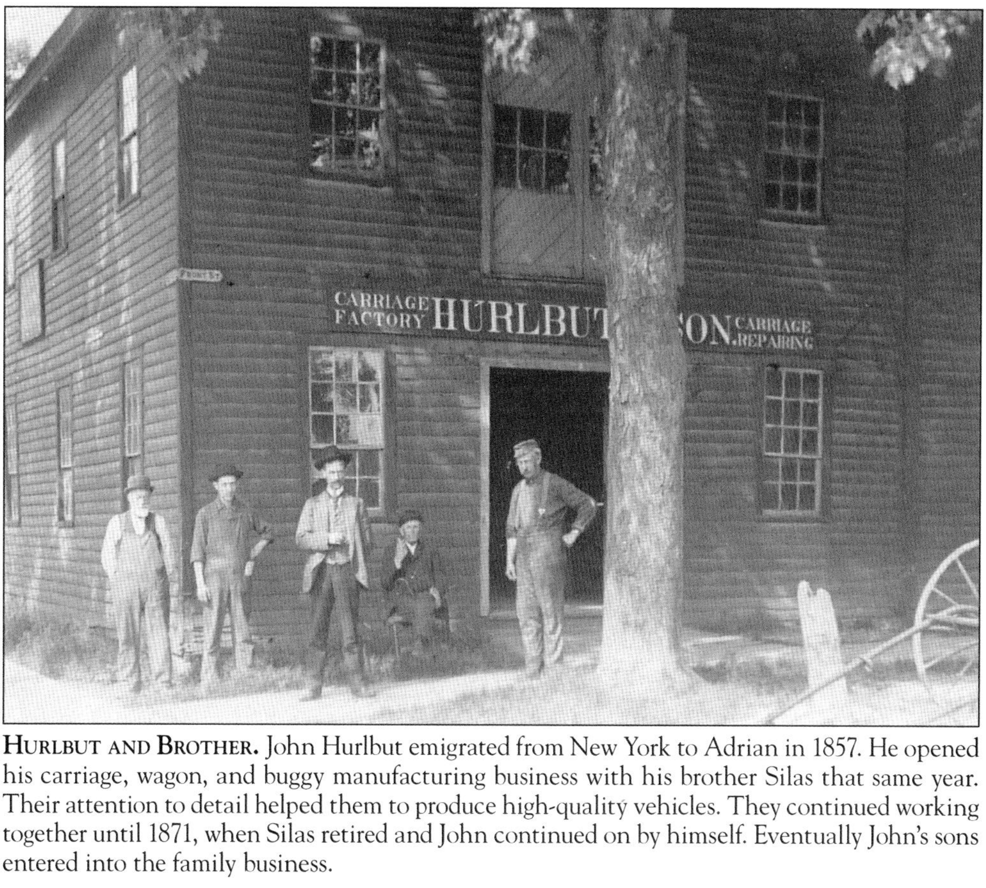

Hurlbut and Brother. John Hurlbut emigrated from New York to Adrian in 1857. He opened his carriage, wagon, and buggy manufacturing business with his brother Silas that same year. Their attention to detail helped them to produce high-quality vehicles. They continued working together until 1871, when Silas retired and John continued on by himself. Eventually John's sons entered into the family business.

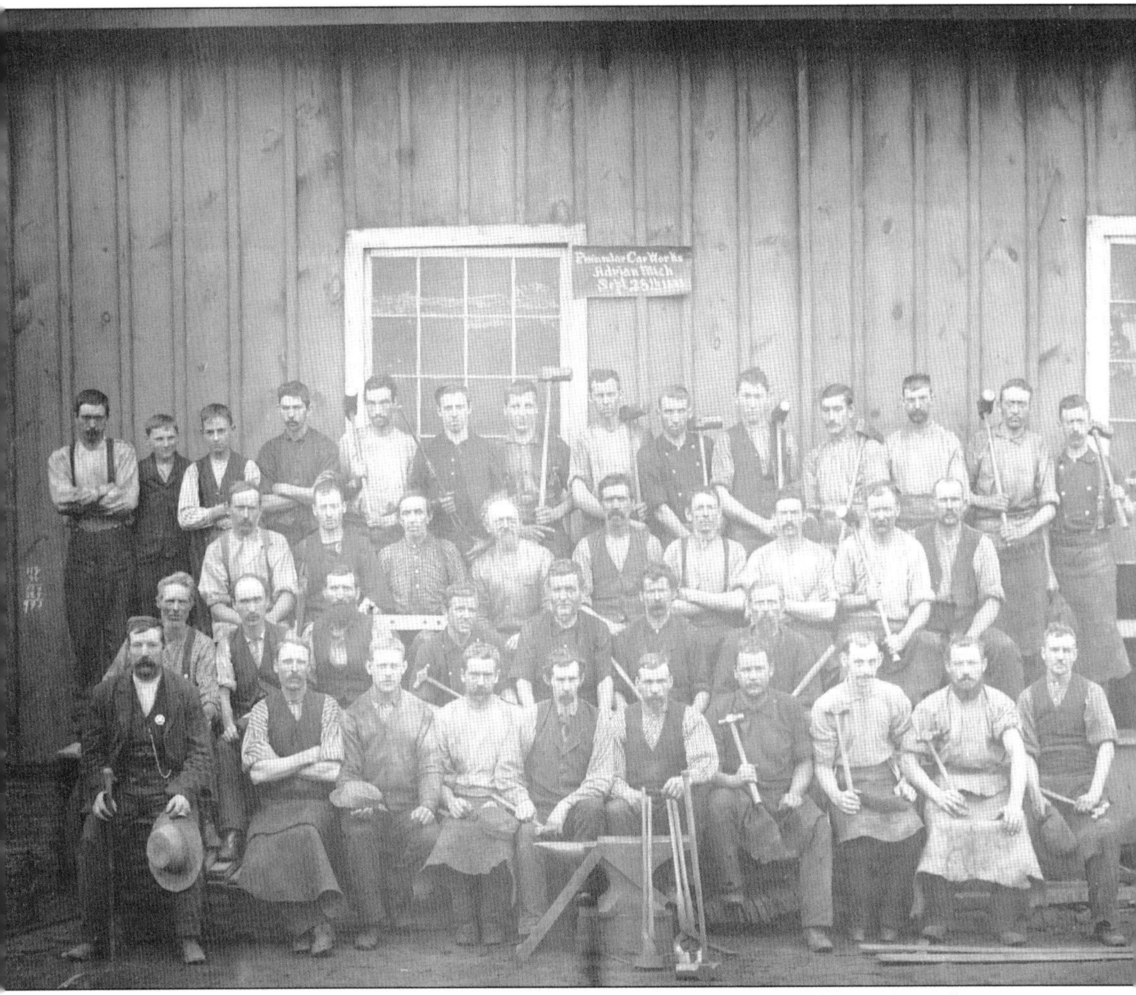

MICHIGAN PENINSULAR CAR COMPANY. Through the incorporation of several small companies, the Michigan Peninsular Car Company was formed by 1892. Peninsular had three car-building factories for the railroads and employed 5,000 men in this sector of its business. One of these factories was in Adrian and constructed large coal cars and boxcars for the railroads. The company survived the Panic of 1893 but eventually shifted to making automobiles after World War I.

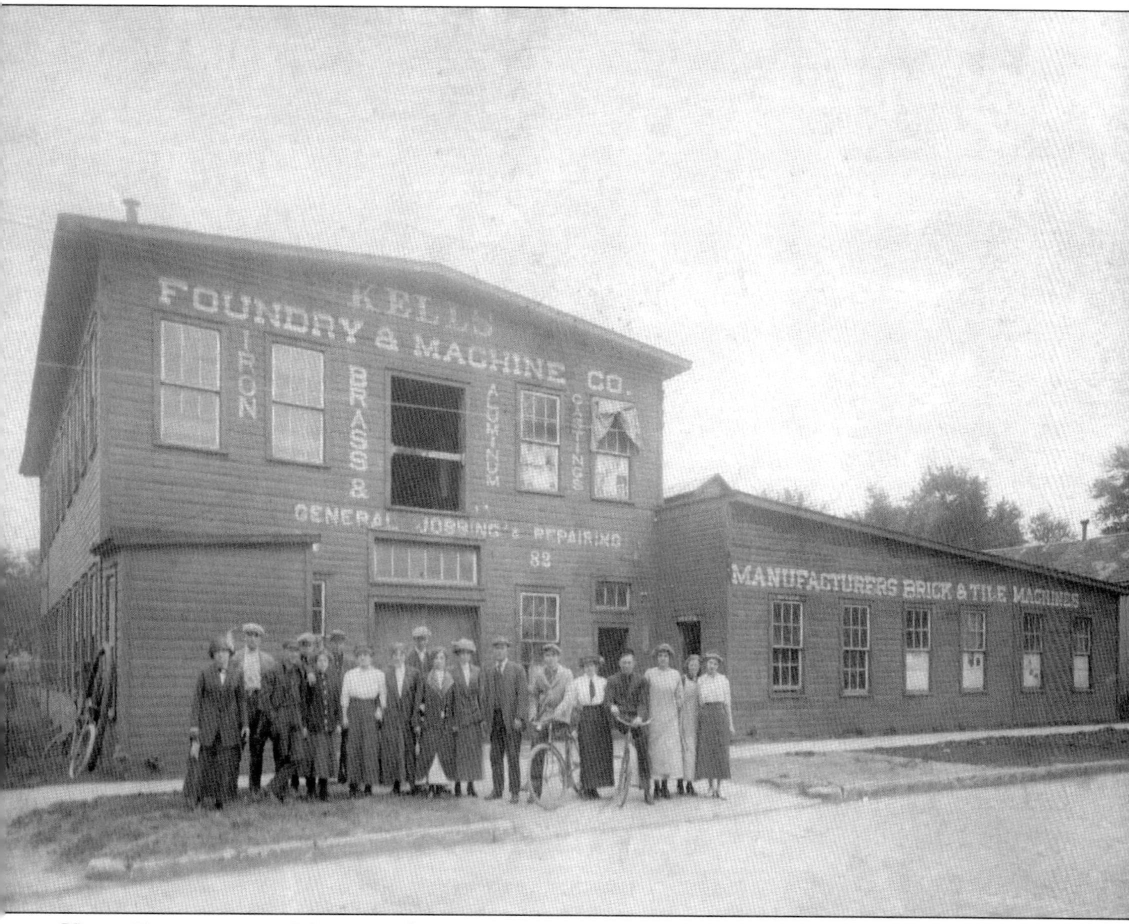

KELLS FOUNDRY AND MACHINE COMPANY. In 1882, Phillip Kells went into business with his three sons by opening a foundry and machine shop. This company became well known for its manufacture of augurs and brick and tile making machines. Due to misfortune, the family sold the business, and by 1906 Walter Cook was the sole proprietor. He expanded into the production of cement block machines.

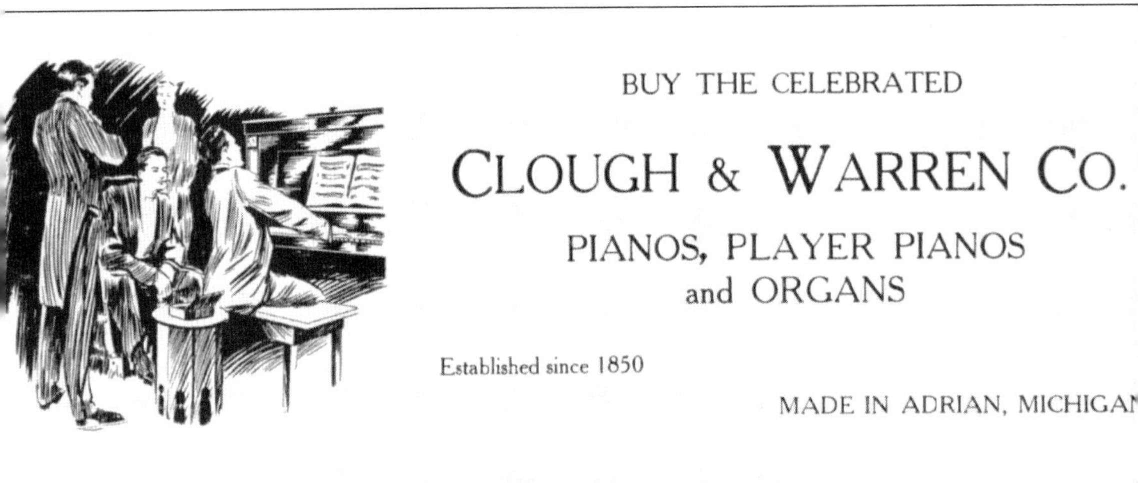

Clough and Warren Piano and Organ Company. Established in Detroit in 1850, this company expanded to include a factory in Adrian. During its lifespan, Clough and Warren created top-of-the-line organs, pianos, and phonograph cabinets using rare, expensive woods with elaborate carvings. Unfortunately, the company did not survive the Great Depression, as luxury items were especially exorbitant.

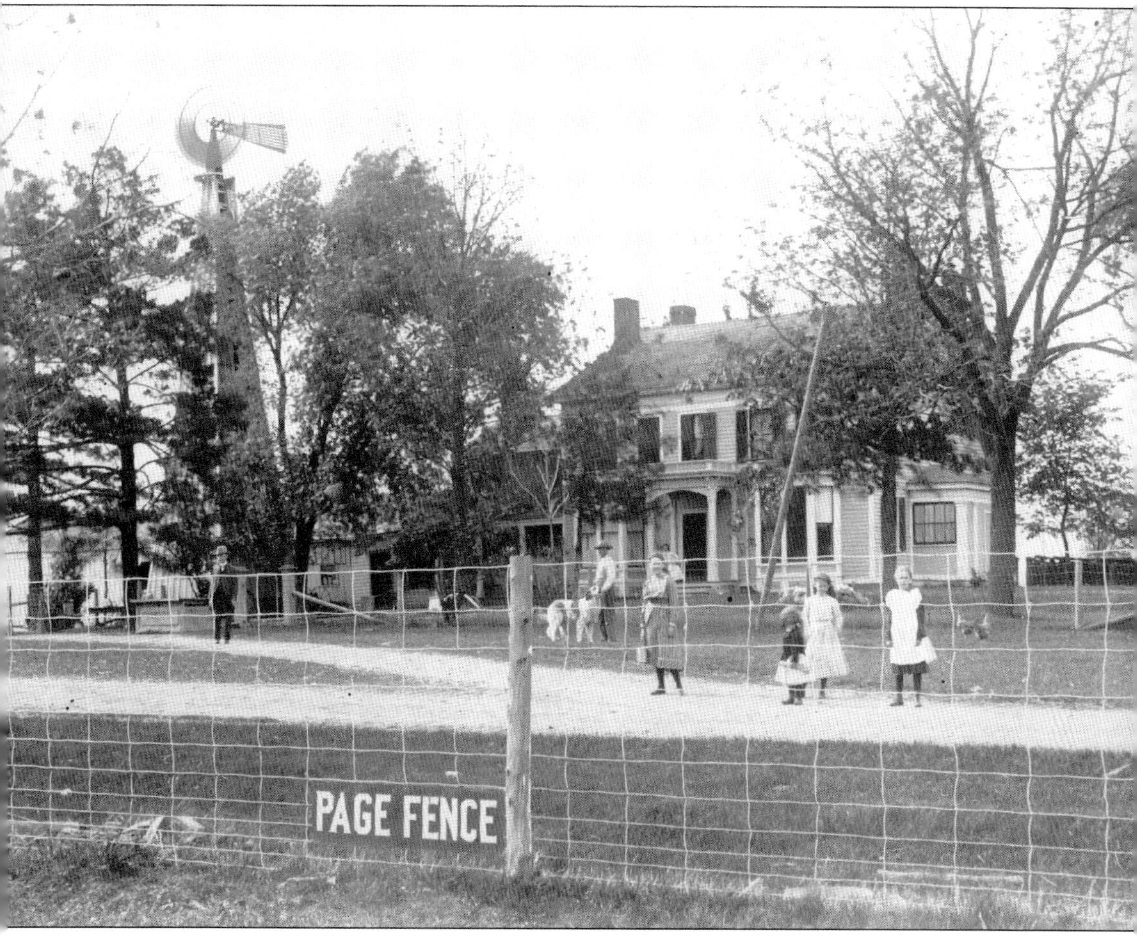

Page Fence. J. Wallace Page incorporated and moved his woven fence business to Adrian in 1889. His innovative fencing was especially useful for enclosing livestock. By the turn of the century, Adrian was called the "fence capital of the world." Page became the most successful fence company, not only due to its advertised "bounce back" product, but also because of its creative use of promotion, such as sponsoring its own baseball team and deer park.

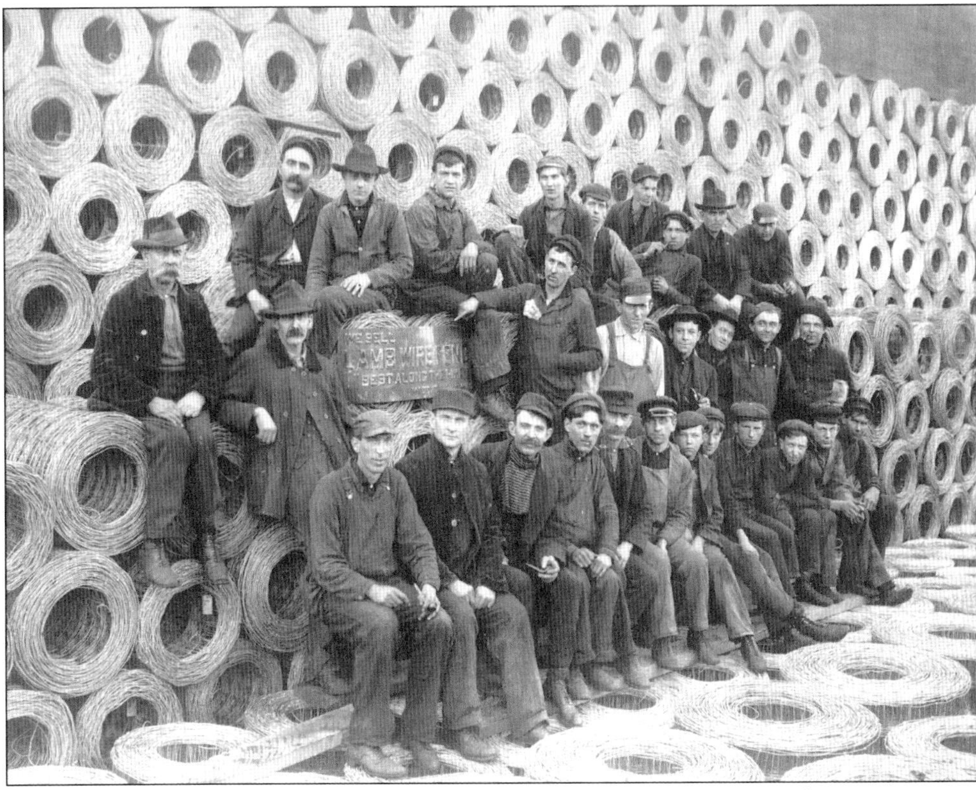

LAMB FENCE COMPANY. In 1897, the Lamb brothers relocated their woven fence company to Adrian near the railroad tracks of the Wabash. Within a decade, they had over 100 employees and were the second-largest fence company in the city. Lamb Fence had a monopoly granted by the Michigan Railroad Commission, being the only right-of-way fencing used by the industry. Above is a group photograph of the workers, and an interior shot of a worker at either Lamb or Page is seen below.

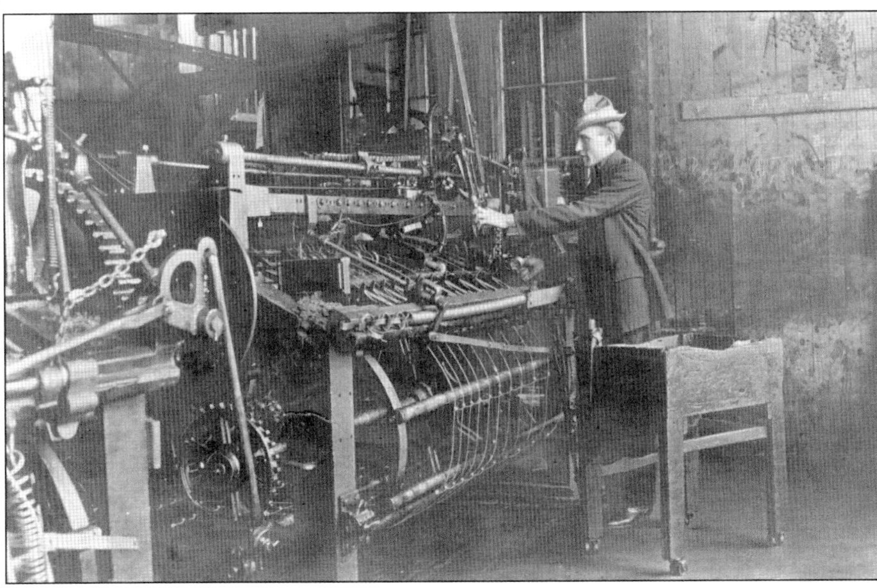

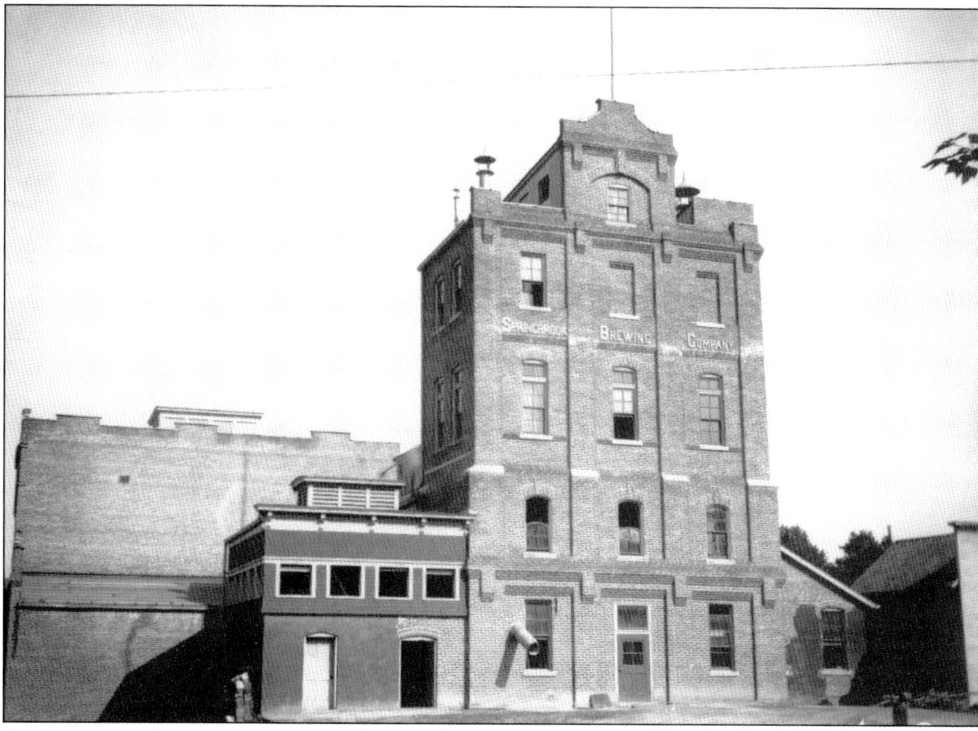

SPRINGBROOK BREWING COMPANY. One of the social traditions that German immigrants brought with them was family-style drinking, especially of pilsners. In 1859, R.A. Kaiser opened his beer-brewing company in Adrian to provide for the local population. Within a decade, the city had another brewery, the Adrian City Brewing Company. In 1903, both organizations merged, took the new name of Springbrook, and opened a new and improved factory, seen above. Some workers are pictured below.

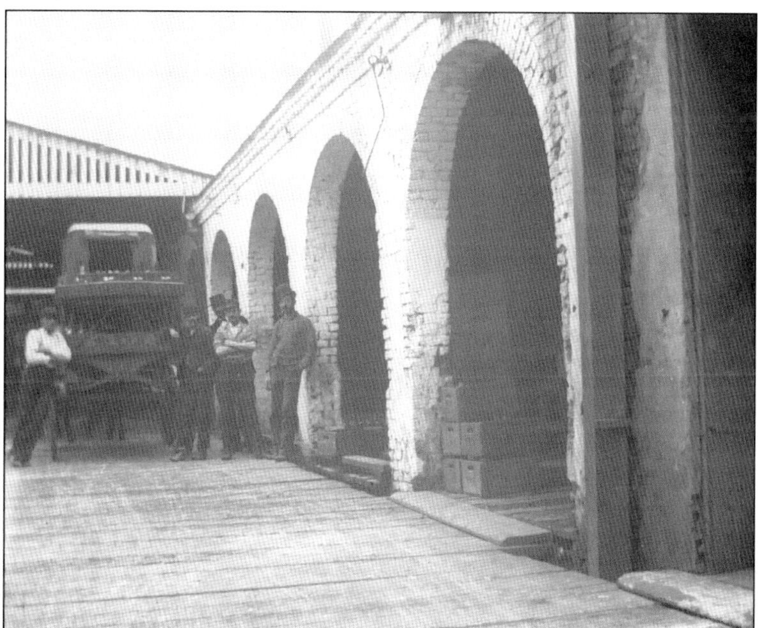

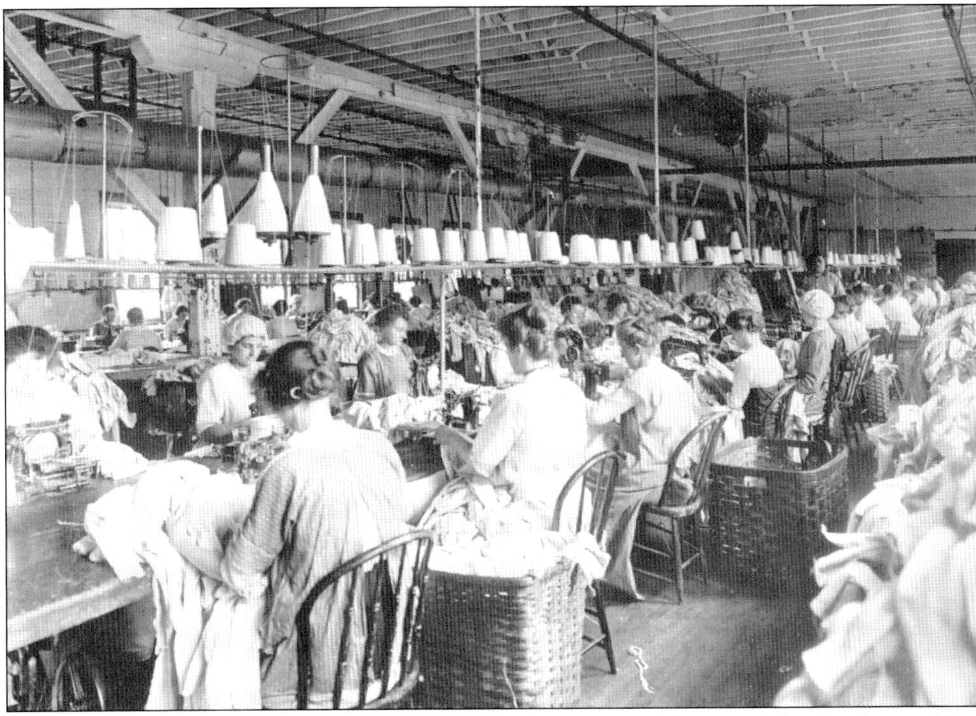

ADRIAN KNITTING COMPANY. In 1900, George Lewis came to Adrian with his brother and had incorporated the Adrian Knitting Company by 1901. The manufacture of heavyweight cotton underwear for children was its niche market under the name of Adrian Knitted Products. Soon, over 100 people were in the employ of Adrian Knitting, and its workforce was primarily female, as can be seen in these two photographs.

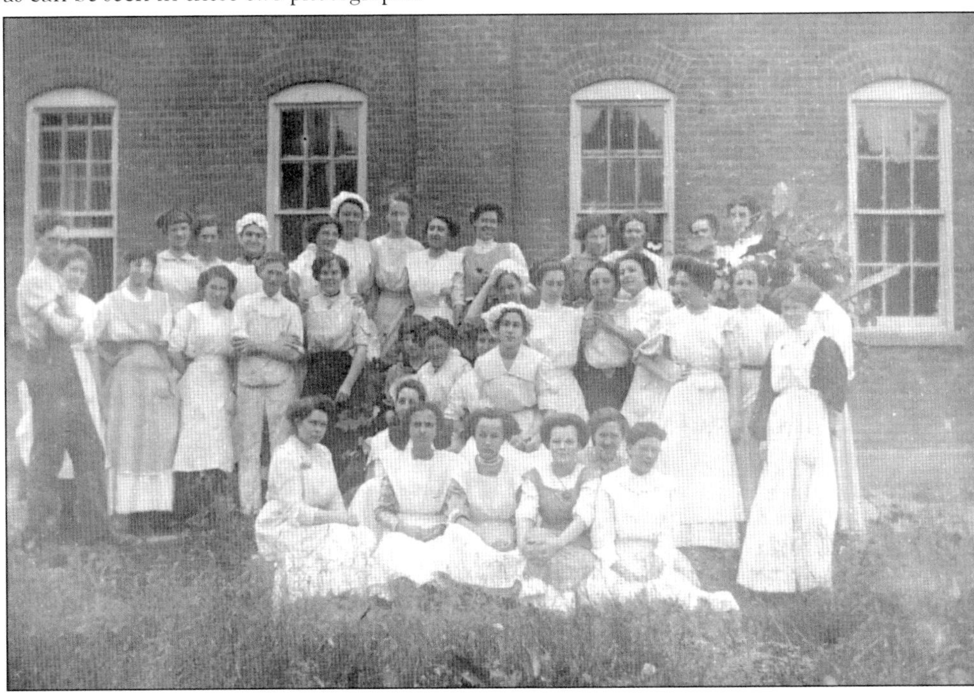

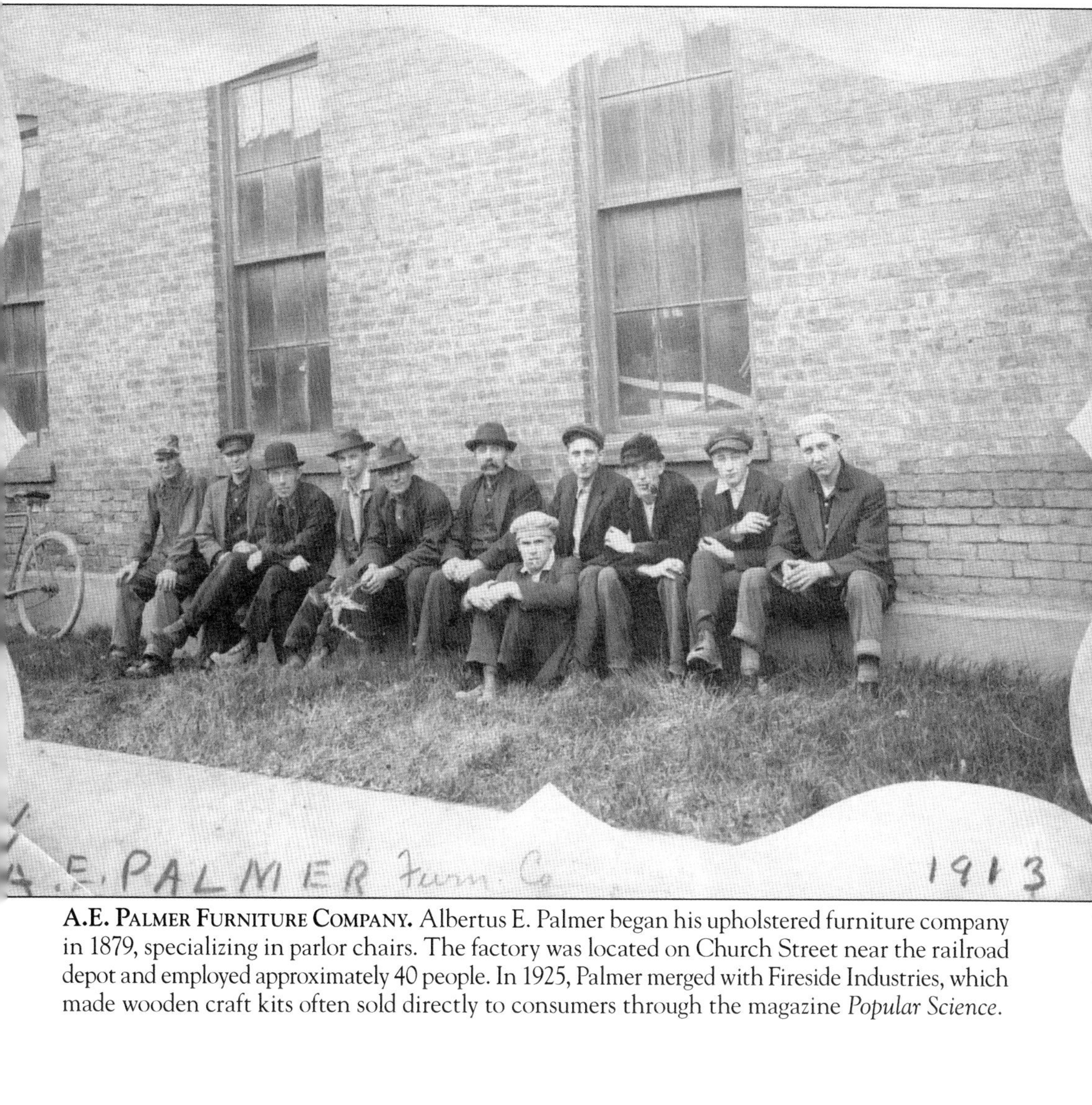

A.E. Palmer Furniture Company. Albertus E. Palmer began his upholstered furniture company in 1879, specializing in parlor chairs. The factory was located on Church Street near the railroad depot and employed approximately 40 people. In 1925, Palmer merged with Fireside Industries, which made wooden craft kits often sold directly to consumers through the magazine *Popular Science*.

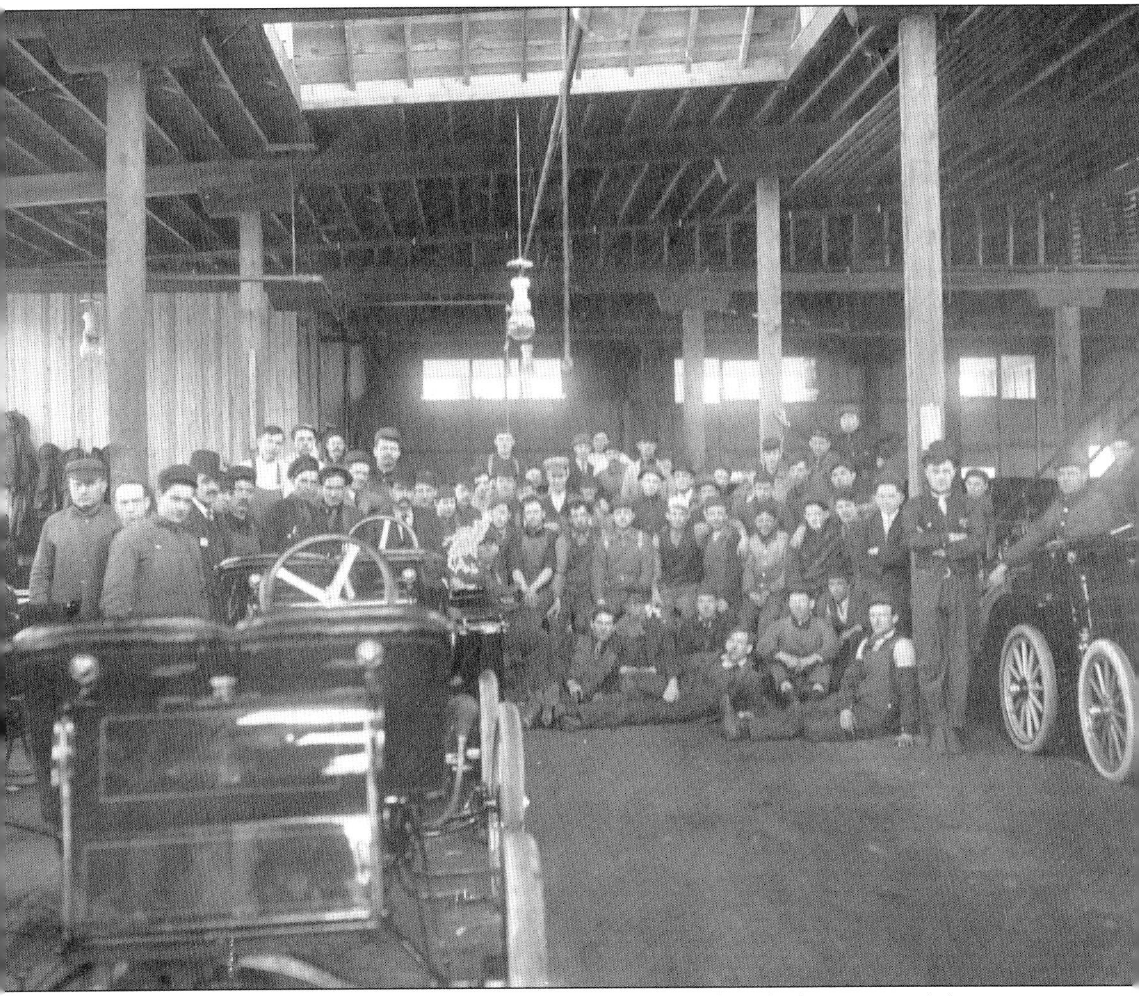

INTERIOR AUTOMOBILE FACTORY. In the early 20th century, Adrian had two automobile companies, the Church Company and the Lion Motor Company, which attempted to diversify the industry of the area. The Church Company produced both the Murray and Lenawee cars between 1901 and 1908. Through the time of its existence, only about 237 cars were sold. This interior factory shot is either from the Church Company or Lion Motor Company.

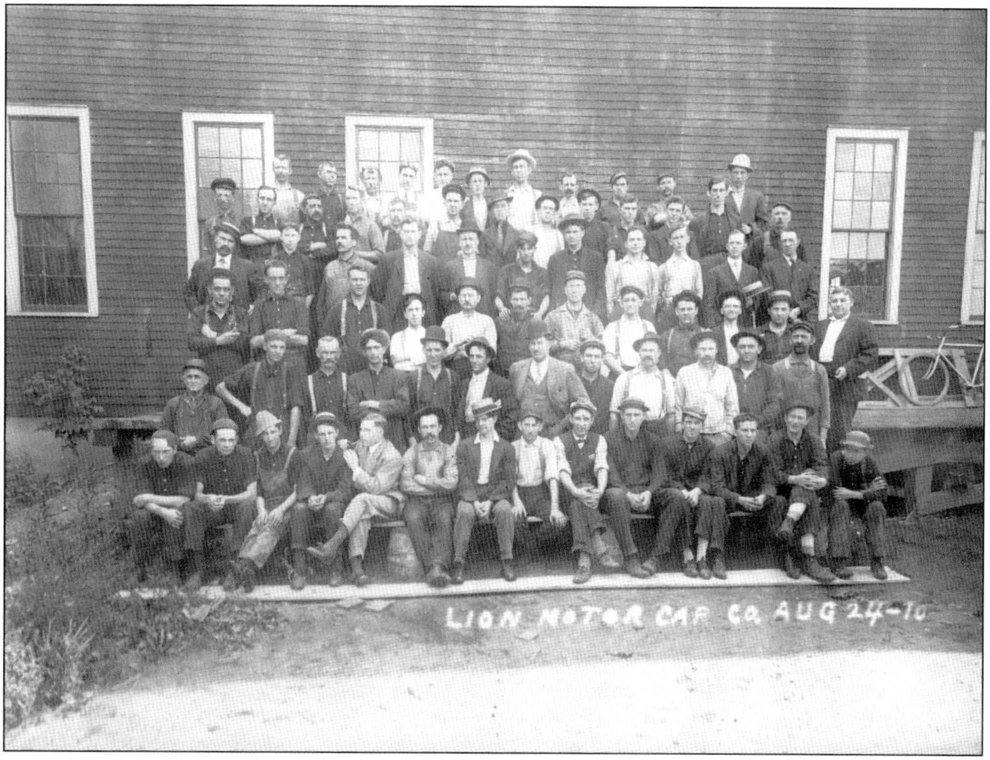

Lion Motor Company. Begun by Henry Bowen and Fred Postal, this automobile company existed from 1909 until 1912 in Adrian. The popular Lion automobile styles included a touring car and a roadster, both with a 40-horsepower engine. Unfortunately, a fire at the factory in 1912 caused the company to go out of business. Above is a photograph of its workers, and below is the factory.

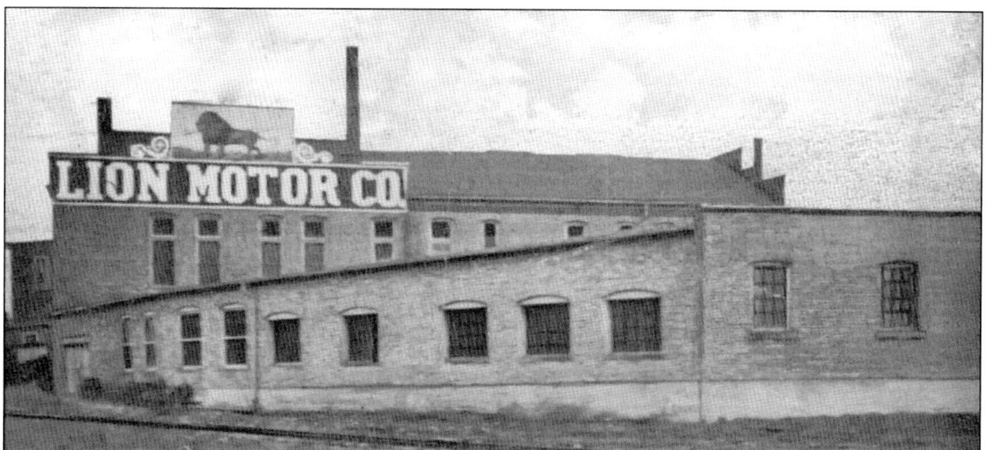

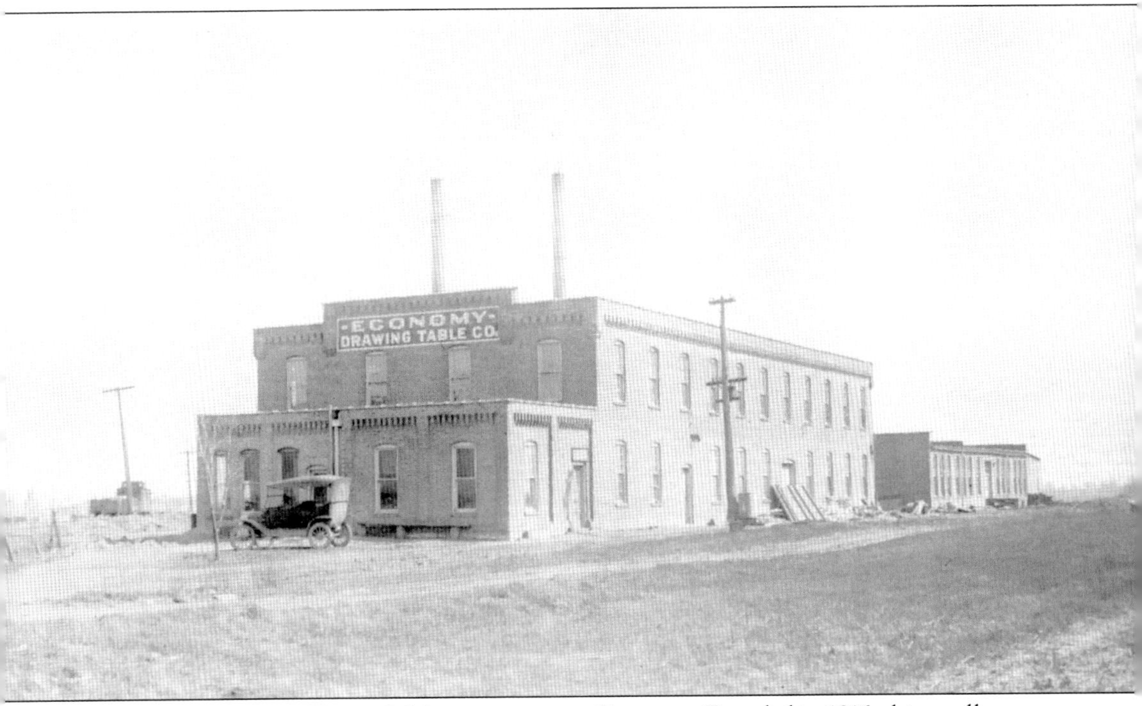

Economy Drawing Table & Manufacturing Company. Founded in 1916, this small company employed approximately 30 people. The primary focus was building filing cabinets and drafting tables. Companies could order this furniture out of either wood or steel. There were a variety of styles to choose from, and this manufacturer would also build to specifications for its customers. In 1926, Kewaunee Manufacturing Company bought the firm and expanded into laboratory furniture.

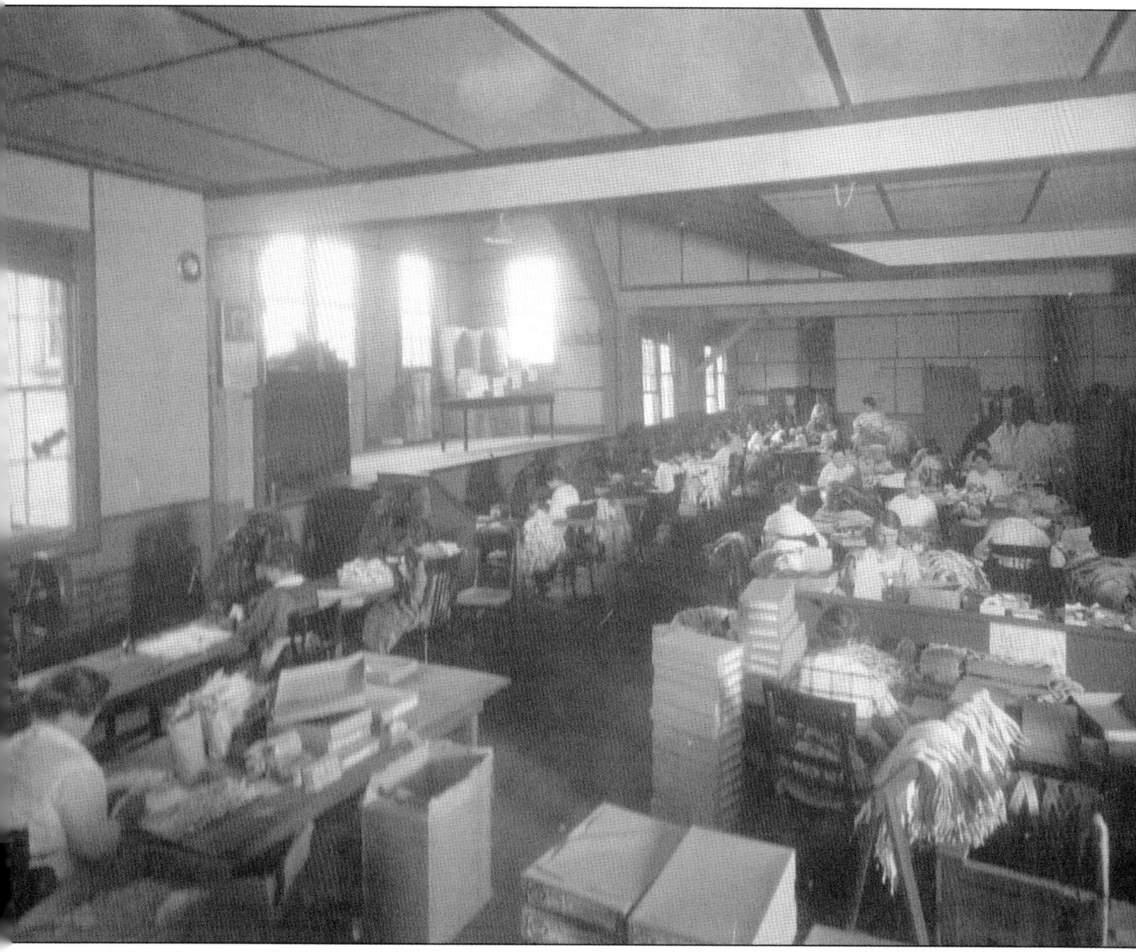

Nu-Way Stretch Suspender Company. Ollie Mott purchased a department store in Adrian in 1906, which he operated until 1914. Mott purchased the patent for an innovative way to make suspenders and had the Nu-Way Stretch Company up and running by 1914 in the town of Dundee. He relocated the factory to Adrian by 1919. The firm made not only Nu-Way and Excello suspenders, but also garters, hose supporters, and corset tie-ons until the 1960s.

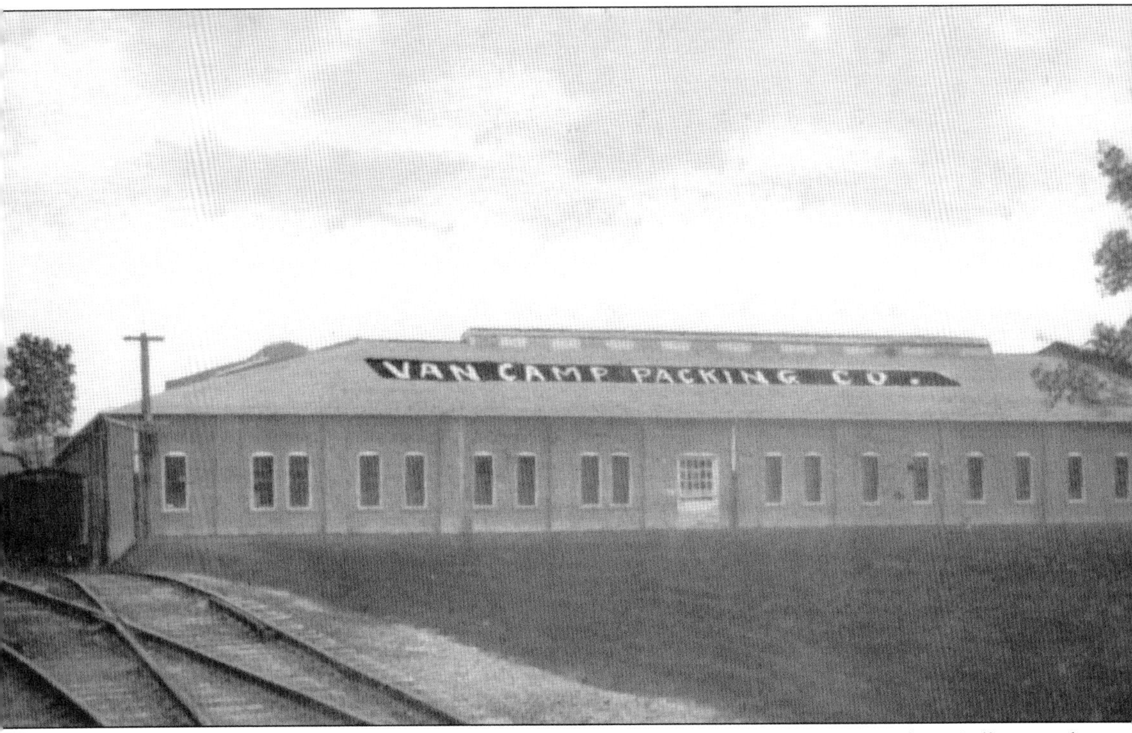

VAN CAMP PACKING COMPANY. The origins of this company date to 1861, when Gilbert and Hester Van Camp began canning fruits and vegetables for their own Indianapolis grocery store. They especially became well known for their pork and beans. By 1921, the firm had 14 plants. Its factory in Adrian was opened in 1911 to produce condensed milk. Lenawee County had 20,000 dairy cows at this time.

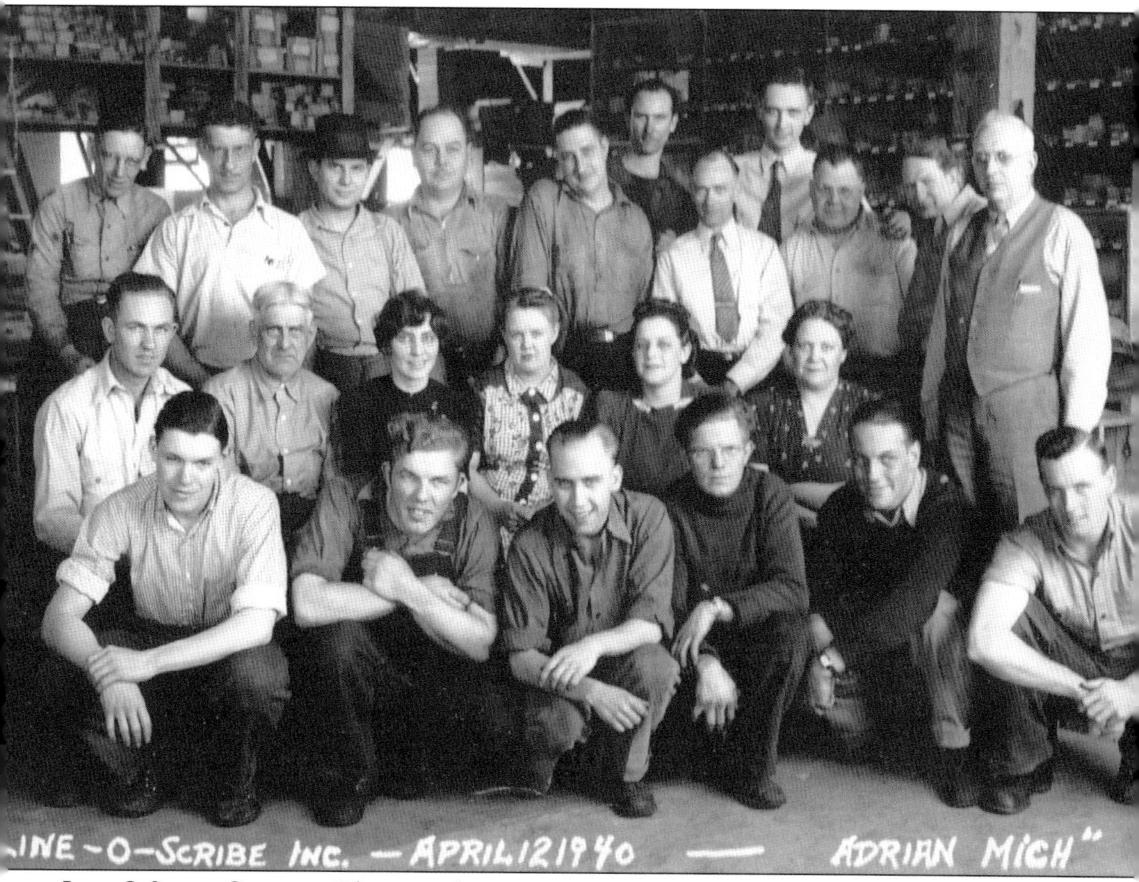

Line-O-Scribe Company. This manufacturing company opened in Adrian in 1928. It produced a wide variety of printing presses for purchase, especially those used by businesses to make price tags, window display pieces, posters, and counter cards. It was perhaps a victim of its own success, being bought out by the Morgan Sign Machine Company of Chicago, Illinois, in 1931. These machines were made through the 1960s.

Bibliography

Ashlee, Laura, ed. *Traveling through Time: A Guide to Michigan's Historical Markers*. Ann Arbor: University of Michigan Press, 2005.

Baker, Moses, ed. *Manual of American Waterworks*. New York: Engineering News, 1888.

Barnard, F.A. *American Biographical History of Eminent and Self-Made Men*. Cincinnati: Western Biographical Publishing Company, 1878.

Besse, Henry. *Church History*. Cleona, PA: Holzapfel Publishing Company, 1908.

Bonner, Richard, ed. *Memoirs of Lenawee County Michigan*. Madison, WI: Western Historical Association, 1909.

——— and William Whitney. *History and Biographical Record of Lenawee County*. Adrian: W. Stearns and Company, 1879.

Bradstreet's Book of Commercial Ratings: Michigan. New York: Bradstreet Company, 1904.

Brown, Charles, ed. *Adrian City Directory 1870*. Adrian: Adrian Times and Expositor, 1870.

Burton, Clarence, ed. *The City of Detroit: 1701–1922*. Detroit: S.J. Clarke Publishing Company, 1922.

Chapin, Henry, ed. *Adrian City Directory for 1885–1886*. Adrian: Henry Chapin, 1885.

Cherry, Dan, ed. *The Best of the Brooklyn Exponent Attic*. Brooklyn, MI: The Brooklyn Exponent, 2006.

Elliot, A.H. and W. Jerome Harrison. *The International Annual of Anthony's Photographic Bulletin*. Vol. 2. New York: E. & H.T. Elliot & Company, 1890.

Fuller, George, ed. *Historic Michigan*. Dayton, OH: National Historical Association, 1924.

Hare, Jack. *Celebration of Fools: An Inside Look at the Rise and Fall of JC Penney*. New York: William Hare, 2004.

Heilprin, Angelo and Louis Heilprin, eds. *Lippincott's New Gazetteer*. Philadelphia: J.B. Lippincott Company, 1906.

King, William, ed. *The History of Homeopathy and its Institutions in America*. New York: The Lewis Publishing Company, 1905.

Lindquist, Charles. *Adrian: The City that Worked*. Adrian: Lenawee County Historical Society, 2004.

———. *Lenawee County: A Harvest of Pride and Promise*. Chatsworth, CA: Windsor Publications, Inc., 1990.

Michigan Bureau of Labor and Industrial Statistics. *Seventeenth Annual Report of the Bureau of Labor and Industrial Statistics*. Lansing, MI: Wynkoop Hallenbeck Crawford Co., 1900.

———. *Twenty-Fourth Annual Report of the Bureau of Labor and Industrial Statistics*. Lansing, MI: Wynkoop Hallenbeck Crawford Co., 1907.

———. *Thirty-Second Annual Report of the Bureau of Labor and Industrial Statistics*. Lansing, MI: Wynkoop Hallenbeck Crawford Co., 1915.

———. *Thirty-Fifth Annual Report of the Bureau of Labor and Industrial Statistics*. Lansing, MI: Wynkoop Hallenbeck Crawford Co., 1918.

Michigan Department of Public Instruction. *Sixty-Fourth Annual Report of the Superintendent of the State of Michigan*. Lansing, MI: Wynkoop Hallenbeck Crawford Co., 1900.
Michigan Legislature. *Public Acts and Joint and Concurrent resolutions of the Legislature of the State of Michigan Regular Session of 1879, with an appendix*. Lansing, MI: W.S. George & Company, 1879.
Michigan Miner. Vol. 4, no. 7, p. 19. Saginaw, MI: Michigan Miner, 1902.
Michigan Public Utilities Commission. *Orders and Opinions of the Michigan Public Utilities Commission*. Fort Wayne, IN: Fort Wayne Printing Company, 1922.
Michigan Railroad Commission. *Twenty-Fifth Annual Report of the Commissioner of Railroads of the State of Michigan*. Lansing, MI: Robert Smith Printing Company, 1897.
Michigan Secretary of State. *Michigan and Its Resources*. Lansing, MI: Robert Smith Printing Company, 1893.
Michigan State Board of Corrections and Charities. *Sixth Biennial Report of the Michigan State Board of Corrections and Charities*. Lansing, MI: W.S. George & Company, 1882.
Mull, Carol. *The Underground Railroad in Michigan*. Jefferson, NC: McFarland & Company, 2010.
Nordin, Dennis. *Rich Harvest: A History of the Grange: 1867-1900*. Baton Rouge: University Press of Mississippi, 1974.
Order of the Eastern Star—Grand Chapter Michigan. *Proceedings 1919*. Grand Rapids. MI: Grand Chapter Michigan O.E.S., 1919.
Pilcher, Elijah. *Protestantism in Michigan*. Detroit: R.D.S. Tyler and Company, 1878.
Polk, R.L., ed. *Adrian City Directory 1921*. Detroit: R.L. Polk & Company, 1921.
———, ed. *Michigan State Gazetteer and Business Directory 1877*. Detroit: R.L. Polk & Company, 1877.
Poor's Directory of Railway Officials and Railway Directors. New York: Poor's Railroad Manual, 1890.
Rubenstein, Bruce and Lawrence Ziewacz. *Michigan: A History of the Great Lakes State*. Wheeling, IL: Harlan Davidson Inc., 2002.
Scott, Irving. *Inland Lakes of Michigan*. Lansing, MI: Wynkoop Hallenbeck Crawford Co., 1921.
Smith, William. *Historical Sketches of Education in Michigan*. Lansing, MI: W.S. George and Company, 1881.
Spillane, Daniel. *History of American Pianoforte*. New York: D. Spillane, 1890.
Spring, Joel. *The American School: 1642–2000*. Boston: McGraw-Hill, 2001.
State Industrial Home for Girls. *Seventh Biennial Report of 1891–1892*. Lansing, MI: Robert Smith Printing Company, 1892.
Tendrick Frank, Lisa. *Women in the American Civil War*, vol. 2. Santa Barbara: ABC-CLIO Inc., 2008.